8/22

D0471967

How Students Learn

SCIENCE IN THE CLASSROOM

Committee on *How People Learn*, A Targeted Report for Teachers

M. Suzanne Donovan and John D. Bransford, *Editors*

Division of Behavioral and Social Sciences and Education

NATIONAL RESEARCH COUNCIL
OF THE NATIONAL ACADEMIES

THE NATIONAL ACADEMIES PRESS
Washington, D.C.
www.nap.edu

THE NATIONAL ACADEMIES PRESS • 500 Fifth Street, N.W. • Washington, D.C. 20001

NOTICE: The project that is the subject of this report was approved by the Governing Board of the National Research Council, whose members are drawn from the councils of the National Academy of Sciences, the National Academy of Engineering, and the Institute of Medicine. The members of the committee responsible for the report were chosen for their special competences and with regard for appropriate balance.

This study was supported by Award No. R215U990024 between the National Academy of Sciences and the U.S. Department of Education. Any opinions, findings, conclusions, or recommendations expressed in this publication are those of the author(s) and do not necessarily reflect the views of the organizations or agencies that provided support for the project.

Library of Congress Cataloging-in-Publication Data

National Research Council (U.S.). Committee on How People Learn, A Targeted Report for Teachers.
  How students learn : history, mathematics, and science in the classroom / Committee on How People Learn, A Targeted Report for Teachers ; M. Suzanne Donovan and John D. Bransford, editors.
     p. cm.
  "Division of Behavioral and Social Sciences and Education."
  Includes bibliographical references and index.
  ISBN 0-309-07433-9 (hardcover) — ISBN 0-309-08948-4 (pbk.) —
ISBN 0-309-08949-2 (pbk.) — ISBN 0-309-08950-6 (pbk.) 1. Learning. 2.
Classroom management. 3. Curriculum planning. I. Donovan, Suzanne.
II. Bransford, John. III. Title.
  LB1060.N38 2005
  370.15'23—dc22

                              2004026246

Additional copies of this report are available from the National Academies Press, 500 Fifth Street, N.W., Lockbox 285, Washington, DC 20055; (800) 624-6242 or (202) 334-3313 (in the Washington metropolitan area); Internet, http://www.nap.edu

Printed in the United States of America.

Copyright 2005 by the National Academy of Sciences. All rights reserved.

Suggested citation: National Research Council. (2005). *How Students Learn: Science in the Classroom*. Committee on *How People Learn*, A Targeted Report for Teachers, M.S. Donovan and J.D. Bransford, Editors. Division of Behavioral and Social Sciences and Education. Washington, DC: The National Academies Press.

Chess Game
Fish is Fish

THE NATIONAL ACADEMIES
Advisers to the Nation on Science, Engineering, and Medicine

The **National Academy of Sciences** is a private, nonprofit, self-perpetuating society of distinguished scholars engaged in scientific and engineering research, dedicated to the furtherance of science and technology and to their use for the general welfare. Upon the authority of the charter granted to it by the Congress in 1863, the Academy has a mandate that requires it to advise the federal government on scientific and technical matters. Dr. Bruce M. Alberts is president of the National Academy of Sciences.

The **National Academy of Engineering** was established in 1964, under the charter of the National Academy of Sciences, as a parallel organization of outstanding engineers. It is autonomous in its administration and in the selection of its members, sharing with the National Academy of Sciences the responsibility for advising the federal government. The National Academy of Engineering also sponsors engineering programs aimed at meeting national needs, encourages education and research, and recognizes the superior achievements of engineers. Dr. Wm. A. Wulf is president of the National Academy of Engineering.

The **Institute of Medicine** was established in 1970 by the National Academy of Sciences to secure the services of eminent members of appropriate professions in the examination of policy matters pertaining to the health of the public. The Institute acts under the responsibility given to the National Academy of Sciences by its congressional charter to be an adviser to the federal government and, upon its own initiative, to identify issues of medical care, research, and education. Dr. Harvey V. Fineberg is president of the Institute of Medicine.

The **National Research Council** was organized by the National Academy of Sciences in 1916 to associate the broad community of science and technology with the Academy's purposes of furthering knowledge and advising the federal government. Functioning in accordance with general policies determined by the Academy, the Council has become the principal operating agency of both the National Academy of Sciences and the National Academy of Engineering in providing services to the government, the public, and the scientific and engineering communities. The Council is administered jointly by both Academies and the Institute of Medicine. Dr. Bruce M. Alberts and Dr. Wm. A. Wulf are chair and vice chair, respectively, of the National Research Council.

www.national-academies.org

COMMITTEE ON *HOW PEOPLE LEARN*: A TARGETED REPORT FOR TEACHERS

JOHN D. BRANSFORD (*Chair*), College of Education, University of Washington
SUSAN CAREY, Department of Psychology, Harvard University
KIERAN EGAN, Department of Education, Simon Fraser University, Burnaby, Canada
SUZANNE WILSON, School of Education, Michigan State University
SAMUEL S. WINEBURG, Department of Education, Stanford University

M. SUZANNE DONOVAN, *Study Director*
SUSAN R. MCCUTCHEN, *Research Associate*
ALLISON E. SHOUP, *Senior Project Assistant*
ELIZABETH B. TOWNSEND, *Senior Project Assistant*

Preface

This book has its roots in the report of the Committee on Developments in the Science of Learning, *How People Learn: Brain, Mind, Experience and School* (National Research Council, 1999, National Academy Press). That report presented an illuminating review of research in a variety of fields that has advanced understanding of human learning. The report also made an important attempt to draw from that body of knowledge implications for teaching. A follow-on study by a second committee explored what research and development would need to be done, and how it would need to be communicated, to be especially useful to teachers, principals, superintendents, and policy makers: *How People Learn: Bridging Research and Practice* (National Research Council, 1999). These two individual reports were combined to produce an expanded edition of *How People Learn* (National Research Council, 2000). We refer to this volume as *HPL.*

The next step in the work on how people learn was to provide examples of how the principles and findings on learning can be used to guide the teaching of a set of topics that commonly appear in the K-12 curriculum. This work focused on three subject areas— history, mathematics, and science—and resulted in the book *How Students Learn: History, Mathematics, and Science in the Classroom.* Each area was treated at three levels: elementary, middle, and high school.

This volume includes the subset of chapters from that book focused on science, along with the introduction and concluding chapter for the larger volume. However the full set of chapters can be found on the enclosed CD.

Distinguished researchers who have extensive experience in teaching or in partnering with teachers were invited to contribute the chapters. The committee shaped the goals for the volume, and commented—sometimes extensively—on the draft chapters as they were written and revised. The principles of *HPL* are embedded in each chapter, though there are differences from one chapter to the next in how explicitly they are discussed.

Taking this next step to elaborate the *HPL* principles in context poses a potential problem that we wish to address at the outset. The meaning and relevance of the principles for classroom teaching can be made clearer with specific examples. At the same time, however, many of the specifics of a particular example could be replaced with others that are also consistent with the *HPL* principles. In looking at a single example, it can be difficult to distinguish what is necessary to effective teaching from what is effective but easily replaced. With this in mind, it is critical that the teaching and learning examples in each chapter be seen as illustrative, not as blueprints for the "right" way to teach.

We can imagine, by analogy, that engineering students will better grasp the relationship between the laws of physics and the construction of effective supports for a bridge if they see some examples of well-designed bridges, accompanied by explanations for the choices of the critical design features. The challenging engineering task of crossing the entrance of the San Francisco Bay, for example, may bring the relationship between physical laws, physical constraints, and engineering solutions into clear and meaningful focus. But there are some design elements of the Golden Gate Bridge that could be replaced with others that serve the same end, and people may well differ on which among a set of good designs creates the most appealing bridge.

To say that the Golden Gate Bridge is a good example of a suspension bridge does not mean it is the only, or the best possible, design for a suspension bridge. If one has many successful suspension bridges to compare, the design features that are required for success, and those that are replaceable, become more apparent. And the requirements that are uniform across contexts, and the requirements that change with context, are more easily revealed.

The chapters in this volume highlight different approaches to addressing the same fundamental principles of learning. It would be ideal to be able to provide two or more "*HPL* compatible" approaches to teaching the same topic. However, we cannot provide that level of specific variability in this volume. We encourage readers to look at chapters in other disciplines as well in order to see more clearly the common features across chapters, and the variation in approach among the chapters..

This volume could not have come to life without the help and dedication of many people, and we are grateful to them. The financial support of our sponsors, the U.S. Department of Education and the members of the President's Circle of the National Academy of Sciences, was essential. We appreciate both their support and their patience during the unexpectedly long period required to shape and produce so extensive a volume with so many different contributors. Our thanks to C. Kent McGuire, former assistant secretary of education research and improvement for providing the initial grant for this project, and to his successor and now director of the National Institute for Education Sciences, Grover J. Whitehurst; thanks are due as well to Patricia O'Connell Ross, Jill Edwards Staton, Michael Kestner, and Linda Jones at the Department of Education for working with us throughout, and providing the time required to produce a quality product.

This report is a somewhat unusual undertaking for the National Research Council in that the committee members did not author the report chapters, but served as advisers to the chapter authors. The contributions of committee members were extraordinary. In a first meeting the committee and chapter authors worked together to plan the volume. The committee then read each draft chapter, and provided extensive, and remarkably productive, feedback to chapter authors. As drafts were revised, committee members reviewed them again, pointing out concerns and proposing potential solutions. Their generosity and their commitment to the goal of this project are noteworthy.

Alexandra Wigdor, director of the Division on Education, Labor, and Human Performance when this project was begun, provided ongoing guidance and experienced assistance with revisions. Rona Brière brought her special skills in editing the entire volume. Our thanks go to Allison E. Shoup, who was senior project assistant, supporting the project through much of its life; to Susan R. McCutchen, who prepared the manuscript for review; to Claudia Sauls and Candice Crawford, who prepared the final manuscript; and to Deborah Johnson, Sandra Smotherman, and Elizabeth B. Townsend, who willingly provided additional support when needed. Kirsten Sampson Snyder handled the report review process, and Yvonne Wise handled report production—both challenging tasks for a report of this size and complexity. We are grateful for their help.

This report has been reviewed in draft form by individuals chosen for their diverse perspectives and technical expertise, in accordance with procedures approved by the National Research Council's Report Review Committee. The purpose of this independent review is to provide candid and critical comments that will assist the institution in making its published report as sound as possible and to ensure that the report meets institutional standards for objectivity, evidence, and responsiveness to the study charge. The review comments and draft manuscript remain confidential to protect the integrity of the deliberative process. We thank the following individuals for their review of this report: Jo Boaler, Mathematics Education, School of Education, Stanford University; Miriam L. Clifford, Mathematics Department, Carroll College, Waukesha, Wisconsin; O.L. Davis, Curriculum and Instruction, The

University of Texas at Austin; Patricia B. Dodge, Science Teacher, Essex Middle School, Essex Junction, Vermont; Carol T. Hines, History Teacher, Darrel C. Swope Middle School, Reno, Nevada; Janis Lariviere, UTeach— Science and Mathematics Teacher Preparation, The University of Texas at Austin; Gaea Leinhardt, Learning Research and Development Center and School of Education, University of Pittsburgh; Alan M. Lesgold, Office of the Provost, University of Pittsburgh; Marcia C. Linn, Education in Mathematics, Science, and Technology, University of California, Berkeley; Kathleen Metz, Cognition and Development, Graduate School of Education, University of California, Berkeley; Thomas Romberg, National Center for Research in Mathematics and Science Education, University of Wisconsin–Madison; and Peter Seixas, Centre for the Study of Historical Consciousness, University of British Columbia.

Although the reviewers listed above have provided many constructive comments and suggestions, they did not see the final draft of the report before its release. The review of this report was overseen by Alan M. Lesgold, University of Pittsburgh. Appointed by the National Research Council, he was responsible for making certain that an independent examination of this report was carried out in accordance with institutional procedures and that all review comments were carefully considered. Responsibility for the final content of this report rests entirely with the authors, the committee, and the institution.

John D. Bransford, *Chair*
M. Suzanne Donovan, *Study Director*

Contents

Handwritten annotation: 3 Learning Principles / 4 Learning Environments / Design Characteristics of

Part I History
(on enclosed CD; not printed in this volume)

Part II Mathematics

(on enclosed CD; not printed in this volume)

Part III Science

A Final Synthesis:
Revisiting the Three Learning Principles

How Students Learn

SCIENCE IN THE CLASSROOM

1

Introduction

M. Suzanne Donovan and John D. Bransford

More than any other species, people are designed to be flexible learners and, from infancy, are active agents in acquiring knowledge and skills. People can invent, record, accumulate, and pass on organized bodies of knowledge that help them understand, shape, exploit, and ornament their environment. Much that each human being knows about the world is acquired informally, but mastery of the accumulated knowledge of generations requires intentional learning, often accomplished in a formal educational setting.

Decades of work in the cognitive and developmental sciences has provided the foundation for an emerging science of learning. This foundation offers conceptions of learning processes and the development of competent performance that can help teachers support their students in the acquisition of knowledge that is the province of formal education. The research literature was synthesized in the National Research Council report *How People Learn: Brain, Mind, Experience, and School.*[1] In this volume, we focus on three fundamental and well-established principles of learning that are highlighted in *How People Learn* and are particularly important for teachers to understand and be able to incorporate in their teaching:

1. Students come to the classroom with preconceptions about how the world works. If their initial understanding is not engaged, they may fail to grasp the new concepts and information, or they may learn them for purposes of a test but revert to their preconceptions outside the classroom.

2. To develop competence in an area of inquiry, students must (a) have a deep foundation of factual knowledge, (b) understand facts and ideas in the context of a conceptual framework, and (c) organize knowledge in ways that facilitate retrieval and application.

3. A "metacognitive" approach to instruction can help students learn to take control of their own learning by defining learning goals and monitoring their progress in achieving them.

A FISH STORY

The images from a children's story, *Fish Is Fish*,[2] help convey the essence of the above principles. In the story, a young fish is very curious about the world outside the water. His good friend the frog, on returning from the land, tells the fish about it excitedly:

> "I have been about the world—hopping here and there,"
> said the frog, "and I have seen extraordinary things."
> "Like what?" asked the fish.
> "Birds," said the frog mysteriously. "Birds!" And he told the
> fish about the birds, who had wings, and two legs, and
> many, many colors. As the frog talked, his friend saw the
> birds fly through his mind like large feathered fish.

The frog continues with descriptions of cows, which the fish imagines as black-and-white spotted fish with horns and udders, and humans, which the fish imagines as fish walking upright and dressed in clothing. Illustrations below from Leo Lionni's *Fish Is Fish* © 1970. Copyright renewed 1998 by Leo Lionni. Used by permission of Random House Children's Books, a division of Random House, Inc.

Principle #1: Engaging Prior Understandings

What Lionni's story captures so effectively is a fundamental insight about learning: *new understandings are constructed on a foundation of existing understandings and experiences.* With research techniques that permit the study of learning in infancy and tools that allow for observation of activity in the brain, we understand as never before how actively humans engage in learning from the earliest days of life (see Box 1-1). The understandings children carry with them into the classroom, even before the start of formal schooling, will shape significantly how they make sense of what they are

BOX 1-1 The Development of Physical Concepts in Infancy

Research studies have demonstrated that infants as young as 3 to 4 months of age develop understandings and expectations about the physical world. For example, they understand that objects need support to prevent them from falling to the ground, that stationary objects may be displaced when they come into contact with moving objects, and that objects at rest must be propelled into motion.[3]

In research by Needham and Baillargeon,[4] infants were shown a table on which a box rested. A gloved hand reached out from a window beside the table and placed another box in one of two locations: on top of the first box (the possible event), and beyond the box—creating the impression that the box was suspended in midair. In this and similar studies, infants look reliably longer at the impossible events, suggesting an awareness and a set of expectations regarding what is and is not physically possible.

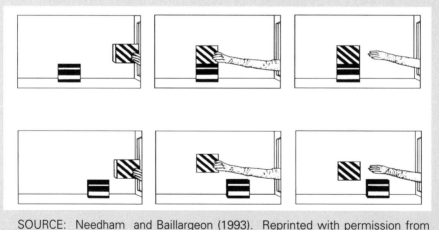

SOURCE: Needham and Baillargeon (1993). Reprinted with permission from Elsevier.

BOX 1-2 Misconceptions About Momentum

Andrea DiSessa[5] conducted a study in which he compared the performance of college physics students at a top technological university with that of elementary schoolchildren on a task involving momentum. He instructed both sets of students to play a computerized game that required them to direct a simulated object (a dynaturtle) so that it would hit a target, and to do so with minimum speed at impact. Participants were introduced to the game and given a hands-on trial that allowed them to apply a few taps with a wooden mallet to a ball on a table before they began.

DiSessa found that both groups of students failed miserably at the task. Despite their training, college physics majors—just like the elementary school children—applied the force when the object was just below the target, failing to take momentum into account. Further investigation with one college student revealed that she knew the relevant physical properties and formulas and would have performed well on a written exam. Yet in the context of the game, she fell back on her untrained conceptions of how the physical world works.

taught. Just as the fish constructed an image of a human as a modified fish, children use what they know to shape their new understandings.

While prior learning is a powerful support for further learning, it can also lead to the development of conceptions that can act as barriers to learning. For example, when told that the earth is round, children may look to reconcile this information with their experience with balls. It seems obvious that one would fall off a round object. Researchers have found that some children solve the paradox by envisioning the earth as a pancake, a "round" shape with a surface on which people could walk without falling off.[6]

How People Learn summarizes a number of studies demonstrating the active, preconception-driven learning that is evident in humans from infancy through adulthood.[7] Preconceptions developed from everyday experiences are often difficult for teachers to change because they generally work well enough in day-to-day contexts. But they can impose serious constraints on understanding formal disciplines. College physics students who do well on classroom exams on the laws of motion, for example, often revert to their untrained, erroneous models outside the classroom. When they are confronted with tasks that require putting their knowledge to use, they fail to take momentum into account, just as do elementary students who have had no physics training (see Box 1-2). If students' preconceptions are not addressed directly, they often memorize content (e.g., formulas in physics), yet still use their experience-based preconceptions to act in the world.

Principle #2: The Essential Role of Factual Knowledge and Conceptual Frameworks in Understanding

The *Fish Is Fish* story also draws attention to the kinds of knowledge, factual and conceptual, needed to support learning with understanding. The frog in the story provides information to the fish about humans, birds, and cows that is accurate and relevant, yet clearly insufficient. Feathers, legs, udders, and sport coats are surface features that distinguish each species. But if the fish (endowed now with human thinking capacity) is to understand how the land species are different from fish and different from each other, these surface features will not be of much help. Some additional, critical concepts are needed—for example, the concept of adaptation. Species that move through the medium of air rather than water have a different mobility challenge. And species that are warm-blooded, unlike those that are cold-blooded, must maintain their body temperature. It will take more explaining of course, but if the fish is to see a bird as something other than a fish with feathers and wings and a human as something other than an upright fish with clothing, then feathers and clothing must be seen as adaptations that help solve the problem of maintaining body temperature, and upright posture and wings must be seen as different solutions to the problem of mobility outside water.

Conceptual information such as a theory of adaptation represents a kind of knowledge that is unlikely to be induced from everyday experiences. It typically takes generations of inquiry to develop this sort of knowledge, and people usually need some help (e.g., interactions with "knowledgeable others") to grasp such organizing concepts.[8]

Lionni's fish, not understanding the described features of the land animals as adaptations to a terrestrial environment, leaps from the water to experience life on land for himself. Since he can neither breathe nor maneuver on land, the fish must be saved by the amphibious frog. The point is well illustrated: learning with understanding affects our ability to apply what is learned (see Box 1-3).

This concept of learning with understanding has two parts: (1) factual knowledge (e.g., about characteristics of different species) must be placed in a conceptual framework (about adaptation) to be well understood; and (2) concepts are given meaning by multiple representations that are rich in factual detail. Competent performance is built on neither factual nor conceptual understanding alone; the concepts take on meaning in the knowledge-rich contexts in which they are applied. In the context of Lionni's story, the general concept of adaptation can be clarified when placed in the context of the specific features of humans, cows, and birds that make the abstract concept of adaptation meaningful.

BOX 1-3 Learning with Understanding Supports Knowledge Use in New Situations

In one of the most famous early studies comparing the effects of "learning a procedure" with "learning with understanding," two groups of children practiced throwing darts at a target underwater.[9] One group received an explanation of refraction of light, which causes the apparent location of the target to be deceptive. The other group only practiced dart throwing, without the explanation. Both groups did equally well on the practice task, which involved a target 12 inches under water. But the group that had been instructed about the abstract principle did much better when they had to transfer to a situation in which the target was under only 4 inches of water. Because they understood what they were doing, the group that had received instruction about the refraction of light could adjust their behavior to the new task.

use of meaningful patterns to remember facts + details

This essential link between the factual knowledge base and a conceptual framework can help illuminate a persistent debate in education: whether we need to emphasize "big ideas" more and facts less, or are producing graduates with a factual knowledge base that is unacceptably thin. While these concerns appear to be at odds, knowledge of facts and knowledge of important organizing ideas are mutually supportive. Studies of experts and novices—in chess, engineering, and many other domains—demonstrate that experts know considerably more relevant detail than novices in tasks within their domain and have better memory for these details (see Box 1-4). But the reason they remember more is that what novices see as separate pieces of information, experts see as organized sets of ideas.

Engineering experts, for example, can look briefly at a complex mass of circuitry and recognize it as an amplifier, and so can reproduce many of its circuits from memory using that one idea. Novices see each circuit separately, and thus remember far fewer in total. Important concepts, such as that of an amplifier, structure both what experts notice and what they are able to store in memory. Using concepts to organize information stored in memory allows for much more effective retrieval and application. Thus, the issue is not whether to emphasize facts or "big ideas" (conceptual knowledge); both are needed. Memory of factual knowledge is enhanced by conceptual knowledge, and conceptual knowledge is clarified as it is used to help organize constellations of important details. Teaching for understanding, then, requires that the core concepts such as adaptation that organize the knowledge of experts also organize instruction. This does not mean that that factual knowledge now typically taught, such as the characteristics of fish, birds, and mammals, must be replaced. Rather, that factual information is given new meaning and a new organization in memory because those features are seen as adaptive characteristics.

Yes

BOX 1-4   **Experts Remember Considerably More Relevant Detail Than Novices in Tasks Within Their Domain**

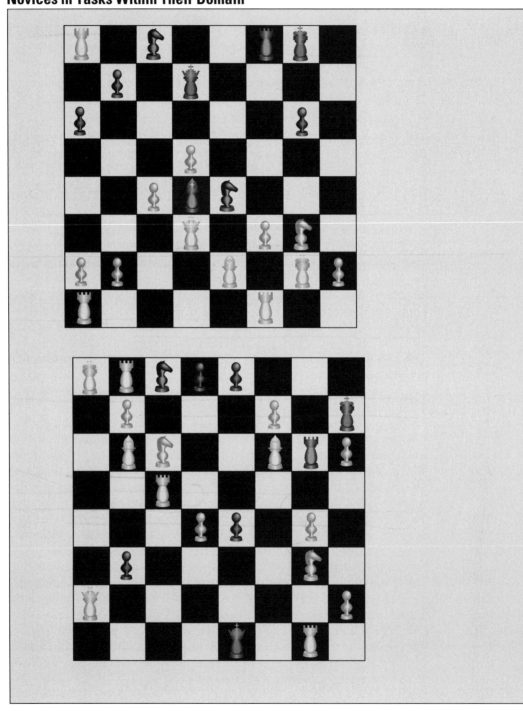

In one study, a chess master, a Class A player (good but not a master), and a novice were given 5 seconds to view a chess board position from the middle of a chess game (see below).

After 5 seconds the board was covered, and each participant attempted to reconstruct the board position on another board. This procedure was repeated for multiple trials until everyone received a perfect score. On the first trial, the master player correctly placed many more pieces than the Class A player, who in turn placed more than the novice: 16, 8, and 4, respectively. (See data graphed below.)

However, these results occurred only when the chess pieces were arranged in configurations that conformed to meaningful games of chess. When chess pieces were randomized and presented for 5 seconds, the recall of the chess master and Class A player was the same as that of the novice—they all placed 2 to 3 positions correctly. The apparent difference in memory capacity is due to a difference in pattern recognition. What the expert can remember as a single meaningful pattern, novices must remember as separate, unrelated items.

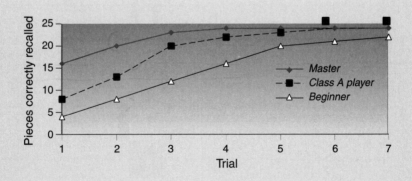

SOURCE: Chase and Simon (1973). Reprinted with permission from Elsevier.

Principle #3: The Importance of Self-Monitoring

Meta-Cognition

Hero though he is for saving the fish's life, the frog in Lionni's story gets poor marks as a teacher. But the burden of learning does not fall on the teacher alone. Even the best instructional efforts can be successful only if the student can make use of the opportunity to learn. Helping students become effective learners is at the heart of the third key principle: a "metacognitive" or self-monitoring approach can help students develop the ability to take control of their own learning, consciously define learning goals, and monitor their progress in achieving them. Some teachers introduce the idea of metacognition to their students by saying, You are the owners and operators of your own brain, but it came without an instruction book. We need to learn how we learn.

"Meta" is a prefix that can mean after, along with, or beyond. In the psychological literature, "metacognition" is used to refer to people's knowledge about themselves as information processors. This includes knowledge about what we need to do in order to learn and remember information (e.g., most adults know that they need to rehearse an unfamiliar phone number to keep it active in short-term memory while they walk across the room to dial the phone). And it includes the ability to monitor our current understanding to make sure we understand (see Box 1-5). Other examples include monitoring the degree to which we have been helpful to a group working on a project.[10]

BOX 1-5 Metacognitive Monitoring: An Example

Read the following passage from a literary critic, and pay attention to the strategies you use to comprehend:

If a serious literary critic were to write a favorable, full-length review of How Could I Tell Mother She Frightened My Boyfriends Away, Grace Plumbuster's new story, his startled readers would assume that he had gone mad, or that Grace Plumbuster was his editor's wife.

Most good readers have to back up several times in order to grasp the meaning of this passage. In contrast, poor readers tend to simply read it all the way through without pausing and asking if the passage makes sense. Needless to say, when asked to paraphrase the passage they fall short.

SOURCE: Whimbey and Whimbey (1975, p. 42).

metacognition / meta-memory

In Lionni's story, the fish accepted the information about life on land rather passively. Had he been monitoring his understanding and actively comparing it with what he already knew, he might have noted that putting on a hat and jacket would be rather uncomfortable for a fish and would slow his swimming in the worst way. Had he been more engaged in figuring out what the frog meant, he might have asked why humans would make themselves uncomfortable and compromise their mobility. A good answer to his questions might have set the stage for learning about differences between humans and fish, and ultimately about the notion of adaptation. The concept of metacognition includes an awareness of the need to ask how new knowledge relates to or challenges what one already knows—questions that stimulate additional inquiry that helps guide further learning.[11]

The early work on metacognition was conducted with young children in laboratory contexts.[12] In studies of "metamemory," for example, young children might be shown a series of pictures (e.g., drum, tree, cup) and asked to remember them after 15 seconds of delay (with the pictures no longer visible). Adults who receive this task spontaneously rehearse during the 15-second interval. Many of the children did not. When they were explicitly told to rehearse, they would do so, and their memory was very good. But when the children took part in subsequent trials and were not reminded to rehearse, many failed to rehearse even though they were highly motivated to perform well in the memory test. These findings suggest that the children had not made the "metamemory" connection between their rehearsal strategies and their short-term memory abilities.[13]

Over time, research on metacognition (of which metamemory is considered a subset) moved from laboratory settings to the classroom. One of the most striking applications of a metacognitive approach to instruction was pioneered by Palincsar and Brown in the context of "reciprocal teaching."[14] Middle school students worked in groups (guided by a teacher) to help one another learn to read with understanding. A key to achieving this goal involves the ability to monitor one's ongoing comprehension and to initiate strategies such as rereading or asking questions when one's comprehension falters. (Box 1-5 illustrates this point.) When implemented appropriately, reciprocal teaching has been shown to have strong effects on improving students' abilities to read with understanding in order to learn.

Appropriate kinds of self-monitoring and reflection have been demonstrated to support learning with understanding in a variety of areas. In one study,[15] for example, students who were directed to engage in self-explanation as they solved mathematics problems developed deeper conceptual understanding than did students who solved those same problems but did not engage in self-explanation. This was true even though the common time limitation on both groups meant that the self-explaining students solved fewer problems in total.

Helping students become more metacognitive about their own thinking and learning is closely tied to teaching practices that emphasize self-assessment. The early work of Thorndike[16] demonstrated that feedback is important for learning. However, there is a difference between responding to feedback that someone else provides and actively seeking feedback in order to assess one's current levels of thinking and understanding. Providing support for self-assessment is an important component of effective teaching. This can include giving students opportunities to test their ideas by building things and seeing whether they work, performing experiments that seek to falsify hypotheses, and so forth. Support for self-assessment is also provided by opportunities for discussion where teachers and students can express different views and explore which ones appear to make the most sense. Such questioning models the kind of dialogue that effective learners internalize. Helping students explicitly understand that a major purpose of these activities is to support metacognitive learning is an important component of successful teaching strategies.[17]

Supporting students to become aware of and engaged in their own learning will serve them well in all learning endeavors. To be optimally effective, however, some metacognitive strategies need to be taught in the context of individual subject areas. For example, guiding one's learning in a particular subject area requires awareness of the disciplinary standards for knowing. To illustrate, asking the question "What is the evidence for this claim?" is relevant whether one is studying history, science, or mathematics. However, what counts as evidence often differs. In mathematics, for example, formal proof is very important. In science, formal proofs are used when possible, but empirical observations and experimental data also play a major role. In history, multiple sources of evidence are sought and attention to the perspective from which an author writes and to the purpose of the writing is particularly important. Overall, knowledge of the discipline one is studying affects people's abilities to monitor their own understanding and evaluate others' claims effectively.

LEARNING ENVIRONMENTS AND THE DESIGN OF INSTRUCTION

The key principles of learning discussed above can be organized into a framework for thinking about teaching, learning, and the design of classroom and school environments. In *How People Learn*, four design characteristics are described that can be used as lenses to evaluate the effectiveness of teaching and learning environments. These lenses are not themselves research findings; rather, they are implications drawn from the research base:

(margin annotation: examples of self-assessment)

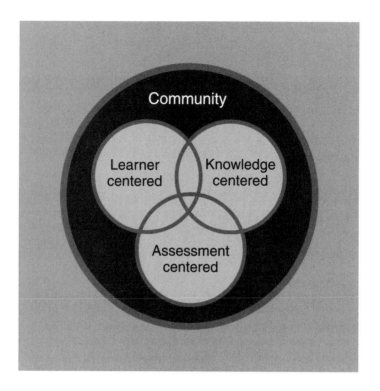

FIGURE 1-1 *Perspectives on learning environments.*

- The *learner-centered lens* encourages attention to preconceptions, and begins instruction with what students think and know.
- The *knowledge-centered lens* focuses on what is to be taught, why it is taught, and what mastery looks like.
- The *assessment-centered lens* emphasizes the need to provide frequent opportunities to make students' thinking and learning visible as a guide for both the teacher and the student in learning and instruction.
- The *community-centered lens* encourages a culture of questioning, respect, and risk taking.

These aspects of the classroom environment are illustrated in Figure 1-1 and are discussed below.

Learner-Centered Classroom Environments

Instruction must begin with close attention to students' ideas, knowledge, skills, and attitudes, which provide the foundation on which new learning builds. Sometimes, as in the case of Lionni's fish, learners' existing ideas lead to misconceptions. More important, however, those existing conceptions can also provide a path to new understandings. Lionni's fish mistakenly projects the model of a fish onto humans, birds, and cows. But the fish does know a lot about being a fish, and that experience can provide a starting point for understanding adaptation. How do the scales and fins of a fish help it survive? How would clothing and feathers affect a fish? The fish's existing knowledge and experience provide a route to understanding adaptation in other species. Similarly, the ideas and experiences of students provide a route to new understandings both about and beyond their experience.

Sometimes the experiences relevant to teaching would appear to be similar for all students: the ways in which forces act on a falling ball or feather, for example. But students in any classroom are likely to differ in how much they have been encouraged to observe, think about, or talk about a falling ball or feather. Differences may be larger still when the subject is a social rather than a natural phenomenon because the experiences themselves, as well as norms regarding reflection, expression, and interaction, differ for children from different families, communities, and cultures. Finally, students' expectations regarding their own performances, including what it means to be intelligent, can differ in ways that affect their persistence in and engagement with learning.

Being learner-centered, then, involves paying attention to students' backgrounds and cultural values, as well as to their abilities. To build effectively on what learners bring to the classroom, teachers must pay close attention to individual students' starting points and to their progress on learning tasks. They must present students with "just-manageable difficulties"—challenging enough to maintain engagement and yet not so challenging as to lead to discouragement. They must find the strengths that will help students connect with the information being taught. Unless these connections are made explicitly, they often remain inert and so do not support subsequent learning.

Knowledge-Centered Classroom Environments

While the learner-centered aspects of the classroom environment focus on the student as the starting point, the knowledge-centered aspects focus on what is taught (subject matter), why it is taught (understanding), how the knowledge should be organized to support the development of expertise (curriculum), and what competence or mastery looks like (learning goals). Several important questions arise when one adopts the knowledge-centered lens:

- What is it important for students to know and be able to do?
- What are the core concepts that organize our understanding of this subject matter, and what concrete cases and detailed knowledge will allow students to master those concepts effectively?
- [The knowledge-centered lens overlaps with the assessment-centered lens (discussed below) when we ask], How will we know when students achieve mastery?[18] This question overlaps the knowledge-centered and assessment-centered lenses.

An important point that emerges from the expert–novice literature is the need to emphasize *connected* knowledge that is organized around the foundational ideas of a discipline. Research on expertise shows that it is the organization of knowledge that underlies experts' abilities to understand and solve problems.[19] Bruner, one of the founding fathers of the new science of learning, has long argued the importance of this insight to education:[20]

> The curriculum of a subject should be determined by the most fundamental understanding that can be achieved of the underlying principles that give structure to a subject. Teaching specific topics or skills without making clear their context in the broader fundamental structure of a field of knowledge is uneconomical. . . . An understanding of fundamental principles and ideas appears to be the main road to adequate transfer of training. To understand something as a specific instance of a more general case—which is what understanding a more fundamental structure means—is to have learned not only a specific thing but also a model for understanding other things like it that one may encounter.

Knowledge-centered and learner-centered environments intersect when educators take seriously the idea that students must be supported to develop expertise over time; it is not sufficient to simply provide them with expert models and expect them to learn. For example, intentionally organizing subject matter to allow students to follow a path of "progressive differentiation" (e.g., from qualitative understanding to more precise quantitative understanding of a particular phenomenon) involves a simultaneous focus on the structure of the knowledge to be mastered and the learning process of students.[21]

In a comparative study of the teaching of mathematics in China and the United States, Ma sought to understand why Chinese students outperform students from the United States in elementary mathematics, even though teachers in China often have less formal education. What she documents is that Chinese teachers are far more likely to identify core mathematical concepts (such as decomposing a number in subtraction with regrouping), to plan instruction to support mastery of the skills and knowledge required for conceptual understanding, and to use those concepts to develop clear connections across topics (see Box 1-6).

If identifying a set of "enduring connected ideas" is critical to effective educational design, it is a task not just for teachers, but also for the developers of curricula, text books, and other instructional materials; universities and other teacher preparation institutions; and the public and private groups involved in developing subject matter standards for students and their teachers. There is some good work already in place, but much more needs to be done. Indeed, an American Association for the Advancement of Science review of middle school and high school science textbooks found that although a great deal of detailed and sophisticated material was presented, very little attention was given to the concepts that support an understanding of the discipline.[22]

The four science chapters in this volume describe core ideas in teaching about light, gravity, genetics and evolution that support conceptual understanding and that connect the particular topic to the larger discipline. Because textbooks sometimes focus primarily on facts and details and neglect organizing principles, creating a knowledge-centered classroom will often require that a teacher go beyond the textbook to help students see a structure to the knowledge, mainly by introducing them to essential concepts. These chapters provide examples of how this might be done.

Assessment-Centered Classroom Environments

Formative assessments—ongoing assessments designed to make students' thinking visible to both teachers and students—are essential. Assessments are a central feature of both a learner-centered and a knowledge-centered classroom. They permit the teacher to grasp students' preconceptions, which is critical to working with and building on those notions. Once the knowledge to be learned is well defined, assessment is required to monitor student progress (in mastering concepts as well as factual information), to understand where students are in the developmental path from informal to formal thinking, and to design instruction that is responsive to student progress.

An important feature of the assessment-centered classroom is assessment that supports learning by providing students with opportunities to revise and improve their thinking.[23] Such assessments help students see their own progress over time and point to problems that need to be addressed in instruction. They may be quite informal. A physics teacher, for example, reports showing students who are about to study structure a video clip of a bridge collapsing. He asks his students why they think the bridge collapsed. In giving their answers, the students reveal their preconceptions about structure. Differences in their answers provide puzzles that engage the students in self-questioning. As the students study structure, they can mark their changing understanding against their initial beliefs. Assessment in this sense provides a starting point for additional instruction rather than a summative ending. Formative assessments are often referred to as "classroom-based assessments" because, as compared with standardized assessments, they are most likely to occur in the context of the classrooms. However, many classroom-based assessments are summative rather than formative (they are used to provide grades at the end of a unit with no opportunities to revise). In addition, one can use standardized assessments in a formative manner (e.g., to help teachers identify areas where students need special help).

Ultimately, students need to develop metacognitive abilities—the habits of mind necessary to assess their own progress—rather than relying solely on external indicators. A number of studies show that achievement improves when students are encouraged to assess their own contributions and work.[24] It is also important to help students assess the kinds of strategies they are using to learn and solve problems. For example, in quantitative courses such as physics, many students simply focus on formulas and fail to think first about the problem to be solved and its relation to key ideas in the discipline (e.g., Newton's second law). When students are helped to do the latter, their performance on new problems greatly improves.[25]

The classroom interactions described in the following chapters provide many examples of formative assessment in action, though these interactions are often not referred to as assessments. Early activities or problems given to students are designed to make student thinking public and, therefore, observable by teachers. Work in groups and class discussions provide students with the opportunity to ask each other questions and revise their own thinking. In some cases, the formative assessments are formal, but even when informal the teaching described in the chapters involves frequent opportunities for both teachers and students to assess understanding and its progress over time.

Community-Centered Classroom Environments

A community-centered approach requires the development of norms for the classroom and school, as well as connections to the outside world, that support core learning values. Learning is influenced in fundamental ways by the context in which it takes place. Every community, including classrooms and schools, operates with a set of norms, a culture—explicit or implicit—that influences interactions among individuals. This culture, in turn, mediates learning. The principles of *How People Learn* have important im-

BOX 1-6 Organizing Knowledge Around Core Concepts: Subtraction with Regrouping[26]

A study by Ma[27] compares the knowledge of elementary mathematics of teachers in the United States and in China. She gives the teachers the following scenario (p. 1):

> *Look at these questions (52 – 25; 91 – 79 etc.). How would you approach these problems if you were teaching second grade? What would you say pupils would need to understand or be able to do before they could start learning subtraction with regrouping?*

The responses of teachers were wide-ranging, reflecting very different levels of understanding of the core mathematical concepts. Some teachers focused on the need for students to learn the *procedure* for subtraction with regrouping (p. 2):

> *Whereas there is a number like 21 – 9, they would need to know that you cannot subtract 9 from 1, then in turn you have to borrow a 10 from the tens space, and when you borrow that 1, it equals 10, you cross out the 2 that you had, you turn it into a 10, you now have 11 – 9, you do that subtraction problem then you have the 1 left and you bring it down.*

Some teachers in both the United States and China saw the knowledge to be mastered as procedural, though the proportion who held this view was considerably higher in the United States. Many teachers in both countries believed students needed a conceptual understanding, but within this group there were considerable differences. Some teachers wanted children to think through what they were doing, while others wanted them to understand core mathematical concepts. The difference can be seen in the two explanations below.

> *They have to understand what the number 64 means. . . . I would show that the number 64, and the number 5 tens and 14 ones, equal the 64. I would try to draw the comparison between that because when you are doing regrouping it is not so much knowing the facts, it is the regrouping part that has to be understood. The regrouping right from the beginning.*

This explanation is more conceptual than the first and helps students think more deeply about the subtraction problem. But it does not make clear to students the more fundamental concept of the place value system that allows the subtraction problems to be connected to other areas of mathematics. In the place value system, numbers are "composed" of tens. Students already have been taught to compose tens as 10 ones, and hundreds as 10 tens. A Chinese teacher explains as follows (p. 11):

> *What is the rate for composing a higher value unit? The answer is simple: 10. Ask students how many ones there are in a 10, or ask them what the rate for composing a higher value unit is, their answers will be the same: 10. However, the effect of the two questions on their learning is not the*

same. When you remind students that 1 ten equals 10 ones, you tell them the fact that is used in the procedure. And, this somehow confines them to the fact. When you require them to think about the rate for composing a higher value unit, you lead them to a theory that explains the fact as well as the procedure. Such an understanding is more powerful than a specific fact. It can be applied to more situations. Once they realize that the rate of composing a higher value unit, 10 is the reason why we decompose a ten into 10 ones, they will apply it to other situations. You don't need to remind them again that 1 hundred equals 10 tens when in the future they learn subtraction with three-digit numbers. They will be able to figure it out on their own.

Emphasizing core concepts does not imply less of an emphasis on mastery of procedures or algorithms. Rather, it suggests that procedural knowledge and skills be *organized around core concepts.* Ma describes those Chinese teachers who emphasize core concepts as seeing the knowledge in "packages" in which the concepts and skills are related. While the packages differed somewhat from teacher to teacher, the knowledge "pieces" to be included were the same. She illustrates a knowledge package for subtraction with regrouping, which is reproduced below (p. 19).

The two shaded elements in the knowledge package are considered critical. "Addition and subtraction within 20" is seen as the ability that anchors more complex problem solving with larger numbers. That ability is viewed as both conceptual and procedural. "Composing and decomposing a higher value unit" is the core concept that ties this set of problems to the mathematics students have done in the past and to all other areas of mathematics they will learn in the future.

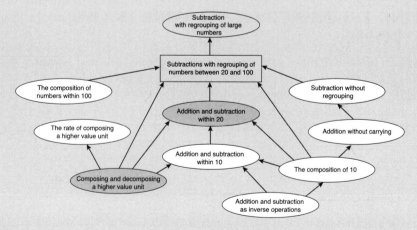

SOURCE: Ma (1999). Illustration reprinted with permission of Lawrence Erlbaum Associates.

plications for classroom culture. Consider the finding that new learning builds on existing conceptions, for example. If classroom norms encourage and reward students only for being "right," we would expect students to hesitate when asked to reveal their unschooled thinking. And yet revealing preconceptions and changing ideas in the course of instruction is a critical component of effective learning and responsive teaching. A focus on student thinking requires classroom norms that encourage the expression of ideas (tentative and certain, partially and fully formed), as well as risk taking. It requires that mistakes be viewed not as revelations of inadequacy, but as helpful contributions in the search for understanding.[28]

Similarly, effective approaches to teaching metacognitive strategies rely on initial teacher modeling of the monitoring process, with a gradual shift to students. Through asking questions of other students, skills at monitoring understanding are honed, and through answering the questions of fellow students, understanding of what one has communicated effectively is strengthened. To those ends, classroom norms that encourage questioning and allow students to try the role of the questioner (sometimes reserved for teachers) are important.

While the chapters in this volume make few direct references to learning communities, they are filled with descriptions of interactions revealing classroom cultures that support learning with understanding. In these classrooms, students are encouraged to question; there is much discussion among students who work to solve problems in groups. Teachers ask many probing questions, and incorrect or naïve answers to questions are explored with interest, as are different strategies for analyzing a problem and reaching a solution.

PUTTING THE PRINCIPLES TO WORK IN THE CLASSROOM

Although the key findings from the research literature reviewed above have clear implications for practice, they are not at a level of specificity that would allow them to be immediately useful to teachers. While teachers may fully grasp the importance of working with students' prior conceptions, they need to know the typical conceptions of students with respect to the topic about to be taught. For example, it may help science teachers to know that students harbor misconceptions that can be problematic, but those teachers will be in a much better position to teach a unit on light if they know specifically what misconceptions students typically exhibit when learning about light.

Moreover, while teachers may be fully convinced that knowledge should be organized around important concepts, the concepts that help organize their particular topic may not be at all clear. History teachers may know that they are to teach certain eras, for example, but they often have little support in identifying core concepts that will allow students to understand the era more deeply than would be required to reproduce a set of facts. To make this observation is in no way to fault teachers. Indeed, as the group involved in this project engaged in the discussion, drafting, and review of various chapters of this volume, it became clear that the relevant core concepts in specific areas are not always obvious, transparent, or uncontested.

Finally, approaches to supporting metacognition can be quite difficult to carry out in classroom contexts. Some approaches to instruction reduce metacognition to its simplest form, such as making note of the subtitles in a text and what they signal about what is to come, or rereading for meaning. The more challenging tasks of metacognition are difficult to reduce to an instructional recipe: to help students develop the habits of mind to reflect spontaneously on their own thinking and problem solving, to encourage them to activate relevant background knowledge and monitor their understanding, and to support them in trying the lens through which those in a particular discipline view the world. The teacher–student interactions described in the chapters of this volume and the discipline-specific examples of supporting students in monitoring their thinking give texture to the instructional challenge that a list of metacognitive strategies could not.

INTENT AND ORGANIZATION OF THIS VOLUME

In the preface, we note that this volume is intended to take the work of *How People Learn* a next step in specificity: to provide examples of how its principles and findings might be incorporated in the teaching of a set of topics that frequently appear in the K–12 curriculum. The goal is to provide for teachers what we have argued above is critical to effective learning—the application of concepts (about learning) in enough different, concrete contexts to give them deeper meaning.

To this end, we invited contributions from researchers with extensive experience in teaching or partnering with teachers, whose work incorporates the ideas highlighted in *How People Learn*. The chapter authors were given leeway in the extent to which the three learning principles and the four classroom characteristics described above were treated explicitly or implicitly. Most of the authors chose to emphasize the three learning principles explicitly as they described their lessons and findings. The four design characteristics of the *How People Learn* framework (Figure 1-2) are implicitly represented in the activities sketched in each of the chapters but often not discussed explicitly. Interested readers can map these discussions to the *How People Learn* framework if they desire.

While we began with a common description of our goal, we had no common model from which to work. One can point to excellent research papers on principles of learning, but the chapters in this volume are far more focused on teaching a particular topic. There are also examples of excellent curricula, but the goal of these chapters is to give far more attention to the principles of learning and their incorporation into teaching than is typical of curriculum materials. Thus the authors were charting new territory as they undertook this task, and each found a somewhat different path.

This volume includes four science chapters. Following the introductory Chapter 2, the science part treats three very different topics: light and shadow at the elementary school level (Chapter 3), gravity at the middle school level (Chapter 4), and genetics and evolution at the high school level (Chapter 5). The sequence of K–12 science topics in the United States is far less predictable than, for example, mathematics. The topics in this part of the volume were chosen at the three grade levels for the opportunities they provide to explore the learning principles of interest, rather than for their common representation in a standard curricular sequences. Light as a topic might just as well appear in middle or high school as in elementary school, for example, and physics is generally taught either in middle school or high school.

The major focus of the volume is student learning. It is clear that successful and sustainable changes in educational practice also require learning by others, including teachers, principals, superintendents, parents, and community members. For the present volume, however, student learning is the focus, and issues of adult learning are left for others to take up.

The willingness of the chapter authors to accept this task represents an outstanding contribution to the field. First, all the authors devoted considerable time to this effort—more than any of them had anticipated initially. Second, they did so knowing that some readers will disagree with virtually every teaching decision discussed in these chapters. But by making their thinking visible and inviting discussion, they are helping the field progress as a whole. The examples discussed in this volume are not offered as "the" way to teach, but as approaches to instruction that in some important respects are designed to incorporate the principles of learning highlighted in *How People Learn* and that can serve as valuable examples for further discussion.

In 1960, Nobel laureate Richard Feynman, who was well known as an extraordinary teacher, delivered a series of lectures in introductory physics that were recorded and preserved. Feynman's focus was on the fundamental principles of physics, not the fundamental principles of learning. But his lessons apply nonetheless. He emphasized how little the fundamental principles of physics "as we now understand them" tell us about the complexity of the world despite the enormous importance of the insights they offer. Feynman offered an effective analogy for the relationship between understanding general principles identified through scientific efforts and understanding the far more complex set of behaviors for which those principles provide only a broad set of constraints:[29]

> We can imagine that this complicated array of moving things which constitutes "the world" is something like a great chess game being played by the gods, and we are observers of the game. We do not know what the rules of the game are; all we are allowed to do is to *watch* the playing. Of course, if we watch long enough, we may eventually catch on to a few of the rules. *The rules of the game* are what we mean by *fundamental physics*. Even if we knew every rule, however, we might not be able to understand why a particular move is made in the game, merely because it is too complicated and our minds are limited. If you play chess you must know that it is easy to learn all the rules, and yet it is often very hard to select the best move or to understand why a player moves as he does. . . . Aside from not knowing all of the rules, what we really can explain in terms of those rules is very limited, because almost all situations are so enormously complicated that we cannot follow the plays of the game using the rules, much less tell what is going to happen next. (p. 24)

The individual chapters in this volume might be viewed as presentations of the strategies taken by individuals (or teams) who understand the rules of the teaching and learning "game" *as we now understand them.* Feynman's metaphor is helpful in two respects. First, what each chapter offers goes well beyond the science of learning and relies on creativity in strategy development. And yet what we know from research thus far is critical in defining the constraints on strategy development. Second, what we expect to learn from a well-played game (in this case, what we expect to learn from well-conceptualized instruction) is not how to reproduce it. Rather, we look for insights about playing/teaching well that can be brought to one's own game. Even if we could replicate every move, this would be of little help. In an actual game, the best move must be identified in response to another party's move. In just such a fashion, a teacher's "game" must respond to the rather unpredictable "moves" of the students in the classroom whose learning is the target.

This, then, is not a "how to" book, but a discussion of strategies that incorporate the rules of the game as we currently understand them. The science of learning is a young, emerging one. We expect our understanding to evolve as we design new learning opportunities and observe the outcomes, as we study learning among children in different contexts and from different backgrounds, and as emerging research techniques and opportunities provide new insights. These chapters, then, might best be viewed as part of a conversation begun some years ago with the first *How People Learn* volume. By clarifying ideas through a set of rich examples, we hope to encourage the continuation of a productive dialogue well into the future.

NOTES

1. National Research Council, 2000.
2. Lionni, 1970.
3. National Research Council, 2000, p. 84.
4. Needham and Baillargeon, 1993.
5. diSessa, 1982.
6. Vosniadou and Brewer, 1989.
7. Carey and Gelman, 1991; Driver et al., 1994.
8. Hanson, 1970.
9. Judd, 1908; see a conceptual replication by Hendrickson and Schroeder, 1941.
10. White and Fredrickson, 1998.
11. Bransford and Schwartz, 1999.
12. Brown, 1975; Flavell, 1973.
13. Keeney et al., 1967.
14. Palincsar and Brown, 1984.
15. Aleven and Koedinger, 2002.
16. Thorndike, 1913.
17. Brown et al., 1983.
18. Wood and Sellers, 1997.
19. National Research Council, 2000, Chapter 2.
20. Bruner, 1960, pp. 6, 25, 31.
21. National Research Council, 2000.
22. American Association for the Advancement of Science Project 2061 Website. http://www.project2061.org/curriculum.html.
23. Barron et al., 1998; Black and William, 1989; Hunt and Minstrell, 1994; Vye et al., 1998.
24. Lin and Lehman, 1999; National Research Council, 2000; White and Fredrickson, 1998.
25. Leonard et al., 1996.
26. National Research Council, 2003, pp. 78-79.
27. Ma, 1999.
28. Brown and Campione, 1994; Cobb et al., 1992.
29. Feynman, 1995, p. 24.

REFERENCES

Aleven, V., and Koedinger, K. (2002). An effective metacognitive strategy—Learning by doing and explaining with a computer-based cognitive tutor. *Cognitive Science, 26*, 147-179.

American Association for the Advancement of Science. (2004). About *Project 2061*. Available: http://www.project2061.org/about/default/htm. [August 11, 2004].

Barron, B.J., Schwartz, D.L., Vye, N.J., Moore, A., Petrosino, A., Zech, L., Bransford, J.D., and Cognition and Technology Group at Vanderbilt. (1998). Doing with understanding: Lessons from research on problem and project-based learning. *Journal of Learning Sciences, 7*(3 and 4), 271-312.

Black, P., and William, D. (1989). Assessment and classroom learning. *Special Issue of Assessment in Education: Principles, Policy and Practice, 5*(1), 7-75.

Bransford, J.D., and Schwartz, D.L. (1999). Rethinking transfer: A simple proposal with multiple implications. *Review of Research in Education, 24*(40), 61-100.

Brown, A.L. (1975). The development of memory: Knowing about knowing and knowing how to know. In H.W. Reese (Ed.), *Advances in child development and behavior* (p. 10). New York: Academic Press.

Brown, A.L., and Campione, J.C. (1994). Guided discovery in a community of learners. In K. McGilly (Ed.), *Classroom lessons: Integrating cognitive theory and classroom practices.* Cambridge, MA: MIT Press.

Brown, A.L., Bransford, J.D., Ferrara, R.A., and Campione J.C. (1983). Learning, remembering, and understanding. In J.H. Flavell and E.M Markman (Eds.), *Handbook of child psychology: Cognitive development volume 3* (pp. 78-166). New York: Wiley.

Bruner, J. (1960). *The process of education.* Cambridge, MA: Harvard University Press.

Carey, S., and Gelman, R. (1991). *The epigenesis of mind: Essays on biology and cognition.* Mahwah, NJ: Lawrence Erlbaum Associates.

Chase, W.G., and Simon, H.A. (1973). Perception in chess. *Cognitive Psychology, 4*(1), 55-81.

Cobb P., Yackel, E., and Wood, T. (1992). A constructivist alternative to the representational view of mind in mathematics education. *Journal for Research in Mathematics Education, 19,* 99-114.

Cognition and Technology Group at Vanderbilt. (1996). Looking at technology in context: A framework for understanding technology and education research. In D.C. Berliner and R.C. Calfee (Eds.), *The handbook of educational psychology* (pp. 807-840). New York: Simon and Schuster-MacMillan.

diSessa, A. (1982). Unlearning Aristotelian physics: A study of knowledge-based learning. *Cognitive Science, 6*(2), 37-75.

Driver, R., Squires, A., Rushworth, P., and Wood-Robinson, V. (1994). *Making sense out of secondary science.* London, England: Routledge Press.

Feynman, R.P. (1995). *Six easy pieces: Essentials of physics explained by its most brilliant teacher.* Reading, MA: Perseus Books.

Flavell, J.H. (1973). Metacognitive aspects of problem-solving. In L.B. Resnick (Ed.), *The nature of intelligence.* Mahwah, NJ: Lawrence Erlbaum Associates.

Hanson, N.R. (1970). A picture theory of theory meaning. In R.G. Colodny (Ed.), *The nature and function of scientific theories* (pp. 233-274). Pittsburgh, PA: University of Pittsburgh Press.

Hendrickson, G., and Schroeder, W.H. (1941). Transfer training in learning to hit a submerged target. *Journal of Educational Psychology, 32,* 205-213.

Hunt, E., and Minstrell, J. (1994). A cognitive approach to the teaching of physics. In K. McGilly (Ed.), *Classroom lessons: Integrating cognitive theory and classroom practice* (pp. 51-74). Cambridge, MA: MIT Press.

Judd, C.H. (1908). The relation of special training to general intelligence. *Educational Review, 36,* 28-42.

Keeney, T.J., Cannizzo, S.R., and Flavell, J.H. (1967). Spontaneous and induced verbal rehearsal in a recall task. *Child Development, 38,* 953-966.

Leonard, W.J., Dufresne, R.J., and Mestre, J.P. (1996). Using qualitative problem solving strategies to highlight the role of conceptual knowledge in solving problems. *American Journal of Physics, 64*, 1495-1503.

Lin, X.D., and Lehman, J. (1999). Supporting learning of variable control in a computer-based biology environment: Effects of prompting college students to reflect on their own thinking. *Journal of Research in Science Teaching, 36*(7), 837-858.

Lionni, L. (1970). *Fish is fish.* New York: Scholastic Press.

Ma, L. (1999). *Knowing and teaching elementary mathematics.* Mahwah, NJ: Lawrence Erlbaum Associates.

National Research Council. (1999). *How people learn: Brain, mind, experience, and school.* Committee on Developments in the Science of Learning. J. D. Bransford, A.L. Brown, and R.R. Cocking (Eds.). Commission on Behavioral and Social Sciences and Education. Washington, DC: National Academy Press.

National Research Council. (2000). *How people learn: Brain, mind, experience, and school, Expanded edition.* Committee on Developments in the Science of Learning and Committee on Learning Research and Educational Practice. J.D. Bransford, A. Brown, and R.R. Cocking (Eds.). Commission on Behavioral and Social Sciences and Education. Washington, DC: National Academy Press.

National Research Council. (2003). *Learning and instruction: A SERP research agenda.* Panel on Learning and Instruction, Strategic Education Research Partnership. M.S. Donovan and J.W. Pellegrino (Eds.). Division of Behavioral and Social Sciences and Education. Washington, DC: The National Academies Press.

Needham, A., and Baillargeon, R. (1993). Intuitions about support in 4 1/2 month-old-infants. *Cognition, 47*(2), 121-148.

Palincsar, A.S., and Brown, A.L. (1984). Reciprocal teaching of comprehension monitoring activities. *Cognition and Instruction, 1*, 117-175.

Thorndike, E.L. (1913). *Educational psychology* (Vols. 1 and 2). New York: Columbia University Press.

Vosniadou, S., and Brewer, W.F. (1989). *The concept of the Earth's shape: A study of conceptual change in childhood.* Unpublished manuscript. Champaign, IL: Center for the Study of Reading, University of Illinois.

Vye, N.J., Schwartz, D.L., Bransford, J.D., Barron, B.J., Zech, L., and Cognitive and Technology Group at Vanderbilt. (1998). SMART environments that support monitoring, reflection, and revision. In D. Hacker, J. Dunlosky, and A. Graessner (Eds.), *Metacognition in educational theory and practice.* Mahwah, NJ: Lawrence Erlbaum Associates.

Whimbey, A., and Whimbey, L.S. (1975). *Intelligence can be taught.* New York: Dutton.

White, B.Y., and Fredrickson, J.R. (1998). Inquiry, modeling, and metacognition: Making science accessible to all students. *Cognition and Instruction, 16*(1), 3-118.

Wood, T., and Sellers, P. (1997). Deepening the analysis: Longitudinal assessment of a problem-centered mathematics program. *Journal for Research in Mathematics Education, 28*, 163-186.

Part III

SCIENCE

Pages 27-394 are not printed in this volume.
They are on the CD attached to the back cover.

9

Scientific Inquiry and
How People Learn

John D. Bransford and M. Suzanne Donovan

Many of us learned science in school by studying textbooks that reported the conclusions of what scientists have learned over the decades. To
know science meant to know the definitions of scientific terms and important discoveries of the past. We learned that an insect has three body parts
and six legs, for example, and that water (H_2O) is a molecule composed of
two hydrogen atoms and one oxygen atom. We learned that the planets in
our solar system revolve around the sun and that gravity holds us to the
earth. To be good at science meant to reproduce such information as accurately and completely as possible. The focus of this kind of instruction was
on *what* scientists know.

Of course, many of us were also introduced to "the scientific method."
This typically involved some variation on steps such as "formulate a hypothesis, devise a way to test the hypothesis, conduct your test, form conclusions
based on your findings, and communicate what you have found." Often
information about the scientific method was simply one more set of facts to
be memorized. But some of us were given opportunities to use the scientific
method to perform hands-on experiments. We might have tested whether
wet or dry paper towels could hold the most weight; whether potential
insulators such as aluminum foil, paper, or wool were the best ways to keep
a potato hot; and so forth. This emphasis on the scientific method was
designed to provide insights into *how* scientists know. Much of this science
instruction—both the "what" and the "how"—was inconsistent with the principles highlighted in *How People Learn* (see Chapter 1).

Two major national efforts conducted during the last decade have provided new guidelines and standards for creating more effective science edu-

cation. The new guidelines include an emphasis on helping students develop (1) familiarity with a discipline's concepts, theories, and models; (2) an understanding of how knowledge is generated and justified; and (3) an ability to use these understandings to engage in new inquiry.[1] At first glance, the traditional science instruction described above appears to fit these guidelines quite well. The first (emphasis on familiarity with a discipline's concepts, theories, models) appears to focus on what scientists know; the second (emphasis on understanding how knowledge is generated and justified) *how* they know. If we let students engage in experimentation, this appears to comport with the third guideline (emphasis on an ability to engage in new inquiry). Like Lionni's fish (see Chapter 1), we can graft the new guidelines onto our existing experience.

But both the new guidelines and the principles of *How People Learn* suggest a very different approach to teaching. Simply telling students what scientists have discovered, for example, is not sufficient to support change in their existing preconceptions about important scientific phenomena.[2] Similarly, simply asking students to follow the steps of "the scientific method" is not sufficient to help them develop the knowledge, skills, and attitudes that will enable them to understand what it means to "do science" and participate in a larger scientific community. And the general absence of metacognitive instruction in most of the science curricula we experienced meant that we were not helped in learning how to learn, or made capable of inquiry on our own and in groups. Often, moreover, we were not supported in adopting as our own the questioning stance and search for both supporting and conflicting evidence that are the hallmarks of the scientific enterprise.

The three chapters that follow provide examples of science instruction that are different from what most of us experienced. They are also consistent with the intent of the guidelines of the National Research Council[3] and the American Association for the Advancement of Science,[4] as well as the principles of *How People Learn*. The authors of these chapters do indeed want to help students learn *what* scientists know and *how* they know, but they go about it in ways that are quite different from more traditional science instruction.

The three chapters focus, respectively, on light (elementary school), physical forces such as gravity (middle school), and genetics and evolution (high school). They approach these topics in ways that support students' abilities to (1) learn new concepts and theories with understanding; (2) experience the processes of inquiry (including hypothesis generation, modeling, tool use, and social collaboration) that are key elements of the culture of science; and (3) reflect metacognitively on their own thinking and participation in scientific inquiry. Important principles of learning and instruction are discussed below.

PRINCIPLE #1: ADDRESSING PRECONCEPTIONS

It is often claimed that "experience is the best teacher." While this is arguably true in many contexts, what we learn from our experience varies considerably in terms of its generality and usefulness. With respect to science, everyday experiences often reinforce the very conceptions of phenomena that scientists have shown to be limited or false, and everyday modes of reasoning are often contrary to scientific reasoning.

Everyday Concepts of Scientific Phenomena

Students bring conceptions of everyday phenomena to the classroom that are quite sensible, but scientifically limited or incorrect. For example, properties are generally believed to belong to objects rather than to emerge from interactions.[5] Force, for instance, is seen as a property of bodies that are forceful rather than an interaction between bodies.[6] As described in Chapter 10, students believe objects to "be" a certain color, and light can either allow us to see the color or not. The notion that white light is composed of a spectrum of colors and that the specific colors absorbed and reflected by a particular object give the object the appearance of a particular color is not at all apparent in everyday experience. Scientific tools (prisms) can break white light into colors. But without tools, students see only white light and objects that appear in different colors (rainbows are an exception, but for the untrained they are a magnificent mystery).

Students enter the study of science with a vast array of such preconceptions based on their everyday experiences. Teachers will need to engage those ideas if students are to understand science. The instructional challenge of working with students' preconceptions varies because some conceptions are more firmly rooted than others. Magnusson and Palincsar (Chapter 10) note that some elementary students in their classrooms believe that shadows are "objects," but this preconception is easily dispelled with fairly simple challenges. Other preconceptions, such as the idea that only shiny objects reflect light, require much more time and effort to help students change their ideas.

It is important to remember that most preconceptions are reasonable based on students' everyday experiences. In the area of astronomy, for example, there is a widespread belief that the earth's seasons are caused by the distance of the earth from the sun rather than by the angle of the earth's axis with respect to the sun, and it is very difficult for students to change these preconceptions.[7] Many experiences support the idea that distance from a heat source affects temperature. The closer we stand to radiators, stoves, fireplaces, and other heat sources, the greater is the heat.

Interestingly, there are also experiences in which we can manipulate the intensity of heat by changing the angle of a heat source—by pointing a hair dryer on one's head at different angles, for example. But without the ability to carefully control distance from the head or the tools to measure small changes in temperature (and without some guidance that helps people think to do this experiment in the first place), the relationship between heat and angle with respect to the heat source can easily be missed.

Everyday Concepts of Scientific Methods, Argumentation, and Reasoning

Students bring ideas to the classroom not only about scientific phenomena, but also about what it means to "do science." Research on student thinking about science reveals a progression of ideas about scientific knowledge and how it is justified.[8] The developmental sequence is strikingly similar to that described in Chapter 2 regarding student reasoning about historical knowledge. Scientific knowledge is initially perceived as right or wrong. Later, discrepant ideas and evidence are characterized as "mere opinion," and eventually as "informed" and supported with evidence.[9] As in history, the sequence in science is more predictable than the timing. Indeed, many students may not complete the sequence without instructional support. In several studies, a large proportion of today's high school students have been shown to be at the first stage (right or wrong) when thinking about various phenomena.[10]

Research has also explored students' reasoning regarding scientific experimentation, modeling, the interpretation of data, and scientific argumentation. Examples of conceptions that pose challenges for understanding the scientific enterprise are summarized in Box 9-1. While research findings have been helpful in identifying problematic conceptions, less is known regarding the pace at which students are capable of moving along the developmental trajectory, or undergoing conceptual change, with effective instructional experiences. The chapters that follow provide many compelling examples demonstrating the kinds of changes in student thinking that carefully designed instructional experiences can support.

Conceptual Change

How People Learn emphasizes that instruction in any subject matter that does not explicitly address students' everyday conceptions typically fails to help them refine or replace these conceptions with others that are scientifically more accurate. In fact, the pioneering research that signaled the tenacity of everyday experience and the challenge of conceptual change was done in the area of science, especially physics.[11] One of the pioneers was

Jim Minstrell, a high school physics teacher and author—along with Pamela Kraus—of Chapter 11. That chapter begins with Minstrell describing an experience in his classroom that prompted him to rethink how he taught physics. He was teaching about universal gravitation and forces at a distance. He found that his students did reasonably well when asked to compute force based on "what if" questions involving a change in the distance of an object from a planet. He found, however, that when asked to think qualitatively about the situation, most of his students were basing their thinking on ideas that were reasonable from their everyday perspective, yet widely discrepant from the ways physicists have learned to think about these situations. For example, when Minstrell asked students to assume that there was no air or friction affecting an object pulling a weight, a number of the students offered that everything would just float away since that is how things work in outer space.

Minstrell notes that this experience raised fundamental questions in his mind, such as what good it is to have students know the quantitative relation or equation for gravitational force if they lack a qualitative understanding of force and concepts related to the nature of gravity and its effects. It became clear that simply teaching students about abstract principles of physics provided no bridge for changing their preconceptions. Minstrell and Kraus discuss ways of teaching physics that are designed to remedy this problem. A study suggesting the advantages of assessing student preconceptions and designing instruction to respond to those preconceptions is summarized in Box 9-2.

The authors of all three of the following chapters pay close attention to the preconceptions that students hold about subject matter. For example, the elementary school students discussed by Magnusson and Palincsar (Chapter 10) had had many years of experience with light, darkness, and shadows—and they brought powerful preconceptions to the classroom. The high school students discussed by Stewart, Cartier, and Passmore (Chapter 12) came with many beliefs about genetics and evolution that are widespread among the adult population, including the beliefs that acquired characteristics can be passed on to offspring, and that evolution is purposeful and proceeds toward a specific goal.

The authors of each chapter focus on issues of conceptual change as a major goal for their instruction. This view of learning is quite different from the more traditional view that learning simply involves the addition of new facts and skills to an existing knowledge base. Understanding scientific knowledge often requires a change in—not just an addition to—what people notice and understand about everyday phenomena.[12]

The chapters that follow focus specifically on creating conditions that allow students to undergo important changes in their thinking and noticing. Everything from the choice of topics to be explored to the procedures for

BOX 9-1   Student Conceptions of Knowledge Generation and Justification in Science

Research into students' thinking about scientific knowledge and processes reveals some common misconceptions and limited understandings (summarized by AAAS[13]):

- **Experimentation:** Upper elementary- and middle-school students may not understand experimentation as a method of testing ideas, but rather as a method of trying things out or producing a desired outcome.[14] With adequate instruction, it is possible to have middle school students understand that experimentation is guided by particular ideas and questions and that experiments are tests of ideas. . . . Students of all ages may overlook the need to hold all but one variable constant, although elementary students already understand the notion of fair comparisons, a precursor to the idea of "controlled experiments"[15]. . . . Students tend to look for or accept evidence that is consistent with their prior beliefs and either distort or fail to generate evidence that is inconsistent with these beliefs. These deficiencies tend to mitigate over time and with experience.[16]

- **Models:** Middle school and high-school students typically think of models as physical copies of reality, not as conceptual representations.[17] They lack the notion that the usefulness of a model can be tested by comparing its implications to actual observations. Students know models can

hypothesis testing and discussion contributes to the successful achievement of this goal. For example, Magnusson and Palincsar note that the study of light allows children to see the world differently and challenge their preconceptions. The examples discussed in the chapters on physics and genetics also illustrate many rich opportunities for students to experience and understand phenomena from new perspectives. Such opportunities for students to experience changes in their own noticing, thinking, and understanding are made possible because of another feature of the programs discussed in these chapters: they all integrate content learning with inquiry processes rather than teaching the two separately. This point is elaborated below.

be changed but changing a model for them means (typical of high-school students) adding new information or (typical of middle-school students) replaing a part that was made wrong (p. 26).

- **Interpretation of Data:** Students of all ages show a tendency to uncritically infer cause from correlations.[18] Some students think even a single co-occurance of antecedent and outcome is always sufficient to infer causality. Rarely do middle-school students realize the indeterminacy of single instances, although high-school students may readily realize it. Despite that, as covariant data accumulate, even high-school students will infer a causal relation based on correlations. Further, students of all ages will make a causal inference even when no variation occurs in one of the variables. For example, if students are told that light-colored balls are used successfully in a game, they seem willing to infer that the color of the balls will make some difference in the outcome even without any evidence about dark-colored balls.

- **Inadequacies in Arguments:** Most high-school students will accept arguments based on inadequate sample size, accept causality from contiguous events, and accept conclusions based on statistically insignificant differences.[19] More students can recognize these inadequacies in arguments after prompting (for example, after being told that the conclusions drawn from the data were invalid and asked to state why).[20]

PRINCIPLE #2: KNOWLEDGE OF WHAT IT MEANS TO "DO SCIENCE"

Feynman characterized the scientific method in three words: observation, reason, and experiment.[21] Einstein emphasized the importance of imagination to scientific advancement, making it possible for the reasoning that follows observation to go beyond current understanding. This view of science extolled by some of its greatest minds is often not recognizable in classroom efforts to teach students how to do science.

We have noted that in the past, teaching the processes, not just the outcomes, of science often involved no more than memorizing and reproducing the steps of an experiment. However, even when science instruction

BOX 9-2 Diagnosing Preconceptions in Physics

A computer-based DIAGNOSER program was designed to help teachers elicit and work with student preconceptions in physics.[22] The program assesses students' beliefs about various physical phenomena and provides recommended activities that help students reinterpret phenomena from a physicist's perspective. The teacher uses the feedback from DIAGNOSER to guide instruction.

Data were collected for students of three teachers at Mercer Island School who used the program and were compared with data for students in a comparable school where the program was not used in physics instruction. Data were collected on Miller Analogies Test math scores for students from both schools, so that individual students were compared with others who had the same level of mathematics achievement. In the figure below, the math scores for both groups on the same mechanics final exam are plotted. The results suggest that students' understanding of important concepts in physics was substantially better in the Mercer Island school, and this result was true for students at all mathematics achievement levels.

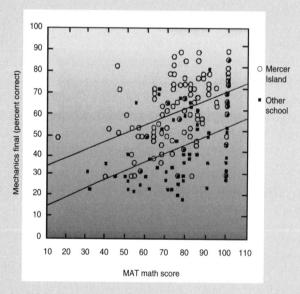

Scores of students from Mercer Island and a comparable school on mechanics final.

is shifted in the direction of engaging in scientific inquiry (as is happening more frequently in today's classrooms), it can be easy to emphasize giving students "recipes for experiments"—hands-on activities that students engage in step by step, carefully following instructions, using measurement tools, and collecting data. These lockstep approaches shortchange observation, imagination, and reasoning. Experimenting may mean that students are asked to conduct a careful sequence of activities in which the number of quarters a wet and dry paper towel can hold is compared in multiple trials, and data are carefully collected and averaged. Yet the question that needs investigation is often unclear, and the reasoning that would lead one to think that either a wet or a dry paper towel would be stronger can remain a mystery to students. As in specific content areas in science, information about the enterprise of science can be passed along to students without an opportunity for them to understand conceptually what that enterprise is about. Indeed, many students believe that everything they learn in science classes is factual; they make no distinction between observation and theory.[23]

The science programs discussed in the following chapters represent a very different approach to scientific inquiry. They do not involve simply setting aside "inquiry time" during which students conduct experiments that are related in some way to the content they are learning. Instead, students learn the content by actively engaging in processes of scientific inquiry. Students may still learn what others have discovered about a phenomenon (see Magnusson and Palincsar's discussions of helping students learn from "second-hand knowledge"). But this is different from typical textbook exercises because the value of reading about others' discoveries is clear to students—it helps them clarify issues that arise in their own inquiry. Reading to answer a question of interest is more motivating than simply reading because someone assigned it. It also changes how people process what they read.[24]

Opportunities to learn science as a process of inquiry (rather than simply having "inquiry times" that are appended to an existing curriculum) has important advantages. It involves observation, imagination, and reasoning about the phenomena under study. It includes the use of tools and procedures, but in the context of authentic inquiry, these become devices that allow students to extend their everyday experiences of the world and help them organize data in ways that provide new insights into phenomena.[25] Crucial questions that are not addressed by lockstep experimental exercises include the following: Where do ideas for relevant observations and experiments come from in the first place? How do we decide what count as relevant comparison groups? How can sciences (e.g., astronomy, paleontology) be rigorously empirical even though they are not primarily experimental? Definitions of what counts as "good science" change as a function of what is being studied and current theorizing about the ideas being investigated. A simple but informative example of how definitions of good scientific methods depend on knowledge of the conceptual issues one is studying is provided in Box 9-3.

One of the most important aspects of science—yet perhaps one of the least emphasized in instruction—is that science involves processes of imagination. If students are not helped to experience this for themselves, science can seem dry and highly mechanical. Indeed, research on students' perceptions of science indicates that "they see scientific work as dull and rarely rewarding, and scientists as bearded, balding, working alone in the laboratory, isolated and lonely.[26] Few scientists we know would remain in the field of science if it were as boring as many students believe.

Generating hypotheses worth investigating was for Einstein an extremely important part of science, where the "imagination of the possible" played a major role. Nobel Laureate Sir Peter Medawar also emphasizes the role of imagining the possible:

> *Like other exploratory processes, [the scientific method] can be resolved into a dialogue between fact and fancy, the actual and the possible; between what could be true and what is in fact the case. The purpose of scientific enquiry is not to compile an inventory of factual information, nor to build up a totalitarian world picture of Natural Laws in which every event that is not compulsory is forbidden. We should think of it rather as a logically particular structure of justifiable beliefs about a Possible World—a story which we invent and criticize and modify as we go along, so that it ends by being, as nearly as we can make it, a story about real life.[27]*

The importance of creative processes in the conduct of science can also be understood by exploring the types of reasoning and investigative choices that have made some scientific investigations particularly productive and feasible. For example, Mendel's critical insight about the discrete nature of heredity was a consequence of his selecting peas for his experiment (see Box 9-4). Other major advances in understanding heredity were equally dependent on scientists finding an approach to investigation that would allow the complexity of the world to be sufficiently simplified to uncover fundamental relationships.[28] This very engaging dimension of the scientific enterprise is hidden when students' inquiry experience is limited to the execution of step-by-step experiments.

The chapters that follow present a variety of ways to help students experience the excitement of doing science in a way that does justice to all stages of the process. The authors describe experiences that allow students to see everyday phenomena with new eyes. They provide opportunities for both inventing and testing models of invisible processes, adopting and sometimes adapting tools to make the invisible visible. Students reason about relationships between theory and data. Furthermore, they do so by creating classroom communities that simulate the important roles of scientific communities in actual scientific practice.[29] This involves paying careful attention to the arguments of others, as well as learning the benefits of group interaction for advancing one's own thinking.

PRINCIPLE #3: METACOGNITION

The third principle of *How People Learn* emphasizes the importance of taking a metacognitive approach to instruction. Much of the research on metacognition focused on the comprehension of text (see Chapter 1) clearly applies to science, where texts can be quite complex and difficult for many students to comprehend. However, more recent research targeted specifically to the monitoring of and reflection on scientific reasoning has also shown promising effects.

A striking example is the work of White and Frederiksen (see Box 9-5), who designed a physics inquiry curriculum called ThinkerTools. The curriculum uses inquiry instruction to engage students in investigations that allow them to confront their misconceptions and develop a scientific understanding of force and motion. Students taught with the ThinkerTools curriculum displayed a deeper conceptual understanding than students taught with a traditional curriculum. This advantage remained even when the ThinkerTools students were in inner-city schools and were compared with students in suburban schools, and when the ThinkerTools students were several years younger. White and Frederiksen later extended the curriculum to include a metacognitive component—what they refer to as "reflective assessment." Students taught with the curriculum including this metacognitive component outperformed those taught with the original curriculum. Gains were particularly striking for lower-achieving students.

Another study, by Lin and Lehman,[30] demonstrates that metacognitive instruction can be effective for college students. In their experiments, students learned about strategies for controlling variables in a complex science experiment that was simulated via computer. As they studied, some received periodic questions that asked them to reflect on—and briefly explain—what they were doing and why; others did not receive these questions. On tests of the extent to which students' knowledge transferred to new problems, those in the metacognitive group outperformed those in the comparison groups.

The authors of the following chapters do not necessarily label their relevant instructional moves as "metacognitive," but they emphasize helping students reflect on their role in inquiry and on the monitoring and critiquing of one's own claims, as well as those of others. They also emphasize that

BOX 9-3 Evaluating the Methods Used in an Experiment

Imagine being asked to evaluate the following experiment and conclusions:

A group of biologists compare data from across the world and note that frogs seem to be disappearing in an alarming number of places. This deeply concerns them, because the frogs may well be an indicator species for environmental changes that could hurt us all. The biologists consider a number of hypotheses about the frogs' disappearance. One is that too much ultraviolet light is getting through the ozone layer.

One group of researchers decides to test the ultraviolet light hypothesis. They use five different species of frogs—an equal number of male and female. Half of the frogs receive constant doses of ultraviolet light for a period of 4 months; this is the experimental group. The other half of the frogs—the control group—are protected so they receive no ultraviolet light.

At the end of the 4 months, the biologists find that there is no difference in death rates between the frogs in the experimental and control groups. This finding suggests that ultraviolet light is probably not the cause of the frogs' demise.

What do you think about the biologists' experiments and conclusions? Are there questions you would want to ask before accepting their conclusions? Are there new experiments that you would want to propose?

This problem has been addressed by hundreds of individuals in classes and workshops.[31] Many of these individuals know a considerable amount about experimental design and typically note a number of strengths and weaknesses about the experiment. Strengths include the fact that it had an experimental/control design that involved several different species of frogs, used stratified random sampling, and so forth. Weaknesses include such concerns as the possibility that the doses of ultra-violet light that were used were too weak; that the light was provided for too short a time (i.e., only 4 months); or that the experimenters did not wait long enough to see the effects of the ultraviolet light, so maybe they should have looked at differences in illness between the two groups rather than comparing the death rates.

Such concerns are valid and relatively sophisticated, but they reflect a lack of knowledge about general principles of biology—principles that raise serious questions about the preceding experiment. In particular, very few people question the fact that only adult frogs were used in the experiment (multimedia materials viewed by participants showed clearly that the frogs were all adults). To understand potential environmental effects on a species, one must look at the life cycle of the species and attempt to identify points in that cycle where the species might be the most vulnerable. For example, when DDT endangered eagles, it did so not by killing the adults but by making the egg shells so brittle that they broke before the offspring could hatch. Overall, what counts as an adequate experimental or empirical design is strongly affected by the current state of knowledge of a particular field. Learning about "the scientific method" in the abstract fails to help students grasp this important idea.

An interesting side note is that people who have participated in the preceding demonstration have been asked whether they ever studied life cycles in school. Almost all have said "yes"; however, they learned about life cycles as isolated exercises (e.g., they were asked to memorize the stages of the life cycle of a fly or mosquito) and never connected this information to larger questions, such as the survival of a species. As a consequence, the idea of life cycles had never occurred to them in the context of attempting to solve the above problem.

In Chapter 1, Bruner's ideas[32] about curriculum organization are discussed; those ideas are highly relevant in this context. For example, he cautions against teaching specific topics or skills without clarifying their context in the broader fundamental structure of the field; rather, students need to attain an understanding of fundamental principles and ideas. Those presented with the frog problem may have learned about life cycles, but their teachers and texts did not explain the importance of this information in the broader structure of the field of knowledge. To paraphrase Whitehead,[33] knowledge that was potentially important for exploring the frog problem remained "inert."

BOX 9-4 The Proof Was in the Peas

Gregor Mendel's major contribution to the field of genetics rested on his choice of peas. Many famous men at the time were conducting experiments in plant breeding, but no general principles had emerged from these experiments. Typically they involved plant organisms that differed on a variety of dimensions, and the offspring were found to be intermediate or, in rare cases, more like one parent plant than the other.

Mendel chose peas for certain critical features: they have both male and female structures and are generally self-fertilizing, but their structure makes it possible to prevent self-fertilization (by removing the anthers before they mature). Numerous varieties of peas were available that differed on certain discrete dimensions; Mendel chose varieties with seeds that were green or yellow, smooth or wrinkled, etc. When the peas were cross-fertilized, they consistently showed one of the two characteristics. When plants with smooth and wrinkled seeds were crossed, they consistently had offspring with smooth seeds. This result suggested that one characteristic is, in Mendel's term, dominant. But when these offspring were self-fertilized and produced their own offspring, characteristics of each of the original parent plants appeared in members of the new generation. The stunning conclusion—that offspring carry genetic information that is recessive but can nonetheless be passed along to future generations—represented a major advance.

To appreciate Mendel's contribution is not just to know the terms he used and the experimental procedures he followed, or even the outcome of his work. It is to understand as well the important role played by his experimental design, as well as the reasoning that led him to design a productive experiment.

being metacognitive about science is different from simply asking whether we comprehend what we read or hear; it requires taking up the particular critical lens through which scientists view the world.

Magnusson and Palincsar provide excellent examples of how metacognitive habits of mind for science require different kinds of questions than people typically ask about everyday phenomena. For example, they note that for young children and for many adults, the assumption that things are as they appear seems self-evident. But science is about questioning the obvious. When we do this, unexpected discoveries often come to light. For example, a scientific mindset suggests that the observation that shiny things reflect light needs to be explained, and this requires explaining why dull objects do not reflect light. As these issues are investigated, it becomes clear that the initial assumption was wrong and that dull objects do indeed reflect light—but at a level that is not always obvious in our everyday experiences. As Magnusson and Palincsar note:

> *Engaging children in science, then, means engaging them in a whole new approach to questioning. Indeed, it means asking them to question. . . . It means questioning the typical assurance we feel from evidence that confirms our prior beliefs, and asking in what ways the evidence is incomplete and may be countered by additional evidence.*

The authors of Chapters 11 and 12 also place a great deal of emphasis on helping students become aware of ways in which scientific inquiry goes beyond peoples' everyday ways of interacting with their environment. The authors attempt to help students compare their personal "ways of knowing" with those developed through centuries of scientific inquiry. Helping students understand the tendency of us all to attempt to confirm rather than rigorously test (and possibly refute) our current assumptions is one example of a metacognitive approach to science instruction. The approach is deepened when we help students learn why and how to create models of phenomena (especially the invisible aspects of phenomena) that can then be put to an empirical test.

The following chapters emphasize another aspect of metacognition as well: helping students learn about themselves as learners. The authors describe classroom activities and discussion that encourage students to reflect on the degree to which they contribute to or detract from group processes, and on the degree to which efforts to communicate findings (e.g., in writing) uncover "holes" in one's thinking that otherwise might remain invisible.

The authors' decisions about the topics they discuss (light, force and gravity, genetics and evolution) were guided in part by the opportunities these topics provide to help students think differently not only about the subject matter, but also about how they "know," and how their everyday approaches to knowing compare with those scientists have developed over the last few centuries.

THE *HOW PEOPLE LEARN* FRAMEWORK

As noted in Chapter 1, authors of the chapters in this volume were not asked to tie their discussion explicitly to the framework of *How People Learn* that suggests classrooms should be learner-centered, knowledge-centered, assessment-centered, and community-centered. Nevertheless, it can be useful to see how this framework applies to their work.

BOX 9-5 Reflective Assessment in ThinkerTools

ThinkerTools is an inquiry-based curriculum that allows students to explore the physics of motion. The curriculum is designed to engage students' conceptions, to provide a carefully structured and highly supported computer environment for testing those conceptions, and to steep students in the processes of scientific inquiry. The curriculum has demonstrated impressive gains in students' conceptual understanding and the ability to transfer knowledge to novel problems.

White and Frederiksen[34] designed and tested a "reflective assessment" component that provided students with a framework for evaluating the quality of an inquiry—their own and that of others. The assessment categories included understanding the main ideas, understanding the inquiry process, being inventive, being systematic, reasoning carefully, applying the tools of research, using teamwork, and communicating well. Students who were engaged in reflective assessment were compared with matched control students who were taught with ThinkerTools, but were asked to comment on what they did and did not like about the curriculum without a guiding framework. Each teacher's classes were evenly divided between the two treatments. There were no significant differences in students' initial average standardized test scores (the Comprehensive Test of Basic Skills was used as a measure of prior achievement) between the classes assigned (randomly) to the different treatments.

Students in the reflective assessment classes showed higher gains both in understanding the process of scientific inquiry and in understanding the physics content. For example, one of the outcome measures was a written inquiry assessment that was given both before and after the ThinkerTools inquiry curriculum was administered. This was a written test in which students were asked to explain how they would investigate a specific research question: "What is the relationship between the weight of an object and the effect that sliding friction has on its motion?"[35] Students were instructed to propose competing hypotheses, design an experiment (on paper) to test the hypotheses, and pretend to carry out the experiment, making up data. They were then asked to use the data they generated to reason and draw conclusions about their initial hypotheses.

Presented below are the gain scores on this challenging assessment for both low- and high-achieving students and for students in the reflective assessment and control classes. Note first that students in the reflective assessment classes gained more on this inquiry assessment. Note also that this was particularly true for the low-achieving students. This is evidence that the metacognitive reflective assessment process is beneficial, particularly for academically disadvantaged students.

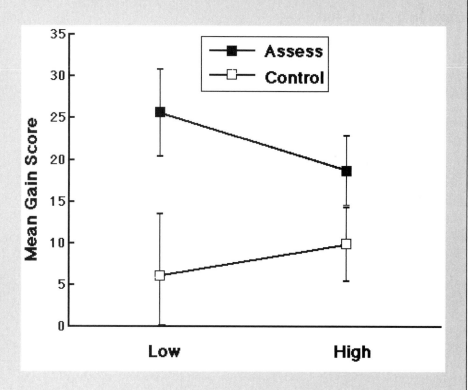

Learner-Centered

All three of the following chapters place a great deal of emphasis on the ideas and understandings that students bring to the classroom. Each begins by engaging students in activities or discussions that draw out what they know or how they know, rather than beginning with new content. Students are viewed as active processors of information who have acquired concepts, skills, and attitudes that affect their thinking about the content being taught, as well as about what it means to do science. Like Lionni's fish (see Chapter 1), students bring preconceptions to class that can shape (or misshape) learning if not addressed. These chapters engage students' ideas so that they can be reexamined, reshaped, and built upon.

Knowledge-Centered

Issues of what should be taught play a fundamental role in each of the chapters that follow. While engaging in inquiry involves a great deal of activity that is under students' control, the authors are quite clear about the knowledge that students need to acquire to understand the topic, and they guide students' inquiry to ensure that the necessary concepts and information (including the terminology) are learned. The chapters emphasize both what scientists know and how they know. But the authors' approaches to instruction make these more than lists of information to be learned and steps to be followed.

Of particular importance, opportunities for inquiry are not simply tacked on to the content of a course; rather, they are the method for learning the content. This sets the stage for a number of important changes in science instruction. Simply having students follow "the scientific method" probably introduces more misconceptions about science than it dispels. First, different areas of science use different methods. Second, as discussed above, lockstep approaches to conducting science experiments exclude the aspects of science that are probably the most gratifying and motivating to scientists—generating good questions and ways to explore them; learning by being surprised (at disconfirmations); seeing how the collective intelligence of the group can supersede the insights of people working solely as individuals; learning to "work smart" by adopting, adapting, and sometimes inventing tools and models; and experiencing the excitement of actually discovering—and sharing with friends—something that provides a new way of looking at the world.

Assessment-Centered

The word "assessment" rarely appears in the three chapters that follow, but in fact the chapters are rich in assessment opportunities. Students are helped to assess the quality of their hypotheses and models, the adequacy of their methods and conclusions, and the effectiveness of their efforts as learners and collaborators. These assessments are extremely important for students, but also help teachers see the degree to which students are making progress toward the course goals and use this information in deciding what to do next. It is noteworthy that these are formative assessments, complete with opportunities for students (and teachers) to use feedback to revise their thinking; they are not merely summative assessments that give students a grade on one task (e.g., a presentation about an experiment) and then go on to the next task.

Community-Centered

The dialogue and discussion in each of the following chapters indicate that the teachers have developed a culture of respect, questioning, and risk taking. Disconfirmation is seen as an exciting discovery, not a failure. A diverse array of thoughts about issues and phenomena is treated as a resource for stimulating conversations and new discoveries—not as a failure to converge immediately on "the right answer." Discussions in class help support the idea of a "learning community" as involving people who can argue with grace, rather than people who all agree with one another (though, as Magnusson and Palincsar suggest, this can take some time and effort to develop).

CONCLUSION

While each of the three chapters that follow has much to offer in demonstrating instructional approaches designed to incorporate important lessons from research on learning, we remind the reader that these chapters are intended to be illustrative. As noted earlier, there are many ways to build a bridge that are consistent with the principles of physics, and this is also true of relationships between course design and general principles of learning. It is the intention of the following chapters to provide approaches and ideas for instruction that other teachers may find useful in their own teaching. Indeed, the approaches are ones that require of teachers a great deal of responsiveness to their students' ideas and thinking. Such approaches to teaching will most likely succeed if teachers understand the principles that drive instruction and incorporate them into their own thinking and teaching, rather than making an effort to replicate what is described in the chapters that follow.

NOTES

1. American Association for the Advancement of Science, 1993; National Research Council, 1996.
2. Carey, 2000.
3. National Research Council, 1996.
4. American Association for the Advancement of Science, 1993.
5. Brosnan, 1990.
6. Driver et al., 1985.
7. Schneps and Sadler, 1987.
8. Benchmarks Online Available: http://www.project2061.org/tools/benchol/bolintro.htm [October 2004].
9. Kitchener, 1983; Perry, 1970.
10. Kitchener, 1983; Kitchener and King, 1981.
11. Clement, 1993; Driver et al., 1985; Pfundt and Duit, 1991.
12. Carey, 2000; Hanson, 1970; National Research Council, 2000.
13. American Association for the Advancement of Science, 1993.
14. Carey et al., 1989; Schauble et al., 1991; Solomon, 1992.
15. Wollman, 1997a, 1997b; Wollman and Lawson, 1977.
16. Schauble, 1990, p. 2.
17. Grosslight et al., 1991.
18. Kuhn et al., 1988.
19. Jungwirth, 1987; Jungwirth and Dreyfus, 1990, 1992.
20. Jungwirth, 1987; Jungwirth and Dreyfus, 1992.
21. Feynman, 1995.
22. Hunt and Minstrell, 1994.
23. Brook et al., 1983.
24. Biswas et al., 2002; Palincsar and Brown, 1984.
25. Petrosino et al., 2003.
26. American Association for the Advancement of Science, 1993.
27. Medawar, 1982.
28. Moore, 1972, Chapter 4.
29. Kuhn, 1989.
30. Lin and Lehman, 1999.
31. Bransford, 2003.
32. Bruner, 1960.
33. Whitehead, 1929.
34. White and Frederiksen, 1998.
35. White and Frederiksen, 2000, p. 2.

REFERENCES

American Association for the Advancement of Science. (1993). *Benchmarks for science literacy*. New York: Oxford University Press.

Biswas, G., Schwartz, D., Bransford, J., and the Teachable Agent Group at Vanderbilt. (2002). Technology support for complex problem solving: From SAD environments to AI. In K.D. Forbus and P.J. Feltovich (Eds.), *Smart machines in education: The coming revolution in educational technology* (pp. 71-97). Menlo Park, CA: AAAI/MIT Press.

Bransford, J.D. (2003). *Frog problem.* Paper presented at the American Physiological Society as the Claude Bernard Distinguished Lecturer of the Teaching of Physiology, San Diego, CA.

Brook, A., Briggs, H., and Bell, B. (1983). *Secondary students' ideas about particles.* Leeds, England: The University of Leeds, Centre for Studies in Science and Mathematics Education.

Brosnan, T. (1990). Categorizing macro and micro explanations of material change. In P.L. Lijnse, P. Licht, W. de Vos, and A.J. Waarlo (Eds.), *Relating macroscopic phenomena to microscopic particles* (pp. 198-211). Utrecht, The Netherlands: CD-p Press.

Bruner, J. (1960). *The process of education.* Cambridge, MA: Harvard University Press.

Carey, S. (2000). Science education as conceptual change. *Journal of Applied Developmental Psychology, 21*(1), 13-19.

Carey, S., Evans, R., Honda, M., Jay, E., and Unger, C. (1989). An experiment is when you try it and see if it works: A study of grade 7 students' understanding of the construction of scientific knowledge. *International Journal of Science Education, 11*, 514-529.

Clement, J. (1993). Using bridging analogies and anchoring institutions to deal with students' preconceptions in physics. *Journal of Research in Science Teaching, 30*(10), 1241-1257.

Driver, R., Guesne, E., and Tiberghien, A. (1985). Some features of children's ideas and their implications for teaching. In R. Driver, E. Guesne, and A. Tiberghien (Eds.), *Children's ideas in science* (pp. 193-201). Berkshire, England: Open University Press.

Feynman, R.P. (1995). *Six easy pieces: Essentials of physics explained by its most brilliant teacher.* Reading, MA: Perseus Books.

Grosslight, L., Unger, C., Jay, E., and Smith, C. (1991). Understanding models and their use in science: Conceptions of middle and high school students and experts. *International Journal of Science Education, 17*(16), 59-74.

Hanson, N.R. (1970). A picture theory of theory meaning. In R.G. Colodny (Ed.), *The nature and function of scientific theories* (pp. 233-274). Pittsburgh, PA: University of Pittsburgh Press.

Hunt, E., and Minstrell, J. (1994). A cognitive approach to the teaching of physics. In K. McGilly (Ed.), *Classroom lessons: Integrating cognitive theory and classroom practice* (pp. 51-74). Cambridge, MA: MIT Press.

Jungwirth, E. (1987). Avoidance of logical fallacies: A neglected aspect of science education and science-teacher education. *Research in Science and Technological Education, 5*, 43-58.

Jungwirth, E., and Dreyfus, A. (1990). Identification and acceptance of a posteriori casual assertions invalidated by faulty enquiry methodology: An international study of curricular expectations and reality. In D. Herget (Ed.), *More history and philosophy of science in science teaching* (pp. 202-211). Tallahassee, FL: Florida State University.

Jungwirth, E., and Dreyfus, A. (1992). After this, therefore because of this: One way of jumping to conclusions. *Journal of Biological Education, 26,* 139-142.

Kitchener, K. (1983). Educational goals and reflective thinking. *The Educational Forum,* 75-95.

Kitchener, K., and King, P. (1981). Reflective judgment: Concepts of justification and their relationship to age and education. *Journal of Applied Developmental Psychology, 2,* 89-116.

Kuhn, D. (1989). Children and adults as intuitive scientists. *Psychological Review, 96,* 674-689.

Kuhn, D., Amsel, E., and O'Loughlin, M. (1988). *The development of scientific thinking skills.* San Diego, CA: Academic Press.

Lin, X.D., and Lehman, J. (1999). Supporting learning of variable control in a computer-based biology environment: Effects of prompting college students to reflect on their own thinking. *Journal of Research in Science Teaching, 36*(7), 837-858.

Medawar, P. (1982*). Plato's republic.* Oxford, England: Oxford University Press.

Moore, J.A. (1972). *Heredity and development* (second edition). Oxford, England: Oxford University Press.

National Research Council. (1996). *National science education standards.* National Committee on Science Education Standards and Assessment, Center for Science, Mathematics, and Engineering Education. Washington, DC: National Academy Press.

National Research Council. (2000). *How people learn: Brain, mind, experience, and school.* Committee on Developments in the Science of Learning and Committee on Learning Research and Educational Practice, Commission on Behavioral and Social Sciences and Education. Washington, DC: National Academy Press.

Palinscar, A.S., and Brown, A.L. (1984). Reciprocal teaching of comprehension-fostering and comprehension monitoring activities. *Cognition and Instruction, 1*(2),117-175.

Perry, W.G., Jr. (1970). *Forms of intellectual and ethical development in the college years.* Fort Worth, TX: HBJ College Publishers.

Petrosino, A., Lehrer, R., and Shauble, L. (2003). Structuring error and experimental variation as distribution in the fourth grade. *Mathematical Thinking and Learning, 5*(2 and 3),131-156.

Pfundt, H., and Duit, R. (1991). *Bibliography: Students' alternative frameworks and science education* (third edition). Kiel, Germany: Institute for Science Education at the University of Kiel.

Schauble, L. (1990). Belief revision in children: The role of prior knowledge and strategies for generating evidence. *Journal of Experimental Child Psychology, 49,* 31-57.

Schauble, L., Klopfer, L.E., and Raghavan, K. (1991). Students' transition from an engineering model to a science model of experimentation. *Journal of Research in Science Teaching, 28,* 859-882.

Schneps, M.H., and Sadler, P.M. (1987). *A private universe* (Video). Cambridge, MA: Harvard Smithsonian Center for Astrophysics.

Solomon, J., Duveen, J., Scot, L., and McCarthy, S. (1992). Teaching about the nature of science through history: Action research in the classroom. *Journal of Research in Science Teaching, 29,* 409-421.

White, B.C., and Frederiksen, J.R. (1998). Inquiry, modeling, and metacognition: Making science accessible to all students. *Cognition and Instruction.* 16(1), 3-117.

White, B.C., and Frederiksen, J.R. (2000). Technological tools and instructional approaches for making scientific inquiry accessible to all. In M.J. Jacobson and R.B. Kozma (Eds.), *Innovations in science and mathematics education* (pp. 321-359). Mahwah, NJ: Lawrence Erlbaum Associates.

Whitehead, A.N. (1929). *The aims of education.* New York: Macmillan.

Wollman, W. (1977a). Controlling variables: Assessing levels of understanding. *Science Education, 61*, 371-383.

Wollman, W. (1977b). Controlling variables: A neo-Piagetian developmental sequence. *Science Education, 61*, 385-391.

Wollman, W., and Lawson, A. (1977). Teaching the procedure of controlled experimentation: A Piagetian approach. *Science Education, 61*, 57-70.

10

Teaching to Promote the Development of Scientific Knowledge and Reasoning About Light at the Elementary School Level

Shirley J. Magnusson and Annemarie Sullivan Palincsar

Children at play outside or with unfamiliar materials look as though they might be answering such questions as: What does this do? How does this work? What does this feel like? What can I do with it? Why did that happen? This natural curiosity and exploration of the world around them have led some people to refer to children as "natural" scientists. Certainly these are the very types of questions that scientists pursue. Yet children are not scientists. Curiosity about how the world works makes engaging children in science relatively easy, and their proclivity to observe and reason (see Chapter 1, Box 1-1) is a powerful tool that children bring to the science classroom. But there is a great deal of difference between the casual observation and reasoning children engage in and the more disciplined efforts of scientists.

How do we help students develop scientific ideas and ways of knowing?[1] Introducing children to the culture of science—its types of reasoning, tools of observation and measurement, and standards of evidence, as well as the values and beliefs underlying the production of scientific knowledge—is a major instructional challenge. Yet our work and that of others suggest that children are able to take on these learning challenges successfully even in the earliest elementary grades.[2]

THE STUDY OF LIGHT

Unlike mathematics, in which topics such as whole-number arithmetic are foundational for the study of rational number, and both are foundational for the study of functions, there is currently little agreement on the selection and sequencing of specific topics in science, particularly at the elementary level.[3] What clearly is foundational for later science study, however, is learning what it means to engage in scientific inquiry—learning the difference between casual and scientific investigations. That learning can be accomplished in the context of many different specific topics.

In this chapter, we choose light as our topic of focus because it affords several benefits. The first is practical: the topic involves relatively simple concepts that children can understand from investigating with relatively simple materials. For example, our bodies and the sun make shadows that can be studied, and similar studies can occur with common flashlights and classroom materials. Pencil and paper, and perhaps some means of measuring distance, are all that is needed for data collection. Children can also study light using simple light boxes (Elementary Science Study's *Optics* unit[4]) in which light bulbs are placed in cardboard boxes containing openings covered with construction paper masks that control the amount of light emanating from the box. Thin slits in the masks make the thin beams of light necessary for studies of reflection and refraction. Multiple wider openings covered with different colored cellophane filters enable investigations mixing colors of light. And again, pencil and paper are all that are needed for data collection showing the paths of light.

In addition, developing scientific knowledge of light challenges us to conceptualize aspects of the world that we do not directly experience—a critical element of much scientific study. For example, light travels, yet we do not see it do so; we infer its travel when we turn on a flashlight in the dark and see a lighted spot across the room.

Developing scientific knowledge often requires conceptual change[5] in which we come to view the physical world in new ways.[6] Students must learn that things are not always what they seem—itself a major conceptual leap. The study of light gives children an accessible opportunity to see the world differently and to challenge their existing conceptions. We see the world around us because light reflects from objects to our eyes, and yet we do not sense that what we see is the result of reflected light.

Some children, moreover, view shadows as objects instead of understanding that shadows are created when light is blocked. Conceptual development is required if they are to understand the relationship among a light source, an object, and the shadow cast by that object. Working with flashlights can provide children an opportunity to challenge directly everyday conceptions about shadows, providing them with a powerful early experience of scientific ways of knowing. Because casual observation of the behavior of light can be misleading, but a relatively accessible investigation of light can be illuminating, the study of light demonstrates the contrast between casual observation and experimentation. For all these reasons, then, the study of light supports children's understanding that relationships in the physical world are not self-evident and that constructing scientific knowledge from observation of the world is different from their everyday reasoning.

Three major instructional challenges parallel the principles of *How People Learn* as they apply to the study of light: (1) providing students with opportunities to develop deep conceptual understanding of targeted aspects of light, and of standards and norms in science for investigating and drawing conclusions (both about light and more generally); (2) supporting students in building or bridging from prior knowledge and experience to scientific concepts; and (3) encouraging children to engage in the kind of metacognitive questioning of their own thinking that is requisite to scientific practice.

Conceptual Understanding

How People Learn suggests that learning for understanding requires the organization of knowledge around core concepts. Thus while light can be studied with tools that are easy to use and opportunities to observe the behavior of light abound, if the classroom activity described in this chapter were simply a set of experiences and observations, it would leave students with little deep knowledge. Experiencing many individual activities (e.g., seeing that light reflects from wood as well as mirrors) does not ensure that students understand the overarching concepts about light outlined below that allow them to predict how light will behave in a wide variety of circumstances. As a result, a major focus in this chapter is on the role of the teacher in guiding students' observations, reasoning, and understanding so that core concepts are grasped.

What conceptual understandings do we consider to be core? As suggested above, grasping the differences between everyday observations and reasoning and those of science is not only core in our approach to teaching about light, but also paramount in providing a foundation for further science study. Salient concepts include the following:

- Standards of the scientific community for understanding and communicating ideas and explanations about how the world works are different from everyday standards. Science requires careful observations that are recorded accurately and precisely, and organized so that patterns can be observed in the data.
- Patterns in observations are stated as knowledge claims.

- Claims are judged on the quality of the evidence supporting or disconfirming them.
- Hypotheses take on the status of claims only after they have been tested.
- Claims are subject to challenge and not considered new scientific knowledge until the scientific community accepts them.

These understandings are foundational for all future study of science.

There are also core concepts regarding the topic of light that we want students to master. These will vary somewhat, however, according to the grade level and the amount of time that will be devoted to the topic. These concepts include the following:

- All objects (experienced in our everyday lives) reflect and absorb light, and some objects also transmit light.
  - Dark or black objects mainly absorb light; light or white objects mainly reflect light.
  - There is an inverse relationship between light reflected from and absorbed by an object: more reflected light means less absorbed light.
- Light reflects from objects in a particular way: the angle of incoming light equals the angle of reflected light.
- What we see is light reflected from objects.
  - There must be a source of light for us to see an object.
  - Sources of illumination can produce light (e.g., the sun) or reflect light (e.g., the moon).
- When an object blocks a source of light, a shadow is formed. Shadows are dark because there is no light reaching them to be reflected to our eyes. The distance of an object from a source of light it blocks determines the size of the object's shadow. The shape of an object's shadow depends on the angle of the object to the light, so the shadow of an object may have more than one shape.
- The color of an object is the color of light reflected from the object.
  - The colors of light come from white light, which can be separated into many colors.
  - The color of an object depends on the extent to which particular colors of light in white light are reflected and absorbed.

Other concepts—such as the nature of light as both a wave and a particle—are beyond what elementary students need to understand. But teachers need to know these core concepts to deal effectively with questions that may arise, as we discuss later in this chapter.

Prior Knowledge

Students bring many prior conceptions about light to the classroom. Some of these are influenced relatively easily. For example, some students believe a shadow is an object, but this conception is not deeply held, and simple experiments with light can provide convincing evidence to the contrary. Other scientifically inaccurate conceptions are not so easily changed by simple experiments.

A very common belief is that light reflects only from shiny objects, such as a mirror or shiny metals. This is hardly surprising; reflections from shiny objects are strikingly obvious, while observing reflection from objects with no apparent shine requires a tool (e.g., a simple device such as a piece of paper strategically placed to show reflected light, or a more sophisticated device such as an electronic meter that measures light energy). In fact, the nature of light has puzzled scientists for centuries.[7] Part of the challenge to our understanding is that the behaviors and effects of light are not easily determined by our senses. Light travels too fast for us to see it traveling, and our observation of light that has traveled great distances, such as light from the sun and other stars, provides no direct evidence of the time it has taken to reach us. Scientists have determined that light exerts pressure, but this is not something we can feel. We see because light is reflected to our eyes, but we have no way of experiencing that directly. We commonly think of color as an intrinsic characteristic of an object because we do not experience what actually occurs: that the color we see is the color of light reflected from the object. Furthermore, grasping this notion requires understanding that white light is made up of colors of light that are differentially absorbed and reflected by objects. If none are reflected, we see black, and if all are reflected, we see white, and this is counter to our experience with colored pigments that make a dark color when mixed together. Finally, perhaps the strongest testimony to the complex nature of light is the fact that scientists use two very different models to characterize light: a particle and a wave.

Because daily experience reinforces ideas that may be quite different from scientific understanding, fostering conceptual change requires supporting students in paying close attention to how they reason from what they observe. For this reason, the approach to teaching we suggest in this chapter provides students with a great many opportunities to make and test knowledge claims, and to examine the adequacy of their own and others' reasoning in doing so. Once again, however, the role of the teacher is critical. As we will see, the prior conceptions with which students work may lead them to simply not notice, quickly dismiss, or not believe what they do not expect to see.

Metacognition

Young children, and indeed many adults, assume that things are as they appear, and no further questioning is required. That light reflects off objects only if they are shiny may appear to be true and in no need of further questioning. Science, however, is about questioning—even when something seems obvious—because explanation is at the heart of scientific activity. Thus the search for an explanation for why shiny objects reflect light must include an answer to the question of why nonshiny objects do not. Such a search, of course, would lead to evidence refuting the notion that only shiny objects reflect light. Engaging children in science, then, means engaging them in a whole new approach to questioning. Indeed, it means asking them to question in ways most of us do not in daily life. It means questioning the typical assurance we feel from evidence that confirms our prior beliefs, and asking in what ways the evidence is incomplete and may be countered by additional evidence. To develop thinking in this way is a major instructional challenge for science teaching.

THE STUDY OF LIGHT THROUGH INQUIRY

With the above principles in mind, we turn now to the learning of science through investigative activity in the classroom, or inquiry-based instruction.[8] Investigations in which students directly observe phenomena, we believe, serve several critical functions. First, when students experiment with light and observe phenomena they do not expect, these discrepant experiences can directly challenge their inaccurate or partially developed conceptions. Students will need many opportunities to observe and discuss the behavior of light that behaves in unexpected ways if they are to develop scientific conceptions of light. Inquiry that is designed to occur over weeks and allows students to work with many different materials can provide that experience. The opportunity for repeated cycles of investigation allows students to ask the same questions in new contexts and new questions in increasingly understood contexts as they work to bring their understanding of the world in line with what scientists think. Equally important, participation in well-designed guided-inquiry instruction provides students with a first-hand experience of the norms of conducting scientific investigation.

But inquiry is a time- and resource-intensive activity, and student investigations do not always lead to observations and experiences that support the targeted knowledge. Therefore, we combine first-hand investigations with second-hand investigations in which students work with the notebook of a fictitious scientist to see where her inquiry, supported by more sophisticated tools, led. This second-hand inquiry provides a common investigative experience that allows the teacher to direct attention to steps in the reasoning process pursued by the scientist that led to the development of core concepts. Moreover, it allows students to see that while scientists engage in a similar type of inquiry, more sophisticated tools, more control over conditions, and larger sample sizes are critical to drawing conclusions that can be generalized with some confidence.

A Heuristic for Teaching and Learning Science Through Guided Inquiry

To aid our discussion of the unfolding of instruction, we present a heuristic—a thinking tool—to support planning, enacting, and evaluating guided-inquiry instruction with elementary school teachers.[9] This heuristic (see Figure 10-1[10]), which shares many features with other researched-based approaches to teaching elementary science through investigation,[11] represents instruction in terms of cycles with phases. The words in all capital letters in Figure 10-1 indicate the phases, and the lines with arrows show the progression from one phase to the next. *Reporting* is a key phase in this conception of instruction; it is the occasion when groups of students report the results of their investigations to their classmates. Students are expected to report on knowledge claims they feel confident in making and providing evidence for those claims from the data they collected during investigation. This expectation lends accountability to students' investigative activity that is often absent when they are simply expected to observe phenomena. To make a claim, students will need precise and accurate data, and to have a

FIGURE 10-1 A cycle of investigation in guided-inquiry science.

claim that is meaningful to the class, they will need to understand the relationship between the question that prompted investigation and the way in which their investigation has enabled them to come up with an answer.

Multiple lines leading from one phase to another indicate the two basic emphases of investigative activity in science: generating knowledge that describes how the world works (outer loop), and generating and testing theories to explain those relationships (inner loop). The reporting phase always marks the end of a cycle of inquiry, at which point a decision is made about whether to engage in another cycle with the same question and investigative context, or to re-engage with a novel investigative context or a new question. Cycles focused on developing knowledge claims about empirical relationships generally precede cycles in the same topic area focused on developing explanations for those relationships. Thinking and discussing explanations may occur in other cycles, but the focus of the cycle represented by the inner loop is on testing explanations.

Each phase in the heuristic presents different learning opportunities and teaching challenges. Each also provides opportunities to focus on ideas describing the physical world (concepts and theories or *content*) as well as the means by which we systematically explore the nature of the physical world (methods and reasoning or *process*).

Each phase requires different types of thinking and activity on the part of the students and the teacher; hence, each has a unique role to play in supporting the development of scientific knowledge and ways of knowing. The following illustrations of teacher and student activity in each phase of instruction are drawn from our work in elementary school classrooms.[12]

The Engage Phase

Description. Each unit of study begins with an engagement phase, which orients thinking and learning in a particular direction. In the elementary classroom, a version of the classic KWL (i.e., what do I Know, what do I Want to learn, what have I Learned) can be a fine way to initiate engagement. In contrast to the typical use of KWL in the language arts, however, to maximize the value of having students identify what they know, teachers should invite students to identify *how* they have come to know the topic area. Doing so can develop students' awareness that "knowing" can mean different things. Does their knowledge arise from something they actually observed? If so, where and when did that occur, and under what circumstances? Or did others observe it and report it to them? If so, how confident were they in what was reported and why? If a student reports knowledge from something written in a book, what other information was provided? Were any data provided to substantiate the claim? How extensive was the information provided regarding what the student reports knowing? This discussion can provide the grist for later comparisons of ways of knowing in everyday life versus in science, history, or the language arts. It also affords teachers an opportunity to draw out and learn about students' prior knowledge, metacognitive awareness, and reasoning abilities. For example, in a class beginning to investigate how light interacts with matter, one student stated that he already knew the answer because he knew that objects were opaque, transparent, or translucent. This statement indicated to the teacher that the student might assume light interacts with an object in only one way, which could limit what he observed. Knowing of this possibility, the teacher would want to monitor for it, and possibly raise questions about the thoroughness of students' observations.

The scientific community defines for itself what knowing in particular ways means. For example, in each discipline (e.g., physics, chemistry, biology), the community defines what are acceptable methods for data collection and what constitutes precise and accurate observation. The community also dictates what constitutes a valuable contribution to the knowledge base. The relative value of a contribution is a function of the extent to which it extends, refines, or challenges particular theories of how the world works. In our everyday world, we do not have a community determining the validity of our thinking or experiences. Thus, the initial conversation when beginning a new area of study provides an important opportunity for the teacher to ascertain children's awareness of the roots of their knowledge, as well as the expectations of the scientific community. For example, when students describe knowing something about the physical world but indicate that their knowledge did not arise from observation or direct experience, the teacher might ask them to think about what they have observed that might be the kind of evidence scientists would expect to have. When students do provide evidence, the teacher might ask them questions about that evidence such as those above, reflecting the norm that systematic study under controlled conditions is a hallmark of the practice of science, and that evidence not obtained under those conditions would lead scientific thinkers to be skeptical about the knowledge claim.

The next step in engagement is to begin to focus the conversation about the topic of study in ways that are likely to support the learning goals. For example, showing students the kinds of materials and equipment available for investigating can lead to a productive conversation about phenomena they can explore. Focusing on ideas that were generated during the KWL activity, the children can be encouraged to suggest ways they might investigate to determine whether those ideas are scientifically accurate (meaning that the claims can be backed by evidence from investigation). Students can also be encouraged to identify what cannot easily be studied within the classroom (because of the nature of the phenomenon or a lack of resources or time) and might be better studied in a second-hand way (i.e., through reading or hearing about what others have studied and concluded from first-hand investigation). For example, we observed a group of third graders studying light who had numerous questions about black holes, the speed of light, and light sources on different planets, all of which they decided were best pursued through second-hand investigation.

At the end of engagement, the students should have a sense of a general question they are trying to answer (e.g., How does light interact with matter?), and should have identified a particular question or questions to be the focus of the first cycle of investigation. To this end, a teacher might (1) focus the class on a particular phenomenon to study and have them suggest specific questions, (2) draw upon conflicting ideas that were identified in the KWL activity and have the class frame a question for study that can inform the conflict, or (3) draw on a question that was identified during the discussion that is a profitable beginning for investigation.

Illustration. What does this kind of beginning look like in a classroom? In a kindergarten classroom,[13] after a brief opportunity for the children to state what they thought they knew about light and how it behaved, the teacher, Ms. Kingsley, arranged for pairs of students to take turns using flashlights in an area of the classroom that had been darkened. This activity provided children an opportunity to become familiar with investigative materials and phenomena that Ms. Kingsley knew would be the focus of later investigation. The children responded to this activity in a variety of ways, from initially becoming focused on finding spiders to dwelling later on the effects they could create with flashlights. For example, one student commented on the colors she saw as she shone the flashlight on the wall in the darkened area: "There's color. When it shines on a color, then it's the color, green, or white, or red, or black. And then you put the light on the ceiling, it's gone." In the following interaction, the children "discover" reflection:

	[Anisha walks forward under the loft, holding the flashlight with her left hand at an angle to the mirror that she holds flat in front of her.]
Anisha	Oh Deanna, look, I can bounce the light.
	[Deanna holds the mirror so light is bouncing directly behind her.]
	Deanna [excitedly] If you look back, maybe you can see the light.

A third student focused on what he saw while holding objects in the beam of light. The following interchange occurred when the students explored with large cardboard cutouts of letters of the alphabet.

| Jeremy | [working with a letter] Ooo, this makes a shadow. A different shadow [than the one he just saw]. [He picks up the letter G and hands it to his partner.] See if the G makes a shadow. |
| Hazel | It does make a shadow. See, look at this. |

When the children described their observations to the class, Ms. Kingsley was able to use those observations to elicit the children's current ideas about light and shadows and how they might investigate those ideas.

In a fourth-grade classroom,[14] the teacher, Ms. Lacey, introduced her students to the study of light by asking them what they wondered about light. The children identified over 100 "wonderings," including questions about how we see, why we see rainbows of color from some glass objects or jewelry, what makes light from the plastic sticks you bend to make them "glow" in the dark, what are black holes, and how fast is the speed of light. The next day, students were given a written assessment about light, presented as an opportunity for them to identify their current thinking about the nature and behavior of light. After reviewing students' responses, Ms. Lacey wrote statements on the board (see Table 10-1) indicating the variety of ideas the class held about light. The variation in views of light exhibited by the students provided a reason to investigate to determine the accuracy of the ideas and the relationships among them.

TABLE 10-1 Fourth Graders' Initial Ideas About Light

Light travels.	Light can be blocked by materials.
Light travels in a curved path.	Light can shine through materials.
Light travels in a straight line.	Light can go into materials.
Light travels in all directions.	Light can bounce off of materials.

Later in the unit on light, Ms. Lacey turned to other wonderings the students had about color and light. In the following excerpt, she ascertains whether students' questions came from what they had been told, read, or observed, and she prompted one student to hypothesize about color from what had previously been learned about the behavior of light.

| Ms. Lacey | I know you guys had a few questions about color, so I'm wondering what you know or would like to know about color? What is it you think you want to learn? Levon? |
| Levon | When I said that my shirt's a light blue, you said how do we know it? And you said we might be able to tell. |

Ms. Lacey	Mm-hmm. You want to know how you know it's blue?
Levon	And you said we might be able to tell how.
Ms. Lacey	Well, I think you want to know why when you see a blue shirt, you—it's blue. Okay. We might be able to figure that out. Tom? What is it you want to know?
Tommy	How you change color with light. I know it's real, cause I seen it.
Ms. Lacey	What did you see?
Tommy	Light makes your shirt be a different color. I want to know how to do that.
Ms. Lacey	Hmm. Jared?
Jared	I'm wondering how light can make color.
Ms. Lacey	How light can make color? You think it does?
Jared	Yeah.
Ms. Lacey	Oh. Marcus?
Marcus	I think light is color.
Ms. Lacey	You think light is color. Hmm. So, is that a hypothesis or is that something you really think?
Marcus	Hypothesis. It's something I heard.
Ms. Lacey	Okay. So we'll see if that's right or not.
Marcus	How does light blend, blend.
Ms. Lacey	How does it . . .
Marcus	Different colors of light blend. Like, in the first-hand, the white light blends with . . .
Ms. Lacey	Do you mean bend? Okay.
Michael	I don't really have a question about color, but I have a question about light. Why do they call light, light?
Ms. Lacey	Ah! Good question.
Marcus	Cause it's, cause it's light, like a light color. You can't even see it.
Michael	And why did they call it that? Why did they call it?
Ms. Lacey	What do you think they should call it?
Michael	Something 'cause it's so light, you can't see it.
Chris	How does color make white?
Ms. Lacey	How does color make white? It does?
Chris	Mm-hmm.

Ms. Lacey	You think so?
Chris	Yeah. I saw it in a book.
Ms. Lacey	So, that is your hypothesis.
Ronny	How does color interact with light?
Jared	How does light, how does light form color?
Ms. Lacey	How does light make color? You think it does?
Jared	How does light form color and make color?
Ms. Lacey	Do you think there's a difference between the word form and make? Or do you think it's the same thing?
Jared	It's kinda the same. Forms like light, or something.
Ms. Lacey	Do you think light forms color?
Jason	Yeah.
Ms. Lacey	What makes you think that it might do that?
Jason	Cause light does.
Ms. Lacey	You just think that? That's a hypothesis you're thinking. Okay.
Andrew	It's not a, I don't have a question, but it's sort of a thought. I read in this book that when colored light reflects off, like, the same color, that it'll reflect off that.
Ms. Lacey	I don't understand what you mean.
Andrew	Okay. If, if there's red light and it reflected off somebody's red shirt . . .
Ms. Lacey	Reflected like off like Jared's shirt?
Andrew	Red, yeah, red shirt.
Ms. Lacey	Okay.
Andrew	And then, to another red shirt and off.
Ms. Lacey	So you think this red light can bounce only if it's on red stuff? Is that what you're thinking?
Andrew	Yeah. Or if it reflects on like green, red light can't reflect on a green object.
Ms. Lacey	Red light can't reflect on a green object? What would happen to it if it wouldn't reflect?
Andrew	It'd stay in. It'll absorb.
Ms. Lacey	You think it might absorb? Could it do anything else?
Andrew	[pause] Transmit?
Ms. Lacey	You think it might transmit? Oh. Jamal? We've got some good ideas here. . . .

A common strategy for engagement not illustrated here is the use of a discrepant event—a phenomenon whose behavior or result is unexpected. For example, if one shines a bright, thin beam of light at an angle into a rectangular block of clear, colorless glass with a frosted surface, one can see that the light interacts with the block in multiple ways. Because the object is transparent, students are not surprised to see light through it, but they may be surprised that the light goes through at an angle (refraction), and they are surprised that light also reflects off the block where it enters and where the refracted light exits the block. We can then ask the question: If light behaves in all these ways with this material, does it do the same with other materials?

While it may be easy to engage children with unfamiliar phenomena or new aspects of familiar phenomena, it is more challenging to support them in developing scientific understanding of the world because scientists often "see" the world differently from what our senses tell us. So using the engagement phase to gain knowledge about the conceptual resources students bring to instruction is just the first step. As the knowledge-building process unfolds in subsequent phases, paying attention to how students use those ideas, promoting the use of particular ideas over others, and introducing new ideas are key. In the next phase, the primary focus shifts from eliciting students' thinking about what the physical world is like to preparing them to investigate it in scientific ways.

The Prepare-to-Investigate Phase

Description. Preparing to investigate is an opportunity for teachers to support children in learning how scientific knowledge is produced. While inquiry often begins with a general question, investigation must be guided by very specific questions. Thus, an important goal of this phase of instruction is to establish the specific question that will be the subject of the subsequent investigation.[15] The question must be specific enough to guide investigation, amenable to investigation by children, and central to the unit of study so that students can construct the desired knowledge of scientific concepts, procedures, and ways of knowing. If the teacher presents a question, it is important that this be done in a way that involves the children in discussion about why the question is important and relevant to understanding the broader topic of inquiry. This discussion provides an opportunity to signal the role of questions in scientific investigation and prompts the metacognitive activity that is the hallmark of any good reasoning. If students suggest a question, or the teacher and students together generate the question, it is still important to check the students' understanding about how the question is relevant to the topic of study.[16]

Once a question has been specified, attention can turn to determining how the question will be investigated. This is a critical issue for scientists, and is no less important for children's developing understanding. The teacher may provide information about procedures to use, students may invent or design procedures, or the teacher and students may work together to determine how investigation should be carried out. Increasingly, there is evidence that children can think meaningfully about issues of methodology in investigation.[17] Nevertheless, it is always important for the teacher to check students' understandings about *why* particular approaches and procedures are useful to answering the question. To this end, the teacher might ask students to describe the advantage of using particular materials or tools over others, or to tell why particular steps or tools are necessary. Then, during the actual investigation, the teacher should periodically reassess students' understanding of what they are doing to ascertain whether accurate understanding was sustained in the face of their actual encounter with phenomena. In addition, the teacher can ask students to evaluate the effectiveness and accuracy of their tools or procedures. These actions support students' metacognitive awareness regarding the question–investigation relationship.

We think of investigation in classrooms as addressing how students should interact with materials, as well as with one another (when investigation is carried out by groups of students). A critical aspect of preparing to investigate is determining with students what they will document and how during their investigation. This may take the form of discussing the extent to which procedures need to be documented (only to a small degree when students are all investigating in the same way, but in detail when groups of students investigate differently), and promoting and illustrating the use of drawings to show investigative setups.

If the amount of data collection has been left undefined, the students will need to consider how they will know when they have collected enough data. The fact that students will have to make and report claims and evidence to their classmates lends greater significance to this issue. Students may find they need to collect more data to have sufficient amounts to convince their classmates of their claim in comparison with what they might have found convincing. Finally, it will be important to have students discuss how to document observations so they are accurate, precise, and informative.

When students are working in groups, assigning them roles can be helpful in supporting them in working together effectively. There are various types of roles that students can adopt during investigation. Possible roles to support effective *management* of the students' activity are Equipment Manager, Timekeeper,[18] and Recorder. These roles are not unique to scientific inquiry, but other roles are. For example, having the required materials does not mean that students will use them effectively; it is necessary to monitor that the correct procedures are being carried out and with care.

In addition, a number of responsibilities attend data collection, such as ensuring that enough data will be collected to fulfill the norms of scientific investigation, determining the level of precision with which observations are to be made (e.g., whether length should be recorded to the centimeter, tenth of a centimeter, or hundredth of a centimeter).[19] These sorts of issues form the basis for *intellectual* roles that students can adopt, in contrast to the management roles discussed above.[20] These roles, rather than being named for a task, are named for the conceptual focus maintained during investigation. For example, one student in a group can assume primary responsibility for pressing the group to evaluate how well procedures are working and being carried out in order to answer the question. Another student can be given primary responsibility for evaluating the extent to which the data being collected are relevant to the question. Finally, another student can be given primary responsibility for checking whether the group has enough data to make a claim in answer to the question.

If the practice of adopting roles is utilized, the prepare-to-investigate phase is used to set this up. Modeling and role-playing are helpful to support students in adopting roles that are new to them. In addition, the formal assignment of roles may change over time because while management roles may always be needed, intellectual roles represent ways of thinking that we want all students to adopt. Thus, the need to formalize such roles should decrease over time as students appropriate them as a matter of course when engaging in scientific investigation.

Finally, it is useful to give some attention to the issue of how data will be recorded. At times it may be best to provide a table and simply have students discuss how they will use it and why it is a useful way to organize their data. At other times it may be best to have the class generate a list of possible means for recording data. Sometimes it may be sufficient to indicate that students should be sure to record their observations in their notebooks, and have the students in their groups decide what approach is best for recording their observations.

Illustration. In the unit on light and shadows, Ms. Kingsley posed to her kindergarteners the question of whether an object's shadow can be more than one shape, following the opportunity they had to explore with flashlights prior to beginning any formal investigation. She knew that not all the children had made shadows during their exploration, so she used part of the discussion in this phase to ascertain students' understanding of how to put objects in the light to make shadows. She showed the class how the materials would be set up, with a light source placed a couple of feet from a wall and a piece of poster paper taped on the wall to allow them to draw the shadows they observed.

During her fourth graders' investigation of the interaction of light and matter, Ms. Lacey bridged from the children's wonderings to a question she introduced: How does light interact with solid objects? She began the preparing-to-investigate phase by ascertaining students' understanding of the question. One boy asked what "interacts" means. She responded that she was interacting with the students, and then asked them to interpret the question without using the word "interact." The students responded with such questions as: "What would it do"? "How does it act"? "How does it behave"? "How do they act together (but not like in a movie)"? Ms. Lacey then solicited questions about other words in the investigation question, and a boy asked, "What is a solid?" Students responded with statements such as: "A solid is not like water."" It's filled in." "It's hard, maybe." "It doesn't bend." At this point, Ms. Lacey picked up a bendable solid, bent it, and asked the students whether it was a solid. Students were divided on whether it was. Ms. Lacey proceeded to review states of matter with the students, discussing properties and examples. She then returned to the preparation for investigating light.

The materials on which the students would shine a flashlight were simple, but there were many of them (more than 20 items), and describing each in order to identify it would have been cumbersome (e.g., blue plastic sheet, colorless plastic sheet, plastic sheet with gold coating on one side). So Ms. Lacey prepared a poster with each type of material mounted on it and numbered. She used the poster to show children the materials with which they would be working, and they discussed the use of the numbers to facilitate documenting their observations.

Ms. Lacey also introduced a new tool to the students: a small rectangular piece of white construction paper, which she called a "light catcher." This tool functioned as a screen to look for reflected or transmitted light. Figure 10-2 shows the setup Ms. Lacey showed the students, with the letters A and B indicating the places where the students expected they might see light.

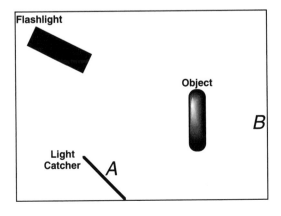

FIGURE 10-2 Investigative setup for studying how light interacts with solid objects.

In addition, the class talked about categorizing objects in terms of how light behaved. Ms. Lacey asked the students what they thought the light might do, and they discussed categorizing the objects based on whether light bounced off, went through, became trapped, or did something else (the students were not sure what this might be, but they wanted to have a category for other possibilities).[21] In the course of that conversation, Ms. Lacey introduced the terms "reflected," "transmitted," and "absorbed," which she stated were terms used by scientists to name the behaviors they had described. There was some discussion about what it meant when an object blocked light: Did that mean light had been absorbed, or was it simply stopped by the material? Ms. Lacey suggested that the class leave that question open, to be discussed again after they had investigated and had the opportunity to observe the light.

Ms. Lacey chose to focus students' recording of their observations by preparing a simple table for them to complete: a column for the number/name of the material and a column each for indicating whether light reflected, transmitted (went through), or was absorbed (trapped by) the material. The use of the table seemed straightforward, so there was little discussion. Ms. Lacey later noticed that most students used the table as though their task was to determine which single column to check for each object. She realized that the students needed guidance to check for each object whether light was reflected, transmitted, or absorbed. The next time Ms. Lacey taught this topic, she made two changes in this phase. First, she was careful to raise the question of whether light could behave in more than one way with a material. Students were divided on whether they thought this was possible, which gave them a reason to investigate and supported them in realizing the need to be thorough in observing light with each object. Second, she asked students how they might provide evidence that light did not interact in particular ways with an object. This discussion led students to realize that they would have information to record in each column of the table, and that what does not happen can be as informative as what does happen.

The Investigate Phase

Description. In this phase, students interact with the physical world, document their observations, and think about what these observations mean about the physical world. The teacher's role is to monitor students' use of materials and interactions with others (e.g., in small groups), as well as attend to the conceptual ideas with which students are working and the ways in which their thinking is similar and different from that of their classmates.

Investigating involves the interaction of content and process. It may appear to students to be more about process because what we observe is a function of when, how, and with what tools we choose to observe. At the same time, what we observe is also a function of what we expect to observe, and how we interpret our observations is clearly influenced by what we already know and believe about the physical world. For example, we have experienced children describing only one type of interaction when shining light on objects because they expected that light could interact in only one way. Thus they described light as only "going through" a piece of clear, colorless plastic wrap even though we could see bright spots of light on the front of the wrap indicating reflected light. Furthermore, students described light as only "being blocked" from a piece of cardboard even though a disc of light the size of the flashlight beam could be seen on the back of the piece of cardboard, indicating that light was going through it.[22]

The teacher determines whether and when to prompt students' awareness of the ways in which their prior knowledge may be influencing their observations. With respect to students' interactions with *materials*, it is important to monitor whether students are using them appropriately. Students invariably use materials in unexpected ways; hence, the teacher needs to observe student activity closely. When students use materials incorrectly, the teacher needs to determine whether to provide corrective feedback. Since it is important for the development of metacognition that students be in the "driver's seat" and not simply follow the teacher's directions, determining whether, when, and how to provide feedback is critical. If the teacher judges that the students' activity is so off the mark that the targeted learning goals will be sacrificed, it is critical to provide prompt corrective feedback. An example in the study of light would be if students measuring angles of the path of light coming into and reflecting off of a mirror were using the protractor incorrectly.

Other cases, however, provide opportunities for students to become aware of gaps in their thinking. An example of this occurred when the teacher in the kindergarten class studying light and shadows noticed that some students were tracing the object directly on their recording paper rather than tracing the object's shadow. When the teacher saw this happening, she joined the group as they were working and began to ask them about their data. In the course of the conversation, she asked them to show her how they had made the shadows, which led them to indicate that some were tracings of the objects themselves, not the shadows. She then asked them, "If our question is about shadows, which drawings show shadows?" The students were able to point to their drawings that were shadows. She then asked, "How could you mark your drawings so that you can tell which ones are shadows, so that when we look for patterns, you'll know which drawings to look at?" They devised a scheme—to draw dots around the drawings that were shadows—and the teacher moved on to another group. Later, when the former group reported, the rest of the class learned about their strategy and how they had dealt with the "mixed" nature of their observations.

Another important category of feedback is when the teacher brings out the norms and conventions of scientific investigation (e.g., holding conditions the same when trials are conducted, measuring from the same reference point, and changing only one variable at a time). Attention to such issues can be prompted by asking students about the decisions they are making about how to investigate. For example, in the fourth-grade investigation of the interaction of light and matter, one group's response to Ms. Lacey's question about what they had found out revealed a lack of attention to the transmission of light. Ms. Lacey handled this in the following way:

Ms. Lacey	When we were preparing to investigate, we said that light might also be transmitted, but I didn't hear you say anything about that. Did you check for that?
Student	No, but we already know light doesn't go through these materials; they block it.
Ms. Lacey	But remember that scientists believe it is important to test out such ideas, and as scientific thinkers, your classmates will be encouraged to look for such evidence. How will you convince them that these materials don't transmit light?

Here Ms. Lacey gave students an important message about the need to rule out possibilities instead of relying on assumptions.

With small-group investigation, in addition to general monitoring to support student collaboration, the teacher needs to be attentive to whether differences in students' ideas create difficulties. In the excerpt below, two kindergarten children in Ms. Kingsley's class are investigating reflection from a mirror. Their initial conflict is due to Brian's interest in placing the mirror so that its back faces the light source. Amanda objects because her exploration during the engage phase revealed that reflection is best from the front of the mirror. She is very interested in seeing the reflection because the class is examining a claim she made from her exploration activity, which was that you can use a mirror to make light "go wherever you want it to."

| Amanda | [tracing line to mirror] This goes to here. The light has to hit the mirror. Then . . . |

Brian	I want it to go that way. [referring to placement of the mirror with its back to the light source]
Amanda	No, the mirror has to face the light source.
Amanda	[turns mirror to face the light source] Lookey! Light, see.
Brian	[turns mirror back around] Lookey, no light, see.
Amanda	But that's because it's not facing that way. [turns mirror to face the light]
Brian	You said you could move it wherever you wanted it to go. So your plan has failed. . . .
Amanda	The light has to do the—okay. This is the light source, right? [*points to source*] This light has to hit the mirror . . . And then, look, look, see . . . Now you think my plan works, see? Watch, see . . .
Brian	[takes hold of mirror] I can't make it go this way! [referring to making the light go behind the mirror] If I take this off [removes mirror from where it rests on their drawing paper], it's going my way. But [puts mirror back onto paper], it's not going my way.
Amanda	The mirror has to face . . . The light has to hit the mirror. [taps mirror with hand] And look: light, light, light. [points to reflected beams of light]
Brian	But you said it could go anywhere. You said it could go anywhere you wanted it to go and I wanted it to go backwards, like this. [referring to making the light go behind the mirror]
Amanda	But the mirror [forcefully places the mirror on their drawing paper] has to face the light source [forceful gesture toward light source], face the light source, and THEN you can move it. [referring to the reflected beam of light]

The interaction of content and process that occurs during investigation means that teachers must be mindful of children's cognitive activity as they undergo and interpret their experiences with the physical world. Teachers should ask students what they are observing and what they think their observations mean about the question under investigation. Sometimes it is useful to ask students *why* they think what they are doing will help them answer the question. In addition, the teacher needs to observe what students observe so students can be prompted to notice important phenomena they might otherwise ignore or be encouraged to pursue observations the teacher believes useful to the knowledge-building process.

When investigative procedures are simple, students are able to focus more of their attention on what the data are and what these data suggest about the question being investigated. When procedures are more complex, students need more time to focus on the meaning of the data apart from the actual investigation. When students design the investigation themselves, they may need to give more attention during the investigation to evaluating how well their plans are working so they can make adjustments. Thus, teachers need to monitor how well children are handling the complexity of the investigation so that sufficient time is allocated to support the knowledge-building process.[23]

Once the data have been collected, students need to analyze them. Identifying patterns is a deductive analytic process in which students work from specific datasets to identify general relationships. From this step, students make knowledge claims, just as scientists would. That is, they make claims about the physical world, using the patterns they identified to generate those claims. We consider this aspect of investigation to be a different instructional phase because the nature of the cognitive activity for the teacher and students has changed. This aspect is discussed as part of the preparing-to-report phase.

Illustration

To illustrate the investigation phase, we draw upon an event that occurred in Ms. Kingsley's kindergarten class during their investigation of light and shadows. Amanda and Rochelle were working together, with Amanda basically directing Rochelle. When Ms. Kingsley checked on them and asked questions to determine their thinking about what they were finding out, it became clear to her that Amanda was quite certain that the shadow from an object could be only one shape, and Rochelle appeared to go along with whatever Amanda thought. While Amanda's thinking was incorrect, Ms. Kingsley chose not to intervene, recognizing that during reporting, the children would have the opportunity to see a wider range of data and possibly reconsider their thinking (see the illustration of the reporting phase).

The following excerpt is from Ms. Lacey's fourth-grade class. This interchange occurred early in the investigation, and Ms. Lacey was checking on a group of three girls that she knew from previous experience had found investigative activity challenging. She began by asking which materials the students had used in their investigation and what they had found out. She learned that one student in the group had been working independently instead of with the other two, and they had not been discussing their results.

Ms. Lacey encouraged them to work together, especially since it would be helpful to have one person holding the flashlight and material, and another person using the light catcher.

Ms. Lacey	[picks up a blue styrofoam object and shines the flashlight on it] What's it doing?
Mandy	Some goes through.
Ms. Lacey	How do you know?
Mandy	Some blue light is on the wall.
Ms. Lacey	Does it do anything else? [Ms. Lacey directs the student to use the light catcher to check other possibilities.]
Mandy	Some is reflected.
Ms. Lacey	Write that down.

Perhaps the most important question asked by the teacher in this excerpt is "How do you know?" This question is at the core of distinguishing systematic research from our everyday sense making. It also sent the message that the students were accountable for their observations, and allowed Ms. Lacey to indicate the need to check for multiple ways in which light might behave with the object.

The Prepare-to-Report Phase

Description

As the activity shifts to a focus on the public sharing of one's findings from investigation (reporting phase), the role of the class as a community of scientific thinkers takes on new meaning. In scientific practice, this phase marks a shift in emphasis from divergent to convergent thinking, and from operating with the values, beliefs, norms, and conventions of the scientific community in the background to operating with them in the foreground.[24] Now it matters a great deal what fellow classmates will think and not just what the investigating group thinks.

In this phase, just as scientists use their laboratory documents to prepare papers for public presentation to the larger scientific community, students use the information and observations in their notebooks to prepare materials for public presentation to their classmates. The public nature of sharing one's claims and evidence means that students need to determine the claim(s) for which there is enough evidence to warrant public scrutiny, and what data they should feature as the compelling evidence backing their own claim(s) and supporting or refuting the claims of others.

Students can use poster-size paper as the medium for reporting, thus allowing the information to be large enough for everyone in the class to see. Posters are expected to include a statement of the group's knowledge claim(s), as well as data backing the claim(s); if groups investigated different questions, the poster should include the question as well. Data may be presented in written, tabular, or graphical form (including figures or graphs), and students may decide to include a diagram of the investigative setup to provide a context for the data. (This is to be expected when students investigated in different ways.) As each group prepares its poster, students should be thinking about how to present their findings to best enable others to understand them, *and* be convinced of the group's claim. Decisions about how to state a claim and what data to include in presenting one's claim provide important learning opportunities.

A major aspect of the teacher's role in this phase is to reflect the norms of the scientific community regarding the development and evaluation of knowledge claims. In the scientific community, for example, there is an expectation that relationships will be stated precisely and backed by unambiguous and reliable data. It should also be recognized that claims can be stated in the negative, thus indicating a relationship that is claimed to be inaccurate—for example, the brightness of the light source does not affect whether light reflects from an object. Such claims help the community narrow its consideration of possible relationships.

Another role of the teacher is to help students attend to issues that may affect the quality of their public presentation. For example, teachers can encourage students to draw as well as write out their ideas to communicate them more effectively. Furthermore, teachers can prompt students to evaluate their poster for its effectiveness in communicating findings. For example: Is it readable? Are things clearly stated? Is there enough information for others to evaluate the claim or be convinced of its validity?

Finally, a key role for the teacher is to monitor the types of claims students are generating and the nature of the evidence they are selecting. The teacher determines whether and to what extent to prompt students' awareness of the role played by process in determining what they observed (e.g., ascertaining students' awareness of imprecise or inaccurate data). With respect to content, the teacher determines whether and when to focus students on particular strategies for interpreting or analyzing their data or to provide additional information to support students in writing claims. It may be necessary for the teacher to help groups reorganize their data to find patterns. For example, Table 10-2 shows two tables. The top table shows the data as they were originally recorded. The order of the columns matches the order of places that students looked to check for light from the flashlight. The order of objects in the first column is simply the order students selected to observe them. The bottom table shows the same data in a similar form,

TABLE 10-2 Data Tables from Initial Recording and with Revisions for Analysis Purposes

Original Data Table and Observations:

Object	On Light Catcher in Front of Object (reflected)	On Back of Object (transmitted)	On Light Catcher Behind Object (absorbed)
Clear glass	dim light	bright light	light shadow
Purple glass	dim purple light	bright purple light	dark purple shadow
Silver wrap	bright light	no light	dark shadow
White plastic sheet	dim light	medium light	medium shadow
White typing paper	bright light	dim light	medium shadow
Black felt	no light	no light	very dark shadow
Orange cardboard	dim orange light	dim reddish light	dark shadow

Reorganized Data Table and Simplified Observations:

Object	On Light Catcher in Front of Object (reflected)	On Back of Object (transmitted)	On Light Catcher Behind Object (absorbed)
Black felt	no light	very dark shadow	no light
Orange cardboard	dim light	dark shadow	dim light
Purple glass	dim light	dark shadow	bright light
White plastic sheet	dim light	medium shadow	medium light
Clear glass	dim light	light shadow	bright light
Silver wrap	bright light	dark shadow	no light
White typing paper	bright light	medium shadow	dim light

but to facilitate looking for patterns, the columns and rows have been reordered, and the data have been simplified (information about color has been removed). This type of reorganization and simplification of data is common for scientists, and may be necessary for students to find patterns from which to make a claim.

Often, the teacher's support is at the level of helping groups figure out how best to state the claim(s) they want to make from their data. It does not include evaluating whether their data support the claim; that is part of the reporting phase and should be shared by the class.

On the other hand, the teacher may choose to support students in making additional claims based on the data they have, particularly in instances where the group has unique data to make a claim that the teacher believes would promote desired knowledge-building for the class. In Ms. Lacey's fourth-grade class, for example, despite students' assumptions that light would behave in only one way with an object, a group had evidence that light behaved in more than one way. Given that this was the only group in the class making such a claim from that body of evidence, Ms. Lacey supported the group to ensure that they would include the claim in their poster so it would be introduced to the whole class.

An alternative approach involves the teacher's questioning students during the prepare-to-investigate phase to lead them to consider the possibility that light may behave in more than one way. The emphasis in this case may be on ruling out the possibility of disconfirming evidence. With this approach, the teacher monitors during the investigation phase whether students are checking for multiple possibilities, and will know whether the students observe light interacting with objects in more than one way.

Illustration. The following excerpt from an investigation of light by third graders shows a typical teacher–student interaction as students attempted to generate knowledge claims.[25] The students were working with light boxes producing narrow beams of light and had been given latitude regarding which questions—identified during the engagement phase—they would like to study. As a result, different groups of students investigated with different types of materials. In the transcript, note that the students did most of the talking. The teacher primarily asked questions to determine the nature of the students' thinking. Note also that the teacher reflected an important norm of scientific activity by asking the students how they planned to represent the observations supporting their claim.

Ms. Sutton	What claim are you working on right now?
Don	We had to change it because we thought that the speed of light would be a [second-hand investigation].
Ms. Sutton	Mm hmm.
Kevin	So, light can reflect off a mirror. Any other object that's not a mirror, like a piece of paper. Let me demonstrate. [Ms. Sutton: Okay.] This is a piece of paper. You see, when the light hits the paper, it disappears. But before it disap-

pears, it hits the paper, it goes through the paper. It disappears.

Ms. Sutton	Hmm. Does *all* the light disappear through the paper?
Kevin	No. Okay, you see all the light that's coming through, from this hole?
Ms. Sutton	Yeah.
Kevin	It goes *to* the piece of paper. It disappears when it hits that piece—that object.
Ms. Sutton	Where do you think it goes?
Don	Through the paper. There's a little light over here. And it stops here because it doesn't have enough power to go anymore.
Ms. Sutton	Okay. Hang on a second. So, you're saying a little bit of light goes through the paper. And you think the rest of the light just disappears?
Kevin	No. The rest of the light that hits the paper disappears from the light—from the object, cause it's not a mirror. But if it hits the mirror it can reflect off of it.
Ms. Sutton	So if it's a mirror, the light goes in another direction, or reflects off. If it's something besides a mirror . . .
Kevin	It doesn't get reflected.
Ms. Sutton	It just disappears, it doesn't reflect?
Kevin	Yep.
Ms. Sutton	Okay. Are you going to try to prove that some way to the group? You have to show some data.
Don	Well, it's not exactly data. We sort of . . .
Kevin	I drew a picture out here.
Ms. Sutton	How could you show that? We could get another piece of paper. Save what you've got so far. How could you show on another piece of paper how the light is different with differ-ent—with the mirror and with the paper? How could you show it? What you just said—so you could show it to the rest of the group?
Kevin	We can draw the top and just say that the light is coming through—put light right here. And then the light through—going out of the box. And then we can put, make like a little part of it

	like this, like the target. And put the paper right here.
Ms. Sutton	So, Kevin is saying, when the light hits the mirror, it looks one way. When the light hits a piece of paper, it looks another way. How could you *show* how it looks those two ways on a piece of paper?
Don	And, another thing is, I sort of drew this thing. That's the light that's over here that goes there. And then when it hits these, it stays there and it doesn't come back.
Ms. Sutton	That's interesting, too. But you guys need to stick to one claim and deal with that. When you think you have evidence for that, if you want to explore something else and have some time, you could do that.

The Report Phase

Description. A critical feature of inquiry-based instruction is the point at which students' findings are publicly shared and discussed. This phase has two parts (see Figure 10-1). First, groups of students who have been investigating together present their claims and evidence, which are discussed by the class in terms of their own merits and in light of the findings presented by previous groups. Second, the class discusses the commonalities and differences among the claims and evidence presented, noting claims that can be rejected, developing a class list of community-accepted claims, and determining claims or questions that need further investigation. In addition to providing occasions for discussing important issues related to the investigative process (e.g., possible errors, missed observations), public reports require students to make and defend statements about their understandings, and provide occasions for examining their own thinking and sense making as well as that of others.[26] In addition, when students publicly share their results, the need for vocabulary and a common language to communicate ideas becomes salient. Thus, there is an important opportunity for the teacher to support and guide students in the use of scientific terms to facilitate their communication.

When students first experience this activity, the teacher plays a pivotal role in communicating and modeling expectations for audience members. This includes establishing and maintaining conversational norms. Despite the fact that children may need to challenge the ideas or work of their classmates, the teacher is key in setting the tone so that this is done with the understanding that the students are all thinking together so they can collectively determine how to understand the aspect of the physical world under investigation. The primary expectations for audience members are to determine whether there is a clearly stated claim that is related to the question under investigation, whether there is evidence backing that claim, and whether the evidence is unambiguous in supporting the claim. The issue of unambiguous support concerns whether there is any evidence—either from other groups or from within the presenting group's data—that would counter the claim. With teacher modeling and practice with the teacher's feedback, students become able to sustain substantive conversations regarding the knowledge they are developing about the physical world.

The reporting phase is particularly complex and rich with opportunities for the teacher to engage in supporting children's thinking and actions. As each group shares its claim(s) and describes the relationship between these claims and their data, the teacher assumes multiple roles: monitoring for understanding, working with the students to clarify ambiguous or incomplete ideas, seeding the conversation with potentially helpful language or ideas, and serving as the collective memory of prior conversations (both in the whole-class context and in the small-group investigation contexts). The challenge in this phase of instruction is to promote the group's advancement toward deeper understanding of the phenomenon under investigation, as well as the nature of scientific ways of knowing, using the fruits of the investigation activity and the collective thinking of the classroom community.

The reporting phase culminates with the whole class discussing the claims that have been shared to determine which if any have sufficiently convincing evidence (and a lack of contradictory evidence) to elevate them to the status of "class claim"—indicating that there is class consensus about the validity of the claim. This discussion of claims typically results in identifying where there is disagreement among claims or contradictory evidence related to particular claims (e.g., when the data presented by one group can also be used to contradict the claim of another), which provides the motivation for the next cycle of investigation.

Illustration. Excerpts from classroom instruction illustrate various aspects of teacher and student activity during this phase. The following transcript is from the beginning of the reporting phase in Ms. Lacey's fourth-grade class. Ms. Lacey introduces students to the class claim chart, on which the class will track the claims that have been introduced and the classroom community's reaction to them. She also forewarns students that they have conflicting views, anticipating the need to prepare the students to hear things from their classmates with which they will not agree.

| Ms. Lacey | And we're going to start making a list of claims. Or we might have a list of—we don't know whether we believe that or not. . . . Some of our claims may end up being "think abouts." We need to think about them some more. . . . |
| | You know what? You guys don't all agree. I've been to every group . . . so you better pay attention. They may not convince you, but you might think to yourself, "aha! I'm gonna try that." Or, "I might need to check that out." |

Ms. Lacey's introduction of the class claim chart sends an important message about the dynamic nature of the inquiry process: reporting is not a culminating activity; it is part of an ongoing activity, the next phase of which will be shaped by what has just transpired. Her decision to alert students to the presence of conflicting ideas provides an authentic purpose for paying attention to one another during the reporting phase and stimulated metacognition.

In the next excerpt, a student questions one of the claims made by the reporting group. The group made a claim that "light can't be trapped" and cited as evidence that "you can't roll it up and throw it." The students' interaction presents the teacher with many issues to which she could react to support the students' development of scientific knowledge and ways of knowing.

Bobby	When you said that you believe that light can't be trapped because it's a gas, you can't roll it up and throw it. What do you mean?
Megan	We mean we can't grab light and throw it at someone.
Heather	It's not solid.
Megan	It's not a liquid, either.
Bobby	So you're saying that light is a gas? How do you know light is a gas?
Heather	Air is a gas, and you can't feel it. Well, you can feel it only when it's blowing. But you can't feel light because it's not blowing.
Bobby	So you guys are saying that you think light is a gas because light is like air?

Ms. Lacey could have pointed out that a claim about light being a gas is unrelated to the focus of this particular investigation; she could have truncated the interaction by providing the information that light is a form of energy, not matter; she could have identified this claim as one that requires further exploration, perhaps in a second-hand way. But Ms. Lacey chose not to interject at all. While this decision has limitations with respect to developing scientific knowledge about light, it has the advantage of giving the students opportunity and responsibility to examine one another's thinking with respect to the norms and conventions of scientific practice, as illustrated by Bobby's pressing the girls to address how they know light is a gas. Such questions can provide opportunities for students particularly interested in a question to pursue it outside of class, or resources might be brought into the class (books or descriptions downloaded from the Internet) that provide information pertinent to the question.

In the next two excerpts, Ms. Lacey responds in two different ways to students' questioning of the reporting group based on her judgment of the reasons for those questions. In the first excerpt, she responds to confusion that she suspects arises from the way students are interpreting language in the phrasing of claims. The excerpt illustrates the language demands involved in both representing one's thinking in a claim and interpreting the claims of others.

Barbie	I'm confused—"we believe light does go in a path." Well, how do you know it goes in a path? It could go different ways. ["*A* path" appears to be interpreted as "*one* path."]
Megan	We tried it on the flashlight. It's just straight. ["*A* path" appears to have meant "a *straight* path."]
Barbie	Cause there's a whole bunch of light. Light can go [other ways] [shows with hand]. ["*A* path" appears to be interpreted as "*one particular* path" instead of many possible paths.]
Megan	We don't believe that.
Ms. Lacey	Can you draw a diagram on the board? [Change from an oral to a written medium may resolve issues due to language demands.]

The girls used a context from their preinstruction assessment—a tree, a person, and the sun—to show two different possibilities regarding the path of light: wavy and straight lines. They drew multiple paths from the sun and pointed to the straight lines as the representations that matched their claim. Ms. Lacey then worked with the class to modify the students' claim about the path of light so that it was consistent with the illustration:

Ms. Lacey	[*to class*] Can you think of some way they could switch that claim to make more sense to us? She's telling us one thing, and they didn't put that one word in. [*to Megan and Heather*] Cause you don't think it goes wavy, you think it goes . . .
Megan	Straight.
Ms. Lacey	How could you change your claim to say that?
Heather	We believe light goes only in a straight path.
Ms. Lacey	[*to class*] Will that make better sense to us?
Class	Yeah.

In the second excerpt, a student struggles to make sense of the claim that light reflects and goes through. Ms. Lacey suspects, because of the student's language, he has difficulty conceptualizing that light can behave in multiple ways simultaneously. As a result, she intervenes, asking a question to help achieve greater clarity regarding the student's confusion:

Megan	Yeah. Stefan?
Stefan	Reflect and go through—on the plastic tray. When you put it on reflect, it reflected off the plastic tray. And when you put it on go through, it went through the plastic tray. But I don't get it. If it reflected off, then how did it go through?
Megan	Well, we put it on an angle and shined it and it went on our screen. And when we put it straight, it went through.
Ms. Lacey	Stefan, are you having a hard time thinking that light can do two things at once? If it reflects off, why did it also go through? Did they explain?

In both of the above examples, as well as in the excerpt at the beginning of this chapter in which a second-grade student objected to a claim about light reflecting from wood, students are revealing that they lack a conception of light that allows it to behave in the ways indicated by other students. Brad does not have a way to think about light that would account for its ability to reflect from wood. Stefan does not have a way to think about light that would account for its ability to simultaneously reflect and pass through an object. How does some of the light "know" to reflect, while other light gets transmitted through the material? These are reasonable issues, and we should not be surprised that the students do not readily accept claims that speak to a reality they do not believe. It is part of the scientific culture to be skeptical about claims that do not fit existing scientific theories, as these claims clearly did not fit the students' preexisting ideas. Indeed, there are numerous examples of scientific papers that presented novel scientific claims and were rejected by top scientific journals because of their inconsistency with prevailing knowledge and beliefs, but later became highly regarded and even prize-winning.[27] Thus when such events occur, it is important for the teacher to recognize that the issue is the fit between the idea presented and the students' conceptual framework. As *How People Learn* suggests, it is precisely in these situations that students' thinking must be fully engaged if they are to develop desired scientific understanding.

There are several ways to proceed in such circumstances. Some research has demonstrated that having students observe relationships can lead them to change their initial thinking about those relationships,[28] or at least come up with alternative ideas.[29] In the case of the second grader who was skeptical about the reflection of light, this would mean setting up the materials so he could observe the reflection from wood that his classmates saw and providing opportunities to examine the reflection from other solids. Other researchers have proposed engaging students in reasoning through a series of phenomena that are closely related,[30] helping students bridge analogous circumstances. In the case of disbelief about light reflecting from wood or other nonshiny solids, this might mean starting with observing instances of reflection that students readily accept (e.g., reflection from a mirror); linking to observations of a very thick mirror, whereby the light beam can be seen traveling through to the silvered back surface of the mirror and reflecting from there; linking to reflection from a less reflective surface, such as lead (a metal, but not shiny); then linking to a similarly less reflective surface but of a different type, such as gray construction paper; and so on. The bridging could go as far as examining reflection from black felt, a material students are initially quite sure does not reflect light, but can be observed to do so if the room is dark enough.[31]

Another approach to addressing the nonacceptance of claims that contradict everyday experience is to tell students that part of learning science means developing new conceptions of reality.[32] This does not necessarily mean discarding existing ideas.[33] However, it does mean that students need to recognize that in a science context, the cultural beliefs and practices that guide knowledge production in the scientific community dictate what knowledge is valued and accepted and hence is considered scientific knowledge,[34] and that they need to operate accordingly in their knowledge-building activity during science instruction.

Despite the challenge of accepting claims that are initially counter to everyday thinking, we have regularly observed students, even very young children, developing new ideas that are counter to their initial thinking. The following example comes from Ms. Kingsley's kindergarten class during their study of light and shadows. The class was discussing two claims that arose from the day's investigation and were posted on the board: (1) an object can make more than one shadow shape, and (2) an object can make only one shadow shape. When Ms. Kingsley asked the class to evaluate the claims in light of the data from students' investigations, which were also posted, Amanda, who had repeatedly stated her view that an object's shadow can be only one shape, gave the following response:

Ms. Kingsley	Okay, look at the evidence we've got here. Does it support the claim that objects make more than one shadow?
Amanda	Both.
Ms. Kingsley	You think it says both Amanda, tell me why.
Amanda	Because um [touching each of the posters with multiple shapes of shadows], all shadow, all shadow, all shadow, all shadow. [touching each of the drawings containing only one shape of shadow] One shadow, one shadow.

Here, Amanda correctly pointed out that the data did not conclusively support one claim over the other, drawing attention to the ambiguity of the results. This provided a reason to investigate further, so the teacher suggested that the class do so the next day. The next excerpt is an exchange that occurred following the next day's investigation. Again, all the groups' data were posted at the front. After examining the data from the second day, all of which showed more than one shadow, Amanda provided a different evaluation of the evidence:

Ms. Kingsley	We need to find out if the documentation supports that a shape can make one shadow or more than one shadow. Does this evidence support the claim . . . [points to the two posted claims]
JT	More!
Derek	One!
Amanda	The first one [an object can make more than one shadow] is true.
Ms. Kingsley	Why?
Amanda	Because one object can make more shadows, see? Because look at all these shadows on the papers. [runs hand along all the posters because they all show multiple shapes of shadows for an object]

Of note is that Ms. Kingsley and the other teachers featured in this section allowed the children to work with the ideas they had, but pressed them to continually reexamine those ideas in light of the results of their own and others' investigations. Amanda needed the time of several cycles of investigation to become convinced of a different idea from the one she initially held. Thus, the cycling process of investigation within the same context is an important aspect of promoting desired development of scientific knowledge and ways of knowing.

Second-Hand Investigation

Our focus thus far has been on the development of understanding through first-hand investigation. Such experiences give students repeated opportunities to articulate and test their reasoning and ideas against one another's first-hand observations, and steep them in the differences between a scientific approach to knowledge building from experience and a more casual everyday approach. However, inquiry-based science instruction can also profitably include learning from text-based resources (as suggested by the *National Science Education Standards*).[35] The study of accumulated knowledge is authentic to scientific practice[36] and involves cognitive activities that have many similarities with first-hand inquiry about the physical world.[37] Second-hand sources can also reliably focus student attention on the core concepts of interest. The question is how to engage students in such activity in a way that keeps them actively engaged intellectually relative to scientific ways of knowing and permits a skeptical stance that is common to a scientific mindset.

To achieve this goal, we developed a novel type of text for inquiry-based instruction, whose use is called a second-hand investigation. These texts are modeled after the notebook of a scientist and so are referred to as notebook texts. They consist of excerpts from the notebook of a fictitious scientist, Lesley Park, who uses her notebook to "think aloud" regarding the inquiry in which she is engaged, sharing with the reader her observations of the phenomenon she is studying, the way in which she has modeled that phenomenon, the nature of her investigation, the data collected in the course of her investigation, and the knowledge claims suggested by the data.[38]

We share excerpts from this instruction to illustrate how text can be approached in an inquiry-based fashion to support students' engagement in scientific reasoning and what role the teacher plays in such activity. The specific notebook text with which the children were working reports on an investigation with materials very similar to those used by the students in studying the interaction of light with matter, although there were several differences in Lesley's investigation, including her use of a light meter to measure the light she observed.

Of note are the various ways that the teacher, Ms. Sutton, supported the students' learning from the text. For example, she led the students in a quick overview of the text during which the students identified the features that signaled this was a scientist's notebook: a header with the scientist's name and date of activity, drawings showing investigative setups, and tables of data. During the reading of the text, a significant amount of time was devoted to examining the relationship between the information in the notebook and the students' own experiences. Ms. Sutton accomplished this by revisiting the claims list arising from the students' own first-hand investigations. The students identified those claims on which there was consensus and those that were still under consideration, but for which there was insufficient evidence. In addition, there were numerous instances in which Ms. Sutton called the students' attention to vocabulary that was introduced in the notebook text and how it compared with terms the students had been using in their own writing and discussion (e.g., Lesley's use of "absorbed" to describe the behavior students referred to as the "blocking" of light).

The following three excerpts illustrate how the text, in combination with the teacher's facilitation, supported the students' engagement in scientific reasoning. In the first excerpt, the students have encountered a table in which Lesley presents data in units she calls "candles."

Ms. Sutton	Okay, it's the readout of how many candles. And right now it's showing the flashlight all by itself has . . .?
Leo	Ten candles.
Ms. Sutton	Ten candles.
Jihad	Could it be like 10.5 or something or 10.3?
Ms. Sutton	I would imagine. Don't you think it could go up or down depending on how bright the light is?
Jihad	So, if she puts zero candles, so that means it doesn't transmit at all?
Ms. Sutton	Yes. Good observation.
Tatsuro	Are there such thing as like, um, a millicandle?

Ms. Sutton mediated the students' sense making with the table. To understand any of the other findings in this table, it was important for the students to recognize that the amount of light from the light source (the flashlight) was "ten candles." This discussion, however, led several students to wonder about this unit of measure. Transferring their knowledge about other units of measure, they inquired about the system from which this unit is derived and how that system "works" (i.e., whether it works like the metric system).

In the next excerpt, the students have encountered Lesley's claim that "all objects reflect and absorb light."

Ms. Sutton	What evidence did you see that would support that [all objects reflect and absorb] even though that wasn't your claim?
Ian	That almost all the objects did and maybe if we used a light meter, we might have found out that every single object did a little.
Ms. Sutton	How about you, Megan?
Megan	Some objects did both things—two different things, but not . . . we didn't, like, kind of find out that for all objects . . .
Ms. Sutton	If you had done more, do you think we might have?
Megan	Maybe.
Ms. Sutton	If you had tested more?
Megan	We didn't do all the objects, yet.

In this exchange, we see how Ms. Sutton related the second-hand investigation to the students' first-hand investigation by calling their attention to the differences between their claims and Lesley's claim. This led to a discussion of two issues: the role of measurement and the sample size. Lesley used a light meter to collect her data, while the children had no means of measurement; they simply described their visual observations as precisely as possible. Ian suggested that with a measuring device, the class's findings might have been consistent with Lesley's. Ms. Sutton introduced the possibility that additional investigation might have yielded a different finding, to which Megan responded that the class had not investigated with all the materials yet. Determining how much evidence is enough to make a broad claim confidently, such as "all objects reflect and absorb light," is fundamental to scientific problem solving.

In the following excerpt, the students entertain other possible explanations for the differences between their findings and Lesley's. In this instance, Lesley is reporting the data for what happens when a flashlight shines on a piece of black felt. She reports that no transmitted light was recorded by her light meter. The majority of students, however, reported having seen transmitted light. Here the class considers why there might be these different findings:

Catherine	When we stuck the lamp like, not like directly next to the black but a little bit up close to the black, it came out a maroon color on the other side.
Ms. Sutton	So we were getting some transmitted. We thought we had some transmitted light, too. She's not getting—detecting that, is she, with her light meter?
Jihad	But she would be more sure because she has a light meter and we don't.
Ms. Sutton	What might cause a difference in results from what you did and from what she did?
Student	She may have had her flashlight back farther and we had ours up very close.
Ms. Sutton	Anything else might have made a difference? Ian?
Ian	She might have either had a weaker flashlight or a thicker piece of felt or something.
Ms. Sutton	Okay, so two things there.
Student	Yeah, or maybe it was because of the light meter.
Ms. Sutton	What about the light meter? How would the light meter make it harder to detect transmitted light?
Tatsuro	Because it's in, measuring in the tens. What if it was like 0.09?
Ms. Sutton	So maybe it's not measuring to the tenth or the millicandle?
Student	Or maybe she's just rounding off.
Ms. Sutton	Maybe she's rounding it off. Maybe the little machine rounds off. Good.
Louise	Or maybe it's because like, in the diagram, it shows it had the sensor pretty far back. Maybe the transmitted light didn't go that far.

In this excerpt, the students began to identify the range of variables that might explain the differences between their outcomes and Lesley's, including differences in the setup, the materials, the strength of the light source, the device used to record the data, and the scientist's decisions regarding the reporting of the data. This exchange is significant to the extent that the students demonstrate an appreciation for the role variables play in the design of an investigation. With this understanding, they are now situated to consider the control of variables that is necessary so that only a single contrast is featured in an experiment.[39]

One final observation about the successful use of text in inquiry-based instruction is the importance of students assuming a skeptical stance rather than simply deferring to the text. The following three excerpts are illustrative. The first two are examples of instances in which students questioned the generality of Lesley's claim that "all objects reflect and absorb light." In the first instance, Kit interjects, "I think that she says 'all' too much. Like she could just say 'most' or she could test more objects because 'all' is kind of a lot because she only tested like, seven." Ms. Sutton responds, "Okay, so you're saying you don't know if she's tested enough to say 'all,' to make that kind of statement."

The second excerpt begins when one student, Katherine, expresses concern that Lesley has not provided sufficient information about the kinds of materials with which she investigated. This leads a second student, Megan, to observe that the objects with which Lesley investigated are quite similar (i.e., they are all "flat") and that Lesley should have selected objects with different characteristics if she wished to make the claim that "all objects absorb and reflect light." Ms. Sutton prompts for more specificity, to which Megan responds, "None of them are kind of like a ball or something that's 3-D. They're all, like, flat . . . because something that's 3-D . . . it gets thicker because if you had a green ball and you shine light through, it would be . . . probably be a darker color because there's two sides to a ball and not just one."

In a related criticism, Kit observes that Lesley needed to consider not only the color of the object she was investigating, but also the material of which it was made:

Kit	I don't think the claim would be as true if the white [objects] were different materials.
Ms. Sutton	Okay, so you would get a—if you had a light meter to measure like she did and you were measuring all the black objects on this list, do you think you still would get different readings? They'd absorb differently? They wouldn't all absorb the same amount?
Students	Yeah . . . yeah. . . .
Ms. Sutton	How many people agree with that, that all the black objects probably wouldn't absorb the same amount of light? Okay, so they're agreeing with you.

SUPPORTING LEARNING THROUGH CYCLES OF INVESTIGATION

Whether students' experiences with investigation are first- or second-hand, the outcome of any single cycle of investigation will not result in development of all the targeted knowledge and reasoning goals for a particular topic of study. Thus, inquiry in any topic area requires multiple cycles of investigation. Discussion of how to design curriculum units with cycles of investigation and the interplay between first- and second-hand experiences is beyond the scope of this chapter. The important point is that students need to have multiple opportunities to learn concepts (i.e., multiple cycles of investigation that provide occasions for dealing with the same concepts) and encounter those concepts in multiple contexts (e.g., reflection is studied in contexts with mirrors, as well as in contexts with other opaque objects). The purpose of this section is to discuss how teachers might think about the development of knowledge across cycles of investigation.

The classroom community determines the fate of any knowledge claim generated by a group. Within and across each cycle, knowledge claims are generated, tested, refuted, tweaked, embraced, discarded, and ignored. (Note that the teacher's guidance is critical to ensure that false claims are not embraced without further exploration and that core claims are understood.) Figure 10-3 illustrates this process. In this case, the class worked with five

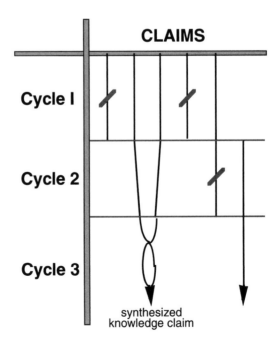

FIGURE 10-3 The development of community knowledge across cycles of investigation.

knowledge claims during Cycle 1 of its investigation. Following the reporting phase, two of these claims were abandoned: one because the child who had initially championed it no longer did so, and the other because there was significant evidence countering it. Three claims survived this first cycle of inquiry: one because there was clear and consistent data supporting it, and the other two because the data were insufficient to make a definitive judgment.

The reporting phase of Cycle 2 of the investigation led to the emergence of a new claim and the abandonment of one of the initial claims because only one of nine groups presented evidence in support of that claim, and the class expressed reservations regarding that group's data collection procedures. The two remaining claims survived, but were revised in ways that suggested they might be related.

Cycle 3 began with the class considering three extant claims. During the reporting phase, the two claims that appeared to be related became combined and synthesized into one claim. This is a significant development from a scientific perspective given the value placed on simplicity and parsimony of claims about the physical world. The final claim, while still in the running, was not accepted by the class, but neither was it rejected.

This progression of events with the community knowledge claims resulting from each cycle is like threads that when woven together create the fabric of scientific knowledge and reasoning on the topic of study. Some threads will dangle, never fully attended to; some will be abandoned; while others will be central to understanding the topic of study and may need to be blended together to create a strong weave. The fate of each thread is determined by classroom community judgments about which claims have the most evidence, account for the greatest range of data, and are simple and concise; that is, the standards for acceptance are values adhered to by scientists in the production of scientific knowledge. Although it can be difficult for teachers to stand by while students initially make scientifically inaccurate claims, the teacher's imposition of the constraints of the scientific community's cultural norms—norms that the students themselves eventually enforce—results in the final set of community claims being scientifically accurate or having indeterminate status with respect to science. Furthermore, whereas dangling threads in a fabric are problematic, they are important to the process of learning science because the reasons for rejecting or abandoning claims form part of the understanding of scientific ways of knowing.

The Development of Conceptual Frameworks

Imagine now that the students have been through several cycles of investigation. What is to prevent these cycles from being experienced as a set of disconnected experiences, resulting in isolated knowledge? How are the students to develop, elaborate, and refine conceptual frameworks from repeated inquiry experiences? We have argued[40] that the "threads that bind" take the form of explicit attention to the relationships among knowledge claims. Conclusions from *How People Learn* tell us that the formulation of a conceptual framework is a hallmark of developing deep understanding, and that a focus on the development of deep understanding is one of the principles distinguishing school reform efforts that result in increases in student achievement from those that do not.[41]

The development of *organized* knowledge is key to the formulation of conceptual frameworks. Developing organized knowledge is enabled by well-designed curriculum materials, but requires specific guidance by teachers as well. Some of that guidance needs to involve pressing students to work from the perspective of the norms for knowledge building in the scientific community. For example, scientists assume that there are regularities in how the world works. If the sky appears gray with no evidence of clouds or the sun, a scientist, who has seen the sun in the sky every other day, will assume that it is still there and infer that something must be blocking it. This perspective dictates different questions than one that does not assume such regularity.

Another area of guidance comes from pressing students to focus on the relationships among the claims they are making. Sorting out these relationships may result in multiple claims being revised into a single claim, as shown in Figure 10-3. Alternatively, revisions may need to be more extensive to fit the expectation of scientists that relationships within a topic area fit together; that is, they are coherent with one another.[42] If we claim that light reflects off the front of a mirror but does not appear to reflect off the back, or if we claim that light can go through glass but does not go through a glass mirror, what is the relationship between those ideas? It is not coherent to claim that light does and does not reflect from a mirror. Similarly, it is not coherent to say that light transmits through glass but not through a glass object (i.e., a mirror). Of course, the coherent view is that light is transmitted through glass, but in the case of a mirror, it is transmitted through the glass part but reflects from the backing that is placed on the glass to make it a mirror. To develop these kinds of perspectives, students must learn concepts in combination, with attention to the relationships among them.

Illustration: The Development of Conceptual Frameworks for Light

In this section we trace the development of student understanding about light over four cycles of investigation in Ms. Lacey's class, guided by the question of how light interacts with matter. This instruction took place over

4 weeks, with each cycle taking about a week of daily instruction. We present concept maps constructed from classroom discourse during the instruction.[43] That is, the maps represent the collective knowledge building that would be evident to the teacher and the class. Transcript excerpts accompany the maps to illustrate the nature of the conversation among the students and teacher.

During Cycle 1, students focused on the differences among objects, assuming that light interacted with each object in only one way. During reporting, they made statements such as: "Light can go through glass if it's clear enough," "Light reflects off mirrors and shiny materials, too," and "We had a solid thing here. It just stopped at the object. It didn't reflect." Students wrestled with whether claims indicating that light could "be blocked" and "stay in" meant the same thing or something different. Figure 10-4 suggests that students thought light could interact with matter in one of three ways.

The question marks in the figure indicate that some individuals or groups asserted the relationships shown, but not all the students accepted these relationships, including one group that provided evidence that light can interact with an object in two ways—a finding that could have dramatically changed the structure of the class's knowledge from what is shown in the figure. This particular group did not recognize the significance of its findings, focusing instead on the one way it should categorize objects from which it had observed multiple interactions. In the following excerpt, the teacher encourages the group to think of its results as a new claim.

Kevin   We saw sort of a little reflection, but we, it had mostly just see-through.

Ms. Lacey So you're saying that some materials could be in two different categories.

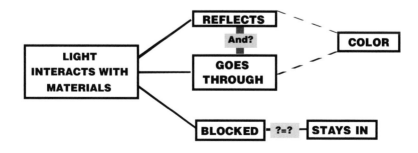

FIGURE 10-4 Community knowledge from the first cycle of investigation (first-hand).

Derek	Yes, because some were really see-through and reflection together, but we had to decide which one to put it in.
Ms. Lacey	Do you think you might have another claim here?
Kevin	Light can do two things with one object.

With the introduction of the idea that light can interact with matter in more than one way, the students embarked upon a second cycle of investigation with the same materials, with the intent of determining which if any objects exhibited the behavior claimed by Kevin and Derek. From this second round of investigation, all groups determined that multiple behaviors can occur with some objects, but there was uncertainty about whether these interactions occur with some types of materials and not others (see Figure 10-5). Nevertheless, the significance of this day's findings is that they represent a different conceptual organization from that of the first cycle (see Figure 10-4) to the extent that light is not confined to behaving in only one way. At the same time, the possibilities for the behavior of light have increased significantly, and only the case of four types of interaction has been ruled out in discussion by the community (following interaction comparing what different groups meant by "blocked" versus "absorbed").

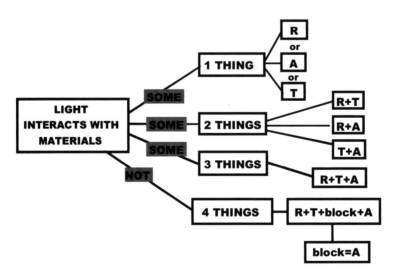

FIGURE 10-5 Community knowledge from the second cycle of investigation (first-hand). R = reflect; T = transmit; A = absorb.

In addition, some students expressed puzzlement about *how* light could interact with a material in more than one way. In response to this question, one group introduced the idea that there was a quantitative relationship among the multiple behaviors observed when light interacted with an object:

Miles   If you said that light can reflect, transmit, and absorb, absorb means to block. How can it be blocked . . . and still go through?

Corey   If just a little bit came through, then most of it was blocked.

Ms. Lacey   Would you draw him a picture, please? [Corey and Andy draw setup.]

Corey   Here's the light, a little being blocked inside, and a little of it comes out . . .

Andy   Some of it's reflecting.

During the third cycle of investigation, in which the students and the teacher interactively read a Lesley Park notebook text about light using reciprocal teaching strategies,[44] the students encountered more evidence that light can interact with matter in multiple ways (see Figure 10-6). This led to conversation concerning how general a claim might be made about the behavior of light:

Andy   Can all objects reflect, absorb, and transmit? Tommy?

Tommy   Most of them.

Andy   Corey?

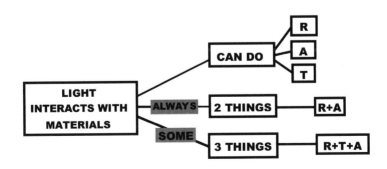

FIGURE 10-6 Community knowledge from the third cycle of investigation (second-hand).

Corey	Yes, because it says right in here, "Light can be reflected, absorbed and transmitted by the same object."
Ms. Lacey	I think we need to clarify something, because you said one thing, Corey, and Miles said something else. Andy's question was "Can *all* objects reflect, absorb, and transmit light?"
Alan	No. It just says light can be reflected, absorbed, and transmitted by the same object. It doesn't say anything about every object.
Ms. Lacey	So you say not all can. Do we have any data in our reading that tells us that not all things absorb, reflect, and transmit?
Tommy	We have evidence that all objects reflect and absorb [referring to a table in the notebook text].

The concept map representing the community's understanding about light up to this point shows greater specification of the prevalence of relationships ("always" versus "sometimes") and a narrowing of the possible relationships that can occur when light interacts with matter: light always reflects and is absorbed.

Lesley's quantitative data about the amount of reflection and transmission of light from an object as measured by a light meter supported additional conversation about the issue of quantitative relationships raised by one group in the previous cycle. However, students did not yet add those ideas to their class claims chart.

In the fourth cycle of investigation, students returned to a first-hand investigation and were now quite comfortable with the idea that light can simultaneously interact with matter in multiple ways. In addition, despite not having tools to compare the brightness of the light, they qualitatively compared the amount of light behaving in particular ways. This is represented in the map in Figure 10-7.

Do all students have the understanding represented in Figure 10-7? The excerpt below suggests that this is unlikely. In this excerpt, a student reveals that he and his partner did not think light would reflect from an object even after the class had established in the previous cycle that light always reflects:

Ms. Lacey	When you saw the blue felt, is that the claim you first thought?
Kenny	Yeah, we learned that this blue felt can do three—reflect, transmit, and absorb—at one, at this one object. And it did. It reflected a little, and transmitted some and it absorbed some.

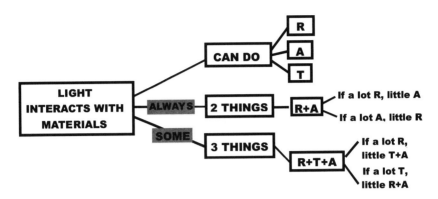

FIGURE 10-7 Community knowledge from the fourth cycle of investigation (first-hand).

Ms. Lacey	And when you started out, what did you think was going to happen?
Kenny	That it was only going to transmit and absorb. We didn't think it would reflect.
Ms. Lacey	What do we know about materials and reflecting?
Class	They always reflect and absorb.

We see the teacher checking on the student's understanding, which is scientifically accurate. But we know that for such a claim—that light reflects off all materials—many experiences may be needed for that knowledge to be robust. Relationships such as this for which we have no direct experience or that are counterintuitive (we see reflected light from objects, not the objects themselves) take time and attention, as well as recursive tacking to knowledge-building processes and the conceptual framework that is emerging from those processes. Conceptual frameworks that represent the physical world in ways we have not experienced (e.g., the electromagnetic spectrum) or are counterintuitive (light is a particle and a wave) pose even greater challenges to the development of scientific knowledge.

THE ROLE OF SUBJECT-SPECIFIC KNOWLEDGE IN EFFECTIVE SCIENCE INSTRUCTION

At the core of teacher decision making featured in this chapter is the need to mediate the learning of individual students. To do this in a way that leads to targeted scientific knowledge and ways of knowing, teachers must be confident about their knowledge of the learning goals. That is, teachers must have sufficient subject matter knowledge, including aspects of the culture of science that guide knowledge production, to fully understand the nature of the learning goals. When students say that light "disappears" into paper but reflects off of mirrors, a teacher's uncertainty about whether that claim is accurate will hamper effective decision making. When students claim an object is opaque and the question at hand is how light interacts with matter, the teacher needs to recognize that the word "opaque" describes the object and not light, and that an opaque object can reflect and absorb light and even transmit some light in certain cases (e.g., a piece of cardboard).

At the same time, having accurate subject matter knowledge is not sufficient for effective teaching. When students claim that light is a gas, it is not sufficient for the teacher to know that light is energy, not a state of matter. The teacher also needs to know what observations of light might convince students that it is not a gas, which in turn is informed by knowing how students think of gases, what their experiences of gas and light have likely been, and what it is possible to observe within a classroom context. This knowledge is part of specialized knowledge for teaching called pedagogical content knowledge because it is derived from content knowledge that is specifically employed to facilitate learning. It is the knowledge that teachers have about how to make particular subject matter comprehensible to particular students.[45]

Pedagogical content knowledge includes knowledge of the concepts that students find most difficult, as well as ways to support their understanding of those concepts. For example, it is difficult for students to understand that the color of objects is the color of light reflected from them because we are not aware of the reflection. Having students use a white screen to examine the color of light reflected from colored objects can reveal this phenomenon in a way that is convincing to them. Pedagogical content knowledge also includes knowledge of curriculum materials that are particularly effective for teaching particular topics. A still valuable resource for the study of light in the elementary grades is the *Optics* kit mentioned earlier that is part of *Elementary Science Study* curriculum materials developed in the 1960s. A teacher's knowledge of these materials and how they can be used to support knowledge building is key to employing them effectively in mediating student learning.

Finally, pedagogical content knowledge includes ways to assess student knowledge. A classic item to determine students' understanding of how we see is a diagram with the sun, a tree, and a person looking at the tree.[46] Students are asked to draw lines with arrows in the diagram to show how the person sees the tree. Arrows should be drawn from the sun to the tree to the person, but it is not uncommon for students to draw arrows from the sun to the person and the person to the tree. Use of this item at the beginning of a unit of study can provide a teacher with a wealth of information on current student thinking about how we see, as well as stimulate students to wonder about such questions.

The more teachers know and understand about how their students think about particular concepts or topics of study, how that thinking might develop and unfold during systematic study of the topic, and how they might ascertain what students' understanding of the topic is at any point in time, the better they are able to optimize knowledge building from students' varied experiences and support students in developing desired scientific knowledge and ways of knowing. When and how to employ particular strategies in the service of supporting such knowledge building is a different issue, but the topic-specific knowledge for teaching that is identified as pedagogical content knowledge is a necessary element if students are to achieve the standards we have set.

CONCLUSION

Science instruction provides a rich context for applying what we know about how people learn. A successful teacher in this context is aware that he or she is supporting students in activating prior knowledge and in building upon and continuing to organize this knowledge so it can be used flexibly to make sense of and appreciate the world around them. To do this well, the teacher must be knowledgeable about the nature of science, including both the products—the powerful ideas of science—and the values, beliefs, and practices of the scientific community that guide the generation and evaluation of these powerful ideas. Furthermore, teachers must be knowledgeable about children and the processes of engaging them in knowledge building, reflecting upon their thinking and learning new ways of thinking.

We have proposed and illustrated a heuristic for conceptualizing instruction relative to the opportunities and challenges of different aspects of inquiry-based instruction, which we have found useful in supporting teachers in effective decision making and evaluation of instruction. We have argued that the development of scientific knowledge and reasoning can be supported through both first- and second-hand investigations. Furthermore, we have proposed that the teacher draws upon a broad repertoire of practices for the purposes of establishing and maintaining the classroom as a learning community, and assessing, supporting, and extending the knowledge building of each member of that community. All of these elements are necessary for effective teaching in the twenty-first century, when our standards for learning are not just about the application of scientific knowledge, but also its evaluation and generation.

NOTES

1. Schwab, 1964.
2. Hapgood et al., in press; Lehrer et al., 2001; Magnusson et al., 1997; Metz, 2004.
3. National Research Council, 2003.
4. These materials, originally developed in the 1960s, can be purchased from Delta Education: http://www.delta-education.com/.
5. Whereas some view conceptual change as referring to a change from existing ideas to new ones, we suggest that new ideas are often developed in parallel with existing ones. The new ideas are rooted in different values and beliefs—those of the scientific community rather than those guiding our daily lives.
6. Chi, 1992.
7. Galili and Hazan, 2000.
8. Our decision to focus on instruction in which investigation is central reflects the national standard that calls for science instruction to be inquiry based.
9. We use the term "guided" inquiry to signal that the teacher plays a prominent role in shaping the inquiry experience, guiding student thinking and activity to enable desired student learning from investigation.
10. Magnusson and Palincsar, 1995.
11. Barnes, 1976; Bybee et al., 1989; Karplus, 1964; Osborne and Freyberg, 1985; Lehrer and Schauble, 2000.
12. All of the instruction featured in this chapter was conducted by teachers who were a part of GIsML Community of Practice, a multiyear professional development effort aimed at identifying effective practice for inquiry-based science teaching.
13. This discussion draws on a study focused on children's self-regulation during science instruction, which took place in a school in a relatively small district (about 4,600 students) that includes a state university. Approximately 45 percent of the students in this district pass the state standardized tests, and 52 percent are economically disadvantaged.
14. This class is in a school in a relatively small district (about 3,000 students) near a major industrial plant in a town with a state university. Approximately 38 percent of the students in this district pass the state standardized tests, and 63 percent are economically disadvantaged.
15. While we are featuring contexts in which there is a single question, teachers could choose to have a context in which children are investigating different questions related to the same phenomenon. However, it is important to recognize the substantially greater cognitive and procedural demands this approach places on the teacher, so it is not something we recommend if a teacher is inexperienced in conducting inquiry-based instruction.
16. Although it can be motivating and conceptually beneficial for students to be placed in the role of generating questions for investigation, the teacher needs to be mindful of the consequences of taking time to investigate questions that may be trivial or peripheral to the unity of study. The teacher may judge the time to be useful as students can still learn a great deal about investigation, but

the teacher also may seek to reshape the question so it is not so conceptually distant as to sidetrack the focus relative to the desired content goals.

17. Hapgood et al., in press; Lehrer et al., 2001; Metz, 2004.

18. This person monitors the time the group is taking for the investigation to support the students in examining how efficiently they are working and deciding whether it is necessary to adjust the tempo of their activity to finish in the allotted time.

19. It is very reasonable for the teacher to discuss these issues with the whole class during the preparing-to-investigate phase and to invite the class to specify procedures. Addressing these matters with the whole class gives the teacher opportunities to model thinking for the benefit of all. However, while this is enabling for students when they are quite new to investigating, it constrains students' development of the knowledge and skills needed to make these decisions independently. Thus it is important for the teacher to give students an opportunity to make these types of decisions on their own during some investigations.

20. Herrenkohl et al., 1999.

21. The students inadvertently interpreted the idea of categorizing to mean that light would behave in only one way with each object. This led many students to stop observing an object as soon as they had identified one way light behaved with it.

22. In both cases, the fact that we can see the object tells us that light is reflected. However, students had not yet established that relationship, so we refer here only to the direct evidence of light.

23. Blumenfeld and Meece, 1988.

24. Magnusson et al., in press.

25. This class is in a moderately sized district (about 16,700) students) in a town with a major university. Approximately 70 percent of the students in this district pass the state standardized tests, and 16 percent are economically disadvantaged.

26. Brown and Campione, 1994; Palincsar et al., 1993.

27. Campanario, 2002.

28. Osborne, 1983.

29. Magnusson et al., 1997.

30. Clement, 1993

31. We observed a group of children in a fourth-grade class working very hard to determine if black felt reflects light. They piled their materials in the bathroom in the classroom, taped around the door to block out any light, and studied the black felt. They were quite proud to report their evidence that it did indeed reflect light.

32. Chi, 1992.

33. Mortimer, 1995.

34. Driver et al., 1994.

35. National Research Council, 1996.

36. Crawford et al., 1996.

37. Magnusson and Palincsar, in press-b.

38. See Magnusson and Palincsar (in press-a) for discussion of the theory and principles underlying the development of these texts; Palincsar and Magnusson (2001), for a more complete description of Lesley's notebook and of research investigating the use of these notebook texts; and Magnusson and Palincsar (in press-b) for a discussion of teaching from these notebook tests.
39. Klahr et al., 2001.
40. Magnusson et al., in press; Palincsar et al., 2001.
41. Newmann et al., 1995.
42. Einstein, 1950.
43. Ford, 1999.
44. Palincsar and Brown, 1984.
45. Magnusson et al., 1999; Wilson et al., 1988.
46. Eaton et al., 1984.

REFERENCES

Barnes, D. (1976). *From communication to curriculum.* Hammondsworth, UK: Penguin Books.

Blumenfeld, P.C., and Meece, J.L. (1988). Task factors, teacher behavior, and students' involvement and use of learning strategies in science. *Elementary School Journal, 88*(3), 235-250.

Brown, A.L., and Campione, J.C. (1994). Guided discovery in a community of learners. In K. McGilly (Ed.), *Classrooms lessons: Integrating cognitive theory and classroom practice* (pp. 229-272). Cambridge, MA: MIT Press.

Bybee, R.W., Buchwald, C.E., Crissman, S., Heil, D.R., Kuerbis, P.J., Matsumoto, C., and McInerney, J.D. (1989). *Science and technology education for the elementary years: Frameworks for curriculum and instruction.* Washington, DC: National Center for Improving Science Education.

Campanario, J.M. (2002). The parallelism between scientists' and students' resistance to new scientific ideas. *International Journal of Science Education, 24*(10), 1095-1110.

Chi, M.T.H. (1992). Conceptual change within and across ontological categories: Examples from learning and discovery in science. In R. Giere (Ed.), *Cognitive models of science: Minnesota studies in the philosophy of science* (pp. 129-186). Minneapolis, MN: University of Minnesota Press.

Clement, J. (1993). Using bridging analogies and anchoring intuitions to deal with students' preconceptions in physics. *Journal of Research in Science Teaching, 30,* 1241-1257.

Crawford, S.Y., Hurd, J.M., and Weller, A.C. (1996). *From print to electronic: The transformation of scientific communication.* Medford, NJ: Information Today.

Driver, R., Asoko, H., Leach, J., Mortimer, E., and Scott, P. (1994). Constructing scientific knowledge in the classroom. *Educational Researcher, 23*(7), 5-12.

Eaton, J.F., Anderson, C.W., and Smith, E.L. (1984). Students' misconceptions interfere with science learning: Case studies of fifth-grade students. *Elementary School Journal, 84,* 365-379.

Einstein, A. (1950). *Out of my later years.* New York: Philosophical Library.

Ford, D. (1999). The role of text in supporting and extending first-hand investigations in guided inquiry science. *Dissertation Abstracts International, 60*(7), 2434.

Galili, I., and Hazan, A. (2000). Learners' knowledge in optics: Interpretation, structure and analysis. *International Journal of Science Education, 22*(1), 57-88.

Hapgood, S., Magnusson, S.J., and Palincsar, A.S. (in press). Teacher, text, and experience: A case of young children's scientific inquiry. *Journal of the Learning Sciences.*

Herrenkohl, L., Palincsar, A.S., DeWater L.S., and Kawasaki, K. (1999). Developing scientific communities in classrooms: A sociocognitive approach. *Journal of the Learning Sciences, 8*(3-4), 451-494.

Karplus, R. (1964). *Theoretical background of the science curriculum improvement study.* Berkeley, CA: Science Curriculum Improvement Study, University of California.

Klahr, D., Chen, Z., and Toth, E. (2001). Cognitive development and science education: Ships that pass in the night or beacons of mutual illumination? In S. Carver and D. Klahr (Eds.), *Cognition and instruction: Twenty-five years of progress* (pp. 75-120). Mahwah, NJ: Lawrence Erlbaum Associates.

Lehrer, R., and Schauble, L. (2000). Modeling in mathematics and science. In R. Glaser (Ed.), *Advances in instructional psychology, vol. 5: Educational design and cognitive science* (pp. 101-159). Mahwah, NJ: Lawrence Erlbaum Associates.

Lehrer, R., Schauble, L., and Petrosino, A.J. (2001). Reconsidering the role of experiment in science education. In K. Crowley, C.D. Schunn, and T. Okada (Eds.), *Designing for science: Implications from everyday, classroom, and professional settings.* Mahwah, NJ: Lawrence Erlbaum Associates.

Magnusson, S.J., and Palincsar, A.S. (1995). The learning environment as a site of science education reform. *Theory into Practice, 34*(1), 43-50.

Magnusson, S.J., and Palincsar, A.S. (in press-a). The application of theory to the design of innovative texts supporting science instruction. In M. Constas and R. Sternberg (Eds.), *Translating educational theory and research into practice.* Mahwah, NJ: Lawrence Erlbaum Associates.

Magnusson, S.J., and Palincsar, A.S. (in press-b). Learning from text designed to model scientific thinking. In W. Saul (Ed.), *Crossing borders in literacy and science instruction: Perspectives on theory and practice.* Newark, DE: International Reading Association.

Magnusson, S.J., Templin, M., and Boyle, R.A. (1997). Dynamic science assessment: A new approach for investigating conceptual change. *Journal of the Learning Sciences, 6*(1), 91-142.

Magnusson, S.J., Borko, H., and Krajcik, J.S. (1999). Nature, sources, and development of pedagogical content knowledge for science teaching. In J. Gess-Newsome and N. Lederman (Eds.), *Science teacher knowledge.* Dordrecht, The Netherlands: Kluwer Academic.

Magnusson, S.J., Palincsar, A.S., and Templin, M. (in press). Community, culture, and conversation in inquiry-based science instruction. In L. Flick and N. Lederman (Eds.), *Scientific inquiry and the nature of science: Implications for teaching, learning, and teacher education.* Dordrecht, The Netherlands: Kluwer Academic.

Metz, K.E. (2004). Children's understanding of scientific inquiry: Their conceptualization of uncertainty in investigations of their own design. *Cognition and Instruction, 22*(2), 219-290.

Mortimer, E.F. (1995). Conceptual change or conceptual profile change? *Science and Education, 4,* 267-285.

National Research Council. (1996). *National science education standards.* National Committee on Science Education Standards and Assessment, Center for Science, Mathematics, and Engineering Education. Washington, DC: National Academy Press.

National Research Council. (2003). *Learning and instruction: A SERP research agenda.* M.S. Donovan and J.W. Pellegrino (Eds.), Panel on Learning and Instruction, Strategic Education Research Partnership. Washington, DC: The National Academies Press.

Newmann, F.M., Marks, H.M., and Gamoran, A. (1995). *Authentic pedagogy: Standards that boost student performance.* (Issue Report #8, Center on Organization and Restructuring of Schools.) Madison, WI: Wisconsin Center for Educational Research, University of Wisconsin.

Osborne, R. (1983). Towards modifying children's ideas about electric current. *Research in Science & Technological Education, 1*(1), 73-82.

Osborne, R., and Freyberg, P. (1985). *Learning in science: The implications of children's science.* Portsmouth, NH: Heinemann.

Palincsar, A.S., and Brown, A.L. (1984). Reciprocal teaching of comprehension-fostering and monitoring activities. *Cognition and Instruction, 1,* 117-175.

Palincsar, A.S., and Magnusson, S.J. (2001). The interplay of first-hand and text-based investigations to model and support the development of scientific knowledge and reasoning. In S. Carver and D. Klahr (Eds.), *Cognition and instruction: Twenty-five years of progress* (pp. 151-194). Mahwah, NJ: Lawrence Erlbaum Associates.

Palincsar, A.S., Anderson, C.A., and David, Y.M. (1993). Pursuing scientific literacy in the middle grades through collaborative problem solving. *Elementary School Journal, 93*(5), 643-658.

Palincsar, A S., Magnusson, S.J., and Hapgood, S. (2001). *Trafficking ideas through the rotaries of science instruction: Teachers' discourse moves and their relationships to children's learning.* Paper presented at the annual meeting of the American Educational Research Association, Seattle, WA.

Schwab, J.J. (1964). Structure of the disciplines: Meanings and significances. In G.W. Ford and L. Pugno (Eds.), *The structure of knowledge and the curriculum* (pp. 6-30). Chicago, IL: Rand McNally.

Wilson, S.M., Shulman, L.S., and Richert, E.R. (1988). '150 different ways' of knowing: Representations of knowledge in teaching. In J. Calderhead (Ed.), *Exploring teachers' thinking.* New York: Taylor and Francis.

11

Guided Inquiry in the Science Classroom

James Minstrell and Pamela Kraus

The story of the development of this piece of curriculum and instruction starts in the classroom of the first author more than 25 years ago. I had supposedly taught my classes about universal gravitation and the related inverse square force law. The students had performed reasonably well on questions of the sort that asked, "What would happen to the force if we increased the distance from the planet?" They supposedly understood something about gravitational forces, resistive forces of air resistance and friction, and the idea of force in general. Then came a rude awakening.

I don't remember why, but we happened to be talking about a cart being pulled across a table by a string attached to a weight over a pulley. The students were becoming confused by the complexity of the situation. So, in an attempt to simplify the context, I suggested, "Suppose there is no friction to worry about, no rubbing, and no friction." Still the students were confused and suggested, "Then there would be so much wind resistance." I waved that notion away as well: "Suppose there were no friction at all and no air resistance in this situation. Suppose there were no air in the room. Now what would be the forces acting on this cart as it was moving across the table?"

I was not prepared for what I heard. Several voices around the room were saying, in effect, "Then things would just drift off the table. The weight and string and cart would all just float away." I was tempted to say, "No, don't think like that." I suppressed that urge and instead asked in a nonevaluative tone, "Okay, so you say things would just float away. How do you know that?" They suggested, "You know, like in space. There is no air, and things just drift around. They aren't held down, because there is no air to hold them down." The students said they knew this because they had heard from the media that in space things are weightless. Indeed, they had seen pictures of astronauts just "floating" around. They had also been told that there is no air in space, and they put the two (no air and weightless) together. But they had no first-hand experiences to relate to what they knew from these external "authorities."

> *If we really want to know what students are thinking, we need to ask them and then be quiet and listen respectfully to what they say. If we are genuinely interested and do not evaluate, we can learn from our students.*

What good is having my students know the quantitative relation or equation for gravitational force if they lack a qualitative understanding of force and the concepts related to the nature of gravity and its effects? They should be able to separate the effects of gravity from the effects of the surrounding air. Later, they should be able to explain the phenomena of falling bodies, which requires that they separate the effects of gravity from those of air. While many physical science books focus on the constancy of gravitational acceleration, most students know that all things do not fall with the same acceleration. They know that a rock reaches the floor before a flat sheet of paper, for example. Not addressing the more common situation of objects falling differently denies the students' common experiences and is part of the reason "school science" may not seem relevant to them. So, we need to separate the effects of air from those of gravity.

> *Learning is an active process. We need to acknowledge students' attempts to make sense of their experiences and help them confront inconsistencies in their sense making.*

Even more fundamental, I want my students to understand and be able to apply the concept of force as an interaction between objects in real-life situations. They should have first-hand experiences that will lead to the reasonable conclusion that force can be exerted by anything touching an object, and also that forces can exist as "actions at a distance" (i.e., without touching the object, forces might be exerted through the mechanisms of gravity, electrostatic force, and magnetic force).

I also want my students to understand the nature of scientific practice. They should be able to interpret or explain common phenomena and design simple experiments to test their ideas. In short, I want them to have the skills necessary to inquire about the world around them, to ask and answer their own questions, and to know what questions they need to ask themselves in the process of thinking about a problematic situation.

Teachers' questions can model the sorts of questions students might ask them-selves when conducting personal inquiry.

Research and best practice suggest that, if we are really clever and care-ful, students will come more naturally to the conceptual ideas and processes we want them to learn. Being clever means incorporating what we have come to understand about how students learn. This chapter describes a series of activities from which the experience of teachers and researchers demonstrates students do learn about the meaning of force and about the nature and processes of science. It also explains how the specific activities and teaching strategies delineated here relate to what we know from re-search on how people learn, as reflected in the three guiding principles set forth in Chapter 1 with regard to students' prior knowledge, the need to develop deep understanding, and the development of metacognitive aware-ness. We attempt to give the reader a sense of what it means to implement curriculum that supports these principles. It is our hope that researchers will see that we have built upon their work in designing these activities and creating the learning environment. We want teachers to get a sense of what it means to teach in such an environment. We also want readers to get an idea of what it is like to be a learner.

The following unit could come before one on forces to explain motion (i.e., Newton's Laws). By the end of this unit, students should have arrived at a qualitative understanding of force as applied in contexts involving buoy-ancy, gravitation, magnetics, and electrostatics. The activities involved are designed to motivate and develop a sense of the interrelationships between ideas and events. The expected outcome includes qualitative understanding of ideas, not necessarily formulas.

THE UNIT: THE NATURE OF GRAVITY AND ITS EFFECTS

Part A: What Gravity Is Not

Getting the Unit Started: Finding Out About Students' Initial Ideas

Teachers need to unconditionally respect students' capacities for learning complex ideas, and students need to learn to respect the teacher as an instructional leader. Teachers will need to earn that respect through their actions as a respectful guide to learning.

For students to understand the following lessons, we need to establish some prerequisite knowledge and dispositions during earlier lessons. Students will need to understand that measurements of a single quantity may vary depending on three factors: the object being measured, the instrument being used, and the person using the instrument. The teacher needs to have enough experience with the class so that the students are confident that the class will achieve resolution over time. Thus, this unit comes about a month or so into the school year. Students need to persevere in learning and trusting that the teacher will help guide them to the big ideas. This should probably not be the students' first experience with guided inquiry. While the set of experiences in Part A below takes a week or more to resolve, prior initial experiences with guided inquiry may take a class period or two, depending on the students' tolerance for ambiguity.

Identifying Preconceptions: What Would Happen If . . . ?

> *Teachers need to know students' initial and developing conceptions. Students need to have their initial ideas brought to a conscious level.*

One way to find out about students' preconceptions for a particular unit is to ask them to give, in writing, their best answers to one or more questions related to the unit. At the beginning of this unit on the nature of gravity and its effects, the teacher poses the following situation and questions associated with Figure 11-1.

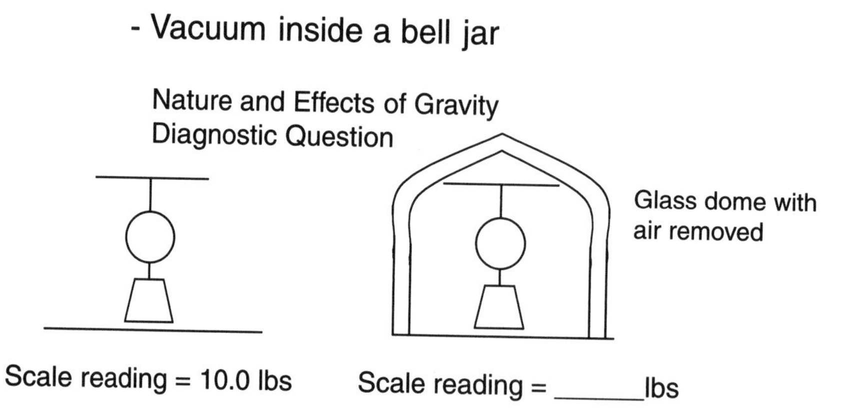

- Vacuum inside a bell jar

Nature and Effects of Gravity
Diagnostic Question

Glass dome with air removed

Scale reading = 10.0 lbs   Scale reading = _____ lbs

FIGURE 11-1 A diagnostic question to use at the beginning of this unit.

Nature and Effects of Gravity, Diagnostic Question 1: Predict the scale reading under the glass dome with air removed.

> *In the diagram with question 1, we have a large frame and a big spring scale, similar to what you might see at the local market. Suppose we put something on the scale and the scale reading is 10.0 lb. Now suppose we put a large glass dome over the scale, frame and all, and seal all the way around the base of the dome. Then, we take a large vacuum pump and evacuate all the air out from under the dome. We allow all the air to escape through the pump, so there is no air left under the glass dome.*
>
> *What would happen to the scale reading with no air under the dome? You may not be able to give a really precise answer, but say what you think would happen to the scale reading, whether it would increase, decrease, or stay exactly the same and if you think there will be a change, about how much? And briefly explain how you decided.*
>
> *I will not grade you on whether your answer is correct. I just want to know your ideas about this situation at this time. We are just at the beginning of the unit. What I care most about is that you give a good honest best attempt to answer at this point in time. I know that some of you may be tempted to say "I don't know," but just give your best answer at this time. I'm pretty sure most all of you can come up with an answer and, most importantly, some rationale to support that answer. Just give me your best answer and reasoning at this point in time. We will be working to investigate this question over the next few days.*

When asked, more than half of students cite answers that suggest they believe air only presses down. Half of those suggest that the scale reading would go to zero in the vacuous environment. About a third of introductory students believe that the surrounding air has absolutely no effect on the scale reading regardless of the precision of the scale. Most of the rest believe that air only pushes up on the object and that it does so with a strong force. Typically, only about one student in a class will suggest that the air pushes up and down but with slightly greater force in the upward direction, the result being a very slight increase in the scale reading for the vacuous environment—a "best answer" at this time.

This question may be more about understanding buoyancy than understanding gravity. However, part of understanding the effects of gravity is learning what effects are *not* due to gravity.

Students need opportunities to explore the relationships among ideas.

Gravitational force is an interaction between any two objects that have mass. In this case, the gravitational force is an interaction between the object on the scale and the earth as the other object. Many students believe gravity is an interaction between the object and the surrounding air. Thus, this has become a first preconception to address in instruction. If teachers fail to address this idea, we know from experience that students will likely not change their basic conceptual understanding, and teachers will obtain the poor results described earlier.

In contrast with the above question, we have seen curricula that attempt to identify students' preconceptions simply by asking students to write down what they know about X. In our experience, this question is so generic that students tend not to pay much attention to it and simply "do the assignment" by writing anything. Instead, preinstruction questions should be more specific to a context, but open up the issues of the discipline as related to that context. These sorts of questions are not easy to create and typically evolve out of several iterations of teaching a unit and finding out through discussions what situations elicit the more interesting responses with respect to the content at hand.

A Benchmark Lesson[1]: Weighing in a Vacuum

In discussion following the posing of this question, I encourage students to share their answers and rationales. Because I am interested in getting students' thinking out in the open, I ask that other students not comment or offer counter arguments at this point, but just listen to the speaker's argument. I, in turn, listen carefully to the sorts of thinking exhibited by the students. I know this will faciliate my helping the class move forward later.

With encouragement and support on my part, some students volunteer to share their answers. Some suggest the scale will go to zero "with no air to hold the object down." Others suggest, "The scale reading will not go to zero but will go down some because gravity is still down and the weight of the air pushes down too, but since air doesn't weigh very much, the downward air won't be down much and the scale reading won't go down much." Some students suggest that the scale reading will increase (slightly or substantially) "because there is no air to hold the object up. It's about buoyancy. The air is like water. Water pushes up and so does air. No air, there is no buoyancy." Still others suggest that the scale reading should stay the same "because air doesn't do anything. The weight is by gravity not by air pressure." And others agree that the scale reading will not change, "but air is pushing on the object. It pushes up and down equally on the object, so there shouldn't be any change." By now several students have usually chimed in to say that one or another of the ideas made sense to them. The ideas are now "owned" by several class members, so we can discuss and even criticize the ideas without criticizing a particular person. It is important to be supportive of free expression of ideas while at the same time being critical of ideas.

Students are more likely to share their thinking in a climate where others express genuine interest in what they have to say. Waiting until one student has completely expressed his or her idea fosters deeper thinking on that speaker's part. Asking speakers critical questions to clarify what they are saying or to help them give more complete answers and explanations fosters their own engagement and learning.

With most of their initial thinking having been expressed, I encourage students to share potentially contradictory arguments in light of the candidate explanations. Students might suggest, "When they vacuum pack peanuts, they take the air away and the weight doesn't go to zero"; or "The weight of the column of air above an object pushes down on the object"; or "Air acts like water and when you lift a rock in water it seems lighter than lifting it out of water, so air would help hold the object up"; or "But, I read where being on the bottom of the ocean is like having an elephant standing on your head, so air must push down if it acts like water"; or "Air is just around things. It doesn't push on things at all, unless there is a wind." Some students begin to say they are getting more confused, for many of these observations and arguments sound good and reasonable.

Once arguments pro and con for most of the ideas have been expressed, it is time to begin resolving issues. Thus far, we have been freely expressing ideas, but I want students to know that science is not based simply on opinion. We can achieve some resolution by appealing to nature; indeed, our inferences should be consistent with our observations of nature. I ask, "Sounds like a lot of good arguments and experiences suggested here, so how can we get an answer? Should we just vote on which should be the right answer and explanation?" Typically, several of the students suggest, "No, we can try it and see what happens. Do you have one of those vacuum things? Can we do the experiment?"

I just happen to have a bell jar and vacuum pump set up in the back room. First, I briefly demonstrate what happens when a slightly inflated balloon (about 2 inches in diameter) is placed under the bell jar and the pump is turned on: the balloon gets larger. I ask the students to explain this result. The students (high school age at least) usually are able to articulate that I did not add air to the balloon, but the air outside the balloon (within the bell jar) was evacuated, so the air in the balloon was freer to expand the balloon.

> *Attention is extremely important to learning.*

We hang a weight on the spring scale, put it under the jar, and seal the edges, and I ask students to "place their bets." This keeps students motivated and engaged. "How many think the scale reading will increase?" Hands go up. "Decrease?" Many hands go up. "Decrease to zero?" A few hands go up. "Stay exactly the same?" Several hands go up. I start the pump.

> *It is important to give students opportunities to apply (without being told, if possible) ideas learned earlier.*

The result surprises many students. The scale reading does not appear to change at all. Some students give a high five. I ask, "What can we conclude about the effects of air on the scale reading?" Some students suggest, "Air doesn't do anything." Sometimes to get past this response, I need to prime the discussion of implications of the results by asking, "Do we know air has absolutely no effect?" A few students are quick to say, "We don't know that it has absolutely no effect. We just know it doesn't have enough effect to make a difference." I ask, "Why do you say that?" They respond, "Remember about measurements, there is always some plus or minus to it. It could be a tiny bit more than it was. It could be a tiny bit less, or it might be exactly the same. We can't tell for sure. Maybe if we had a really, really accurate scale we could tell."

I also want the students to see that conclusions are different from results, so I often guide them carefully to discuss each. "First, what were the actual results of the experiment? What did happen? What did we observe?" Students agree that there was no observable change in the scale reading. "Those were the results. We observed no apparent change in the scale reading."

> *Students should be provided opportunities to differentiate between summarizing observable results and the conclusions generalized from those results.*

Because I want students to understand the role of experimentation in science, I press them for a conclusion: "So, what do we know from this experiment? Did we learn anything?" Although a few students suggest, "We didn't learn anything," others are quick to point out, "There can't be any big changes. We know that the air doesn't have a big effect." At this point, it appears students have had sufficient experience talking about the ideas, so I may try to clarify the distinction between results and conclusions: "Conclusions are different from results. Conclusions are about the meaning of the results, about making sense of what we observed. So, what can we conclude? What do these results tell us about the effects of the air?" With some additional discussion among the students, and possibly some additional clarification of the difference between results and conclusions, most students are ready to believe the following summary of their comments: "If the air has any effect on the scale reading, it is not very large. And apparently gravity is not caused by air pressure pressing things down."

Activity A1

Activity A1 is a simple worksheet asking students to review their answers to questions about their initial ideas, other ideas that have come out in discussion, and the results and conclusions from the preceding benchmark lesson. Typically, I hand this summary sheet out as homework and collect it at the beginning of the next class. By reviewing what students have written, I can identify related issues that need to be discussed further with certain students. Alternatively, I may ask students to check and discuss their answers with each other in groups and to add a page of corrections to their own answers before handing in their original responses. One purpose of this activity is to encourage students to monitor their own learning.

> *Students need opportunities to learn to monitor their own learning.*

Progressing from the preinstruction question through the benchmark discussion takes about one class period. In showing that gravity is not caused by air pressure, we have generated questions about the effects of the surrounding air. Students now want to know the answer to the original question. I used to end the investigations of the surrounding air at this point and move on to investigating factors affecting gravity, but I discovered that students slipped back to believing that air pressed only down or only up. Therefore, we redesigned the curriculum activities to include more time for investigation into the effects of surrounding fluids. Doing so also allows us to incorporate some critical introductory experiences with qualitative ideas about forces on objects. This experience helps lay the groundwork for the later unit on forces, when we will revisit these ideas and experiences. To deepen students' understanding of the effects of surrounding fluids then, we now engage in several elaboration activities wherein students have opportunities to test various hypotheses that came up in the benchmark discussion.

> *Revisiting ideas in new contexts helps organize them in a rich conceptual framework and facilitates application across contexts.*

Opportunities for Students to Suggest and Test Related Hypotheses

In the benchmark lesson, several ideas were raised that need further testing. Some students suggested air only pushed up, others that air only pushed down, still others that air pushed equally or did not push at all. Some suggested that air was like water; others contested that idea. Each of the following activities is intended to give students opportunities to test these ideas in several contexts, recognizable from their everyday world. That is, each activity could easily be repeated at home; in fact, some students may have already done them. One goal of my class is for students to leave seeing the world differently. Groups of three or four students each are assigned to "major" in one of the elaboration activities and then to get around also to investigating each of the other activities more briefly. In every case, they are asked to keep the original bell jar experiment in mind: "How does this activity help us understand the bell jar situation?" With respect to the activity in which they are majoring, they will also be expected to present their results and conclusions to the class.

Elaboration Activity A2: The Inverted Glass of Water. This activity was derived from a trick sometimes done at parties. A glass of water with a plastic card over the opening is inverted. If this is done carefully, the water stays in the glass. Students are asked to do the activity and see what they can learn about the directions in which air and water can push. They are also given the opportunity to explore the system and see what else they can learn.

> *Allowing students freedom to explore may give teachers opportunities to learn. Teachers need to allow themselves to learn.*

My purpose here is to help students see that air can apparently push upward (on the card) sufficiently to support the card and the water. That is usually one conclusion reached by some students. Early in my use of the activity, however, I was surprised by a student who emptied the water and placed the card over the open end of the inverted glass and concluded, "It's the stickiness of water that holds the card to the glass." For a moment I was taken aback, but fortunately other students came to my rescue. They said, "At first we thought it might be because the card just stuck to the wet glass, but then we loaded the card with pennies to see how many pennies the card would hold to the empty glass. We found it would only hold about three pennies before the card would drop off. The water we had in the glass weighs a lot more than three pennies. Stickiness might help, but it is not the main reason the card stays on. The main reason must be the air below the card."

This was such a nice example of suggesting and testing alternative explanations that I now bring up the possibility of the stickiness being all that is needed if this idea does not come up in the group presentation. More recently, other students have tested the stickiness hypothesis by using a rigid plastic glass with a tiny (~1 mm) hole in the bottom. When they fill the glass, put on the card, and invert the glass, they put their finger over the hole. When they move their finger off the hole, the water and card fall. They conclude that the air rushing in the hole pushes down on the water and that the air pushing from under the card is not providing sufficient support. I now make sure I have plastic cups available in case I need to "seed" the discussion.

After making these observations, students are ready to draw the tentative conclusion that the upward push by the air on the card must be what is supporting most of the weight of the water on the card. They note the water must push down on the card, and since the stickiness of the water is not enough to hold the card, there must be a big push up by the air. This conclusion is reached more easily by more mature students than by middle-level students. The latter need help making sense of this argument. Most are willing to say tentatively that it makes sense that the air pushes up and are more convinced after they see the various directions in which air pushes in the other activities.

Elaboration Activity A3: Inverted Cylinder in a Cylinder of Water. This activity was derived from some students describing observations they had made while hand-washing dishes. They had observed what happened when an inverted glass was submerged in a dishpan of water. In activity A3, a narrow cylinder (e.g., 100 ml graduated cylinder) is inverted and floated in a larger cylinder (e.g., 500 ml graduated cylinder) of water. Again, students are asked to see what they can learn about the directions that air and water can push.

I want students to see that air and water can push up and down, and that the deeper one goes in a fluid, the greater is the push in any direction. While doing this activity, students observe that the farther down one pushes the floating cylinder, the more difficult it is to push. Thus, they conclude that the water is pushing upward on the air in the small cylinder, and the push is greater the deeper one goes. Typically, some students cite as additional evidence the observation that the water level in the small cylinder rises within that cylinder the farther down one pushes the small cylinder, thus compressing the air. I commend these students for their careful observation and suggest that other students observe what happens to the level of the water in the inner cylinder. The more the air is compressed, the harder the water must be pushing upward on the air to compress it, and the more the compressed air must be pushing upward on the inside of the small cylinder.

The students appear to have reached the conclusions I hoped for. Although I primed them with relevant questions, they made the observations and reached the conclusions.

Elaboration Activity A4: Leaky Bottle. This activity, like the others, came from experiences students had suggested helped them with their thinking about fluids. A 2-liter plastic soda bottle with three holes in it at three different heights is filled to the top with water and allowed to leak into a basin. Again, students are asked to see what they can learn about the directions in which air and water can push.

> *By listening to students' arguments, the teacher can learn what related experiences make sense to them.*

Here I want students to learn that air and water can push sideways as well as up and down and again, that the push of air and water is greater the deeper one goes. "Suppose there is a tiny drop of water at this opening. In what direction would the air push on it? In what direction would the water in the container push on the droplet?" With some guidance to think about the directions in which air and water push on a tiny droplet right in the opening of one of the holes, the students conclude that the inside water must be pushing outward (sideways) on the droplet, since the droplet comes out. They also observe that the water comes out with different trajectories at the three different-elevation holes. They again see this as evidence that the deeper one goes, the greater is the push by the fluid, in this case sideways. I see some students capping the bottle and observing air going in (bubbles rising) the top hole while water is coming out the lower holes. They conclude that at the top hole, the outside air must push the hypothetical droplet into the water since that is the direction the air goes. Thus, they see that air and water can push sideways and that pressure is greater with depth.

Elaboration Activity A5: Water and Air in a Straw. I think most parents have been embarrassed by their children doing something like this activity while out to dinner. Students place a straw a few centimeters into a container of water and put a finger over the upper end of the straw before withdrawing the straw from the water. Typically, this results in a bit of air in the upper part of the straw and a few milliliters of water staying in the bottom part of the straw. Students are invited to explain.

> *In science, we strive for the simplest hypothesis necessary to explain the phenomenon.*

Observing that the water stays in the straw, some students conclude that the air below the straw helps support the water. Other students may suggest that the air or vacuum above the water may be "sucking" the water up, an alternative hypothesis. This latter hypothesis is probably cued by the situation because virtually all of these students have experienced sucking on a straw to get liquid to rise. Other students counter by turning the straw over while keeping their finger over the one end, now the bottom end. This leaves the water in what is now the top of the straw, with air in the straw below the water. One student suggests, "The air in the straw is now holding up the water. But, see how the water at the end of the straw now goes down a bit into the straw. That means the weight of the water is causing the air in the straw to be compressed slightly, and if we take our finger away, the air in the straw goes out and the water falls because it is not supported." Other students chime in with their experiment of making two bits of water in the straw with a bit of air between them. They have a bubble of air in the bottom of the straw with a bit of water next, then a bubble of air, and finally more water in the top of the straw. These students argue that the middle bubble of air is both pushing up on the bit of water above and pushing down on the bit of water below. The sucking hypothesis, although not completely eradicated, seems less necessary. Thus, most students come to the conclusion that air can push up and down at the same time.

The first time I tried these activities, I had planned them as a "circus lab." After about 10 minutes, I told students to move on to the next station. Most students stayed where they were. It was 40 minutes before I could get the three girls at the straw station to give it up. I now allow students to major in one activity and visit the others. They get engaged in these simple, common activities, and challenged, they need time to come up with and test explanatory ideas. So I now plan for students to have two class periods in which to complete their major activity, briefly visit each of the other activities, and prepare to present their findings to the class. Toward the end of the second period, we may begin class presentations.

On a third day, we finish the presentations and have a class discussion about what we learned. We summarize the similarities and differences in the properties of air and water. Virtually all students now agree that air and water can push up and down and sideways, that is, can push in all directions. Virtually all agree that the deeper one goes in water, the greater is the push in all directions. There is not quite the same strength of agreement that the push by air is greater the deeper one goes. But usually some students will note that the higher one goes up a mountain, the lower is the air pressure. Other students agree with this observation and add their own, such as that this is why airplanes are pressurized. So, they argue, air and water have many similar properties. Students now have sufficient background for me to introduce the technical term "fluid" properties. Both air and water are fluids.

They can exert pressures in all directions, and they appear to have this increase in pressure with depth.

After students have had experiences and come up with ideas to summarize those experiences, it makes sense to introduce a technical term for ease of communication.

What are the differences? With some guidance, students suggest that air is "squishable" and water is not. They know that water is denser, heavier for the same volume, for we studied density earlier in the year. Students also may talk about the stickiness of water to itself and to other things, like the containers it is in. Since the students have summarized the ideas, I can now introduce the technical terms "cohesion" and "adhesion." Now they are ready for another elaboration activity that more closely approximates the initial benchmark activity.

Elaboration Activity A6: "Weighing" an Object in a Fluid Medium. In this activity, I weigh a solid cylinder suspended by a string and ask, "What will happen to the scale reading if I attempt to weigh this object while it is under water?" Virtually all students suggest the scale reading will be lower than when the object is weighed out of the water. They are given an opportunity to test their predictions and are then encouraged to explain the results.

When complex explanations involving several factors are needed for their reasoning, students need more time to put the pieces together.

The scale reading is lower. Some students conclude that the water is pushing up by an amount that is the difference between what the object weighed when out of the water and when in the water. Note, however, that this is going back to the conclusion that water pushes up, with no mention of any downward push. Many textbooks let students off the hook at this point: "This upward force by the water is called the buoyant force." But this prevents a deeper, more useful understanding involving the resolution of the up and down forces, so I press for more: "Tell me about the pushes by the water on this solid, metal cylinder." Several students jump in with claims based on their previous experiences. They introduce their earlier conclusion that the water is pushing on the top and sides as well as on the bottom. I probe for more: "In what directions are those pushes?" Now students are even more eager to apply the ideas that have emerged in the last few days.

A few students say, "The water on top pushes down." Several others add, "The water below pushes up. The water on the sides pushes sideways."

I now ask, "So, how do we explain the observation that the scale reading is less?" Several students are now constructing an explanation. I give them a few minutes to work on their explanations in small groups and then ask them to share their conclusions: "The water pushes up and the water pushes down. But the push up is greater than the push down, 'cuz it is deeper." Some students have it, but others are still struggling. If students do not volunteer consideration of the comparison between the pushes, I may ask the question, "Why should the push from below be larger? Why does that make sense?" Several students respond, "Because the deeper we go the bigger the push."

At this point, several students have represented the application of our recently derived ideas with words. In the interest of deepening the understanding for all students, I suggest they represent the situation with pictures, using arrows to show the directions of the forces and varying the lengths of the arrows to show the magnitude (size) of the forces. I ask each group to take white board and a marking pen and draw such a picture of the submerged metal cylinder. After a few minutes, we compare diagrams and have members of each group describe their drawings and explain the situation. By now, nearly all the groups have drawn the cylinder with a larger arrow up than down. Each of these arrows, they say, represents the size and direction of the push by the water on that part of the cylinder.

Building an Analogy to Understand the Benchmark Experience

Now that it appears the students understand the weighing-in-water situation, I direct them back to the weighing-in-a-vacuum situation. "So, what does all of this tell us about the situation of weighing under the bell jar? If we had a really accurate instrument, what do you think would have happened to the scale reading and why?" A few students begin to construct an analogy: "Weighing in air would be like the weighing in water." I ask, "How so?" One student responds, "The air around the world is kind of like an ocean of air. Down here is like being deep in the ocean of air. On a mountain air doesn't press as hard." Another adds, "Air can push in all directions, just like water. So if water can push up and down on the cylinder, so can air." "But air doesn't push as much [hard], so you don't get as big a difference," says another. With some guidance from me, the students build an analogy: "Weighing in the water is to weighing out of the water (in air) as weighing in the ocean of air is to weighing out of the air, that is in a vacuum." I ask, "So what would happen to the scale reading in the vacuum if we had a very accurate instrument?" One student responds, "The scale reading would be more."

Another adds, "Just like the scale is more when we take the thing out of the water."

> *Building an analogy from a situation students understand to one they do not can build understanding of the new situation.*

Consensus Discussion and Summary of Learning

There are expectations for what students should have learned from the curricular activities performed thus far. Up to this point, I have been attempting to identify students' understandings about the pushes of the surrounding fluid (water or air). In the class, I now guide a discussion aimed at achieving consensus on what we can conclude about water and air from our observations. On the topical content side, learners should know the following:

- Water and air have some similar properties.
  — Fluids (at least water and air) can push in all directions, up, down, sideways.
  — The deeper one goes in the fluid, the greater is the push in any direction.
- Water and air have some different properties.
  — Since water is denser than air, the effects of the pushes by water are greater.
  — Water can stick to itself (cohesion).
  — Water can stick to other materials and things (adhesion).
  — Air is more squishable (compressable) than water.

The learners should have evidence (results) from the class experiences that they can use to support each of these conclusions.

> *Students need opportunities to reflect on and summarize what they have learned.*

Learners also have had an opportunity to practice some habits of mind that are consistent with learning and reasoning in science:

- Inferences come from observations (evidence-based reasoning).
- Controlled experiments can be used to test most of our ideas.

- Dialogue in science means questioning for clarity of observations, ideas, and explanations.
- Dialogue in science means being supportive and encouraging to elicit the ideas of others while at the same time asking critical questions, such as "How do you know?"
- If we persevere, we will likely be able to understand complex situations.

Students need opportunities to monitor their own learning.

If habits of reasoning and action are also among our learning goals, we need to make them as explicit as we make our content goals.

Diagnostic Assessment

At some point after the benchmark lesson and the more focused elaboration lessons, and after the class has begun to develop tentative resolutions for some of the issues raised, it is useful to give students the opportunity to check their understanding and reasoning individually. Although I sometimes administer these questions on paper in large-group format, I prefer to allow the students to quiz themselves when they feel ready to do so. They think they understand, but they need opportunities to check and tune their understanding. To address this need for ongoing formative assessment, I use a computerized tool[2] that assists the teacher in individualizing the assessment and keeping records on student progress. When students feel they are ready, they are encouraged to work through computer-presented questions and problem appropriate to the unit being studied.

Typical questions related to the key ideas of the preceding activities might juxtapose three situations involving weighing a solid object—the solid object in air, in water, and in a vacuum—each object suspended from a string attached to a spring scale. A first question checks on the students' recall of the specific results obtained and asks them to put the expected scale readings in order assuming the scale has the precision needed. A second question checks on the students' reasoning: "What reasoning best justifies the answer you chose?" For this question, I look for responses that suggest "the water pushes up," "the air pushes down," or "air has no effect on scale readings." Have the students fallen back into their preconceptions, or have they made the desired progress?

Other questions extend the students' application of the ideas to new contexts: "Using the ideas of pushes by air and water, explain how the squeezable plant watering container (with the long curved 'straw' on top) works." Another question suggests a special room wherein the air pressure can be increased from normal to much higher: "What would happen to the scale reading and why?" Another asks students to predict what would happen to a scale reading if we attempted to weigh the solid object in alcohol, which is less dense than water but more dense than air.

> *Assessment should help the teacher monitor whether students are still operating on the basis of preconceptions, as well as whether they have attained the learning goal(s).*

For all these questions, I look for evidence to determine whether the students' ideas have changed or they are still showing evidence of believing their original idea that fluids only push up or down or that the weight is proportional to air pressure. Thus, I aim to move students' understanding across the gap from their preconceptions to a more scientific understanding. The assessment allows them to monitor their learning. If there is trouble, they get feedback suggesting they rethink their answer and/or reasoning in light of the class experiences. I thus obtain a report of what sort of problematic thinking students have exhibited and what experiences might help them move farther across the learning gap.

Part B: What Is Gravitational Attraction?

Exploring Similarities and Differences Between Actions at a Distance

In the previous subunit (Part A) the class separated the effects of the surrounding medium from the effects of gravity on static objects. We appear to have taken a bit of a detour into understanding more about the effects of air and water and other fluids on objects submerged in the fluid. Later we will need to return to looking at the effects of the surrounding fluid when we explore falling bodies (Parts C and D). First, however, we explore the concept of "action at a distance," a key notion in understanding gravity.

> *Students should be able to see science as involving many questions as yet unanswered.*

Although there are still many unanswered questions about gravity, the students do know a great deal about what it does and about the variables on which the strength of the gravity force depends. In Part B, now that the students know about some effects that are not due to gravity, we explore some of the effects that are. Because many effects of gravity are so subtle and pervasive (we live and deal with them every day), the students need to explore gravity by comparing and contrasting its effects with some similar effects and causes they can investigate first-hand.

Research has shown that many students do not separate gravitational effects from magnetic or electrostatic effects. But the effects are similar in that they are all "actions at a distance"; that is, one object can affect another without touching it. Actions at a distance can act through materials and even across empty space. The first activity (B1) in this subunit is to construct analogies among the various actions at a distance. The goal is for students to see that the situations are similar, but the properties of the objects or materials on which the influencing objects act are different.

Benchmark Lesson: Making a Torsion Bar Do the Twist

In the classroom, several meter sticks are hanging from their center points from strings attached to the ceiling. They should be hanging so that each meter stick is horizontal and free to rotate horizontally. On the two ends of one meter stick are hanging two identical brass spheres. From the ends of another hang two aluminum spheres, from another two wooden spheres, from another two steel spheres, and from another two foam spheres. Each system should hang fairly still with the meter stick horizontal (though this is sometimes difficult with students moving around the room). Each is arranged to be what is called a "torsion balance" or "torsion bar." The word "torsion" comes from "torque," which means twist. So, we are going to see whether these bars can be made to twist by bringing something near the objects hanging from the ends without touching the objects (see Figure 11-2). Care must be taken not to bump or even touch the bars except to adjust them to remain still at first. Note that, depending on the maturity and coordination of the students, it will likely be necessary to set up and run the experiment as a demonstration after students have made their predictions individually. Some teachers have found that it helps keep the torsion bars still if movement of students around the room is limited, and even the

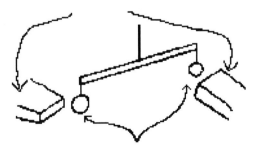

FIGURE 11-2 Torsion bar, spheres, and influencing material.

heating/cooling fan for the room is turned off and windows and doors closed. Even quick hand motions near these delicate balances will cause them to move—possible air effects again. Now the problem:

> *Suppose one end of a magnet is very slowly brought near (but not touching) a sphere on one end of each torsion bar. (Notice that there is a similar situation on the other end of the torsion bar. We will be discussing mainly what happens at one end of the bar, but because of symmetry we can generalize the effect to both ends.)*
> *1. Predict what the torsion bar will do in each case. If you think the bar will twist, tell whether it will go toward or away from the magnet.*
> *When brought near the brass sphere the bar will*
> _____.
> *When brought near the aluminum sphere the bar will*
> _____.
> *When brought near the wooden sphere the bar will*
> _____.
> *When brought near the steel sphere the bar will*
> _____.
> *When brought near the foam sphere the bar will*
> _____.
>
> *2. Briefly explain how you decided which will twist and in what direction.*
>
> *If any will not twist, tell why you think they will not.*

> *To keep students thinking, teachers should not give answers but present opportunities for students to test their answers.*

While students are answering the questions individually, I circulate around the room, making sure that they understand the questions and that I am getting a feeling for the sorts of answers and thinking I will hear during the discussion. When it appears most students have finished answering and explaining, I ask them to share their predictions and explanations with others. One student suggests, "I think all the metal ones will move because metal is attracted to magnets." I ask whether that makes sense to others, and most of the class appears to agree. Another student says he has tried this before and only "silverish" metal things get attracted, not things like gold rings. Another says, "Not all silver things are attracted, 'cuz I've tried to pick up money, and magnets don't pick up quarters, nickels, or dimes." A few others agree. After only a few minutes of this discussion, students are ready to see what happens. So I carefully and slowly bring the magnet near one of the spheres in first one situation and then another until we have tried them all. While doing this, I suggest that the students write down the results of each situation. The results are that only the steel sphere is attracted to the magnet, and none of the others are affected.

In this case, because the students typically know little about various kinds of metals and their properties and because I do not want to lose the focus on actions at a distance, I elect to tell the students about the metals that are attracted to magnets. I suggest that, while most materials have some magnetic properties, only metals containing iron readily show the effects with magnets such as those we are using.

> *Preinstruction assessment should check for specific preconceptions.*

Next I bring out a styrofoam cup that I have been careful to leave in my desk for several days, so it likely will not be electrostatically charged. I ask the students to predict whether the cup will affect any of the spheres on the torsion balances. There are no clear patterns of prediction. Most students appear to be just trying to guess. I immediately show them what happens: the foam cup does not affect any of the objects (unless the spheres themselves happen to have become charged electrically).

> *In guided inquiry, the teacher needs to monitor class ideas as they exist initially and as they develop.*

Then I rub the cup across my hair a couple of times and ask the students what they expect will happen now. Some students say they think the cup will attract the steel "because you magnetized the cup." Others say no, that the cup now has "electrical charge," so it will attract all the metal pieces because "metal conducts electricity." Still others say, "Because the metals conduct the charge away, they won't be affected." Again, given the confusion and, in some cases, lack of experience with the phenomena, it is time to move quickly to doing the experiments. So I bring the charged cup near each sphere. The results are that every sphere is attracted to the cup. One student facetiously suggests, "That's static cling." For now we conclude that all materials are attracted to an object that has been electrostatically charged. In later investigations of electrostatics, I want students to see that there are two kinds of electrostatic charge and the neutral condition, but I elect not to encourage that investigation at this time so we can keep building the action-at-a-distance story.

Next, I "cuddle" the cup in my hands. By gently putting my hands all over the cup and breathing warm, moist air on it, I am discharging it. When I am pretty sure it has been discharged, when I see that it will not pick up a tiny scrap of paper, I go through the test of bringing the cup near but not touching each sphere again, and we find that there is no effect on any of the spheres. (Note that this part of the lesson is tricky, and it takes practice to make sure the cup is no longer charged.) So I cuddle the magnet as well, but it still attracts the steel sphere and no others. I rub the magnet across my hair and test it, again with no effect except with the steel sphere.

> *Students need opportunities to summarize the big ideas that have been developed by the class.*

It is now time to have students summarize and build consensus. Magnets attract steel pieces without touching them, but do not affect any other materials that we can readily see. And the magnet effect cannot be cuddled off. Static-charged foam cups (and other things such as plastic rulers and inflated latex balloons) attract all kinds of materials without touching them, but the charge can be cuddled off. Thus magnets and static-charged objects are similar in that they both influence other things without touching them, and I suggest this is called "action at a distance." I continue to point out that the two phenomena are apparently different kinds of action at a distance, since they affect different kinds of material. Magnets affect materials that contain iron, but static-charged things can affect almost anything made out of almost any material. Finally, the electrical charge can be cuddled off, but the magnetic effect cannot.

> *Technical media can be used to enhance or extend the students' experience.*

What about gravity? It also acts without touching. The students have heard slogans about gravity making things fall here on earth, holding the moon in orbit, and holding the planets in orbit around the sun, but how can I make that abstraction real for them? What does gravity affect? Can it be cuddled away?

> *Thinking needs to be challenged whenever passive media are used.*

I show a piece of film that demonstrates a torsion balance experiment similar to what we have been observing during the first half of the class period. In the film, a meter stick is again used as the torsion bar. In this case,

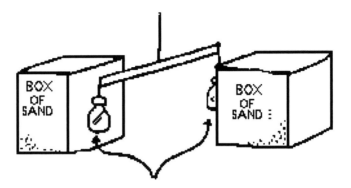

FIGURE 11-3 Experiment illustrating gravitational torsion balance.

quart milk bottles are hung from each end of the bar and adjusted until the bar is horizontal and remaining still. Then a large cardboard box of sand is pulled close (but not touching) to one side of one bottle, and another box of sand is pulled to the other side of the balance but near the other bottle of water (see Figure 11-3). To help students understand the film, I stop it and simulate the situation in one corner of the classroom with bottles and boxes. Then the students watch the film as the bar slowly twists such that the bottles get closer to the boxes. Because the effect is so unbelievable to students and because an indirect measure of the movement of the bar is used in the film, I talk the students through the procedure, the results, and the final conclusion:

Teacher	Do you understand the procedure? How is it like the procedure we used for the magnet situation and the electric charge situation?
Student 1	There are things hanging from the stick in all of 'em.
Student 2	The stick could turn if something made it turn, like a magnet or rubbed foam cup.
Teacher	What is brought into this situation like the magnet or the charged cup?
Student 3	A box of sand?
Student 4	Two boxes of sand.
Teacher	So is there an effect here?
Student 3	No, it is not like the magnet, a box of sand can't cause the bottle to move.

Teachers can foster students' thinking by asking questions, by reflecting students' comments back to them, and by avoiding expressing judgments about whether those comments are right or wrong.

[Partly because students do not believe there should be an effect, and partly because the film uses a subtle way of detecting the movement, most students fail to see the movement at first. I tape a small piece of mirror to the middle of the meter stick with the bottles and shine a flashlight on the mirror. This is also done in the film. A spot of reflected light hits the wall over my shoulder.]

One goal of inquiry-based teaching is to get students to be the ones asking the questions and challenging or bringing up apparently conflicting observations.

Teacher	What would happen to the spot of light if the meter stick twisted?
Student 5	The spot would move. It's like when the light hits my watch and makes a spot and then I move my wrist and make the spot hit somebody in the face. [some laughter]
Teacher	Yes, good example, although it might be distracting, so please don't do it in class. In the film they were shining a light on the mirror in the center of the meter stick. What happened to the light?
Student 5	It moved.
Student 6	Yeah. The light went first one way, then the other.
Student 2	But that would mean that something like a magnet made the stick turn.
Student 4	The box of sand pulled on the bottle of water and made the stick turn.
Student 7	No way, Jose! [laughter] Sand can't pull on water.
Student 3	Yeah maybe they had a magnet or foam cup or something to do it.
Teacher	Good question, lets see how they address that in the film.

[I run the film through the part where they show the effect is not an electrical one, and the voice of the physicist on the film concludes that the bottles moved because of the gravitational attraction between the sand-filled boxes and the bottles of water.]

Student 3   But, how come we can't see that [gravitational attraction] here with our stuff?

Teacher   Another good question. The gravitational effect of a box of sand on a bottle of water is so weak that it requires a very delicate setup. Although Sir Isaac Newton, in 1687, suggested every object in the universe pulled on every other object in the universe, it really wasn't until about a hundred years later that another scientist named Henry Cavendish built a very sensitive torsion balance and was able to see evidence of gravitational attraction happening with ordinary things in a laboratory.

Providing some information from the history of science can help give students perspective on human involvement in the development of ideas.

[When I was at the university I had a chance to repeat Cavendish's experiment. The equipment was so delicate that when a truck went by the building I was in, we had to start the experiment over again. It made the equipment shake, even though we could not even feel or hear the truck. Note that in the film, the experiment is conducted in a mostly vacant building, and the torsion bar is hung from the rafters.]

Teacher   OK, so this was about the best I could do to show you that any thing that has mass will pull on any and every other thing that has mass. This is part of Newton's law of universal gravitation. Even ordinary things like boxes of sand and bottles of water exert a gravitational pull on each other, and they do it without touching each other. Gravity is also an action at a distance. Can we rub it off? No, not unless we could get rid of the mass. But, then we would have nothing, because everything has mass. Let's summarize in a table [which I write on the board and encourage them to record in their notes for the day].

Teacher   So remember these three different sets of

Three different kinds of action at a distance:

Magnetism	Acts at a distance	Acts mostly on iron things	Can't be cuddled away easily
Static electricity	Acts at a distance	Acts on anything (charged or neutral)	Can be cuddled away
Gravity	Acts at a distance	Acts on anything (with mass)	Can't be cuddled away at all

circumstances associated with three different forces that can all act at a distance, even across empty space. We conclude that they all three are "actions at a distance," but they act on different materials. Some we can make come and go under certain circumstances (e.g., cuddling, and I will end class with changing a magnet). So far we have no way of making the gravity go away. And we have some evidence that you might encounter in later classes that gravity is the force that holds planets in their orbits and makes dust and gases in the universe come together to form stars.

If students have had sufficient first-hand experience, short lectures can make sense even to young students.

Mainly for fun and motivation, I show the students that if I beat on an iron bar with a hammer while holding the bar parallel to the earth's magnetic field, I can cause the bar to become a magnet. For fun, I have them chant as I beat on the bar: [bang bang] "uwa," [bang bang] "tafu," [bang bang] "yiyam." As I beat the pairs of hits faster and faster, the chant begins to sound more and more like "ohwhat afool Iam." The bell rings, and the students leave laughing and agreeing with the chant. That concludes the main lesson showing the various types of actions at a distance.

> *Humor can enliven the learning experience and help build positive relationships between students and teachers.*

Factors on Which the Magnitude (Size) of Gravitational Force Depends

The purpose of the next series of lessons is to build a case for students to believe that the magnitude (size) of the gravitational force grows as each of the two interacting masses becomes larger, and that the greater the separation distance between the two masses, the smaller is the gravitational force that each exerts on the other. High school physics students and more mathematically capable middle school students may be able to conclude with analogous experiences from magnetism and electrostatics that the dependence on distance of separation is an inverse square law. For middle school students, teachers can be more successful building cases that yield qualitative relationships as opposed to yielding mathematical relations and especially equations. The following activities include first-hand observations, reasoning from results to formulate conclusions, and analogical reasoning from concrete situations to abstractions not readily accessible through classroom experiences. From these more qualitative experiences, later algebraic formulation of the gravitational force law can make more sense to students.

We saw early in this unit that gravity does not depend on air pressure pressing down on an object. From other prior experiences, students know that we can measure the weight of something fairly precisely using a spring scale (see Figure 11-4). The heavier the object, the greater the spring scale

FIGURE 11-4 Common experiences using a spring scale to weigh objects.

reading will be. But what is the cause of that reading if it is not air pressing down? I could just wave my hands and suggest "gravity," but I want students to have a deeper understanding of gravity by at least understanding the factors on which it depends. I build the case for factors affecting gravity by determining factors that affect magnetic force, and then arguing by analogy about factors affecting gravity.

Students generally love playing with magnets, especially strong ones. I recommend having at least one strong magnet available for each physical science classroom. Among other experiences set up for students' investigations with magnets, one station has a spring scale firmly attached to a heavy brick on a table. A string is tied to the hook on the spring scale. The other end of the string has a loop on which to hang one or more identical paper clips (see Figure 11-5). Set up properly, the magnet attracts the paper clips and the string pulls on the spring scale, registering a reading even without the magnet touching the paper clips. The teacher might ask, "How can the magnet do that?" Most students from the earlier lesson see that the magnet is exerting a force at a distance.

> *Answering such questions as "How do you know?" or "Why do you believe?" helps students build understanding of how knowledge in the discipline is constructed.*

Teacher	What kind of action at a distance is the magnet exerting, and what kind of material does it affect?
Student 1	Magnetic.
Student 2	Magnetism.
Teacher	How do you know?
Student 3	'Cuz the paper clips are made of iron.
Teacher	Did any other action at a distance affect iron?
Student 3	Yeah. Electric force.

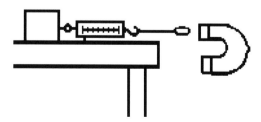

FIGURE 11-5 Apparatus for testing factors that affect magnetic force.

Student 4	And gravity because the paper clips have a little mass.
Student 1	But, I know in this case it's magnetic because there is a magnet.
Student 2	Also, when we set it up we touched the paper clips a lot and that's like cuddling, so there shouldn't be any electric force.
Teacher	Very good. So, we're pretty sure it is magnetic and not electric force. And we are pretty sure it is not gravitational because gravity force is so weak.
Student 3	Yeah, we know all that without even talking about it.
Student 2	So, what's the point?

I see now that I am losing their attention, so I elect to demonstrate the apparatus initially myself. I set it up so there are four paper clips being pulled by but not touching the magnet, and I ask one student to read the spring scale reading and record the reading on the board. I ask another student to carefully measure the distance between the paper clips and the magnet. (Note we are just measuring the separation distance here. With more mature students, we could get into concerns about measuring center-to-center distance as necessary for the force equation.)

I then ask what we might do to make the scale reading lower. Upper elementary and middle school students' intuition suggests that using a weaker magnet would make the scale reading lower. Some also suggest that if we had fewer paper clips, that might do it, too. Other students suggest we might need more paper clips to lessen the force. Since no one has mentioned the separation distance, I ask how it might make the scale reading lower. I ask the students to answer the question for themselves first without saying their answers out loud, so everyone has a chance to do the thinking. Most students suggest moving the magnet farther away will decrease the force and the scale reading.

Quiet can allow each student time to do his or her own thinking.

It appears that the students are now ready to test their predictions and hypotheses. We try a weaker magnet and fewer paper clips, but I allow the distance to get smaller as well. The scale reading rises. Although this is confusing, I want to give students an opportunity to notice and suggest the need to control variables without my having to tell them to do so.

Sometimes, there are emergent goals that need to be addressed before returning to the primary instructional goal. For example, teaching about the content may need to move to the background of the instruction while teaching about the processes of science are brought to the foreground, even though both are always present.

Student 2	See, it's what I thought, less paper clips makes it stronger.
Student 3	No it's what I said. Smaller distance makes it bigger.
Student 4	We got too many things happening.
Student 1	I'm getting lost.
Student 3	It's like we studied before about making fair tests. This isn't a fair test.
Student 4	Oh yeah.
Teacher	OK. Why not, Chris? Why isn't it a fair test? Hang in there Tommy [Student 1]. I think we are about to clear this up. I will have you decide when the argument and results of the experiments make sense to you. The rest of you need to talk to Tommy to convince him of what you are saying. Chris, you were saying?
Student 3	You gotta keep things constant. Like change only one thing and keep other things constant.
Student 4	Oh yeah, like we did before, make a fair test. OK, Tommy?
Student 1	No, I don't remember anything about a fair test.
Student 4	It's like when we said we have to keep all the things [a few students are saying "variables"]. Yeah, we have to keep all the variables the same except one.
Teacher	But, does that help you, Tommy?
Student 1	Not really. What's it got to do with this experiment? That was something we did before when we were studying other stuff.
Student 3	In this experiment we have to keep the number of paper clips the same and the strong magnet the same and change the distance. Only change the distance, if we want to see whether

the distance changes the scale reading. Otherwise, if we change other things too, we will not know whether it is distance or something else that made it bigger.

> *To become learners, independent of authority, students need opportunities to make sense of experiences and formulate rational arguments.*

Student 1	OK. So, what happened?
Student 3	Well, we didn't keep the other things, variables, the same. So, we need to do that to find out what happens.
Teacher	Good, to find out whether that one variable, for example the distance, affects how big the magnetic force is. [At this point, because the apparatus is difficult to control, I demonstrate what does happen when we keep the big magnet and the number of paper clips the same and just decrease the distance between the magnet and paper clips. The scale reading rises.] Now can we tell if varying the distance affects the force?
Student 2	Yeah. It does.
Teacher	How does distance affect force, Tommy? Which way does it go? The smaller the distance . . .
Student 1	The smaller the distance, the bigger the force. Does it get smaller if the distance gets bigger?
Teacher	Good question. Let's try it. [I increase the distance, and the scale reading is lower.] So, what can we conclude now?
Student 1	The bigger the distance the smaller the scale, and the smaller the distance, the bigger the force scale.
Teacher	Good. Now, what do we need to do to test whether the number of paper clips makes a difference in the force?
Student 1	Would we change the paper clips or keep them the same?
Student 2	If you want to test the paper clips, you change the number of paper clips and see if that changes the force.

Student 1	Is that right? Oh! Oh! I get it. So to see if one thing affects the other thing, you change the one thing and see what happens to the other.

The teacher's questions to clarify students' statements help the students become clearer about what they know.

Teacher	That's sounding like you've got the idea of fair test or what is sometimes called "controlling variables," but could you say it again and say what you mean by the word "thing," which you used several times.
Student 1	OK. To see if paper clips affect the scale, the force, you change the number of paper clips and see if the force changes. Right?
Teacher	Yes, good. Now suppose you wanted to see if the strength of the magnet affected the force. What would you do?
Student 1	Change the magnet and see if the force changed.
Teacher	What would you do about the other variables?
Student 2	I'd keep . . . [At this point I interrupt to let Tommy (Student 1) continue his thinking. Meanwhile, other students are getting restless, so I let them go ahead with the apparatus and see what they can find out, which I charge them with demonstrating later for the rest of us. Meanwhile, I continue with Tommy and anyone else who admits to needing some help here.]

All students can learn, but some need more assistance than others, and some need more challenge than others.

Teacher	So, Tommy. What are the factors that we want to investigate here?
Student 1	See if bigger magnets have a bigger force.
Teacher	OK. Anything else?
Student 1	See if more paper clips makes the force reading bigger.

Student 5	And see if distance makes the force bigger or smaller.
Student 1	We already saw that one.
Teacher	If we changed the number of paper clips and we changed the magnet, would we know whether one of these affected the force?
Student 6	Not if we changed both. If we changed both, one or both might be changing the force.
Teacher	So, what do we need to do, Tommy?
Student 1	Oh, do we need to only change one thing, like change the strength of magnet we use and don't change the paper clips?
Student 6	And we'd need to keep the distance the same too right, else that might be changing the force too?
Teacher	Good. So, we think that strength of magnet, the number of paper clips, and the distance might all change the magnetic force. So we just change one of those variables at a time and keep the others constant and see if the force changes and in what direction.

Assuming all the students are familiar with the equipment, sometimes it is more important to help some students focus on the argument while others wrestle with the details of manipulating the equipment.

In a while, I bring the whole class together. I help the students summarize the ideas they have developed and how the controlled experiments helped test those ideas. The group that had the challenge to test factors demonstrates the apparatus and the procedures they used to obtain the following results:

• The more paper clips, the higher the scale reading (keeping magnet and distance constant).
• The stronger the magnet, the higher the scale reading (keeping number of paper clips and distance of separation constant).
• The greater the distance of separation, the lower the scale reading (keeping number of paper clips and strength of the magnet constant).

> *Students need assistance in differentiating between results and conclusions. Results are specific to the experiment, while conclusions generalize across situations.*

From these results we conclude that the magnetic force grows larger with more magnetic "stuff" (paper clips containing iron), with a stronger magnet, or with closer distance of separation between the big magnet and the iron pieces.

Building a Bridge from Understanding Magnetic Action at a Distance to Understanding Gravitational Action at a Distance

> *Analogies can help bridge from the known to the unknown and from the concrete to the abstract.*

I now illustrate two situations on the front board. One is something like the situation we have just investigated, with a large magnet pulling on an iron object and stretching a spring scale. Since this diagram is a bit different from the previous one, I ask students to discuss the similarities and differences. When they appear to see that the situations just seem to be different representations of the same conclusions we drew, I move on to the second diagram. It looks like the first, except that a large sphere represents the earth, and the object is anything that has mass (see Figure 11-6). The spring scale is the same. I ask students how this situation is similar and different from the weighing of a fish depicted in Figure 11-4.

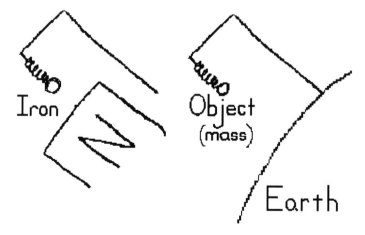

FIGURE 11-6 Diagramming an analogy between magnetism and gravity.

Student 5	Oh, it's like, the earth pulls on the object like the magnet pulls on the piece of iron.
Student 7	They are both actions at a distance.
Student 4	So what. We already knew that.

[So the students appear to recognize the analogous situations. Now comes the difficult part.]

Teacher	From our previous experiments you know on what factors the magnetic force depends. Right?

[There is a chorus of "yes," but I don't trust it because we now have a different diagram, and I want to know if the students are transferring what they know about the previous situation. Students recite the list: "how much iron," "how big (strong) the magnet is," "how far apart they are." Now reasonably assured, I move on.]

Teacher	What are some possible factors on which gravitational force might depend, if it acts similarly to magnetism?
Student 2	Oh. Maybe it depends on the separation distance?
Student 8	Maybe on the mass of the thing, 'cuz that would be like the number of paper clips.
Student 1	Maybe on the strength of the magnet.
Student 3	No, there is no magnet in the gravity situation.
Teacher	OK. Hang on. Tommy [Student 1], there is no magnet in this situation [pointing to the gravitational case], but what might be similar to the strength of the magnet?
Student 1	The strength of the earth?

To build deep understanding of ideas, students need opportunities to transfer the ideas across contexts. Teachers need to check on this transfer of knowledge to new situations.

Teacher	It is kind of like the strength of the earth isn't it. Just like the magnetic force depends on how big and strong the magnet is, the gravitational force might depend on how big, how much mass there is in the earth. Just like the more magnet we have, the bigger the force; the more mass the earth has, the bigger the force. I cannot easily show you, with experiments, on what factors the gravity force depends. But by what is called an "analogy," we can make a good guess at the factors gravity depends on. If gravity action at a distance acts like magnetic action at a distance, it should depend on how much there is of each of the two objects interacting and on how big the separation distance is. By careful experiments with sensitive apparatus like the Cavendish torsion balance we saw before, scientists have verified that the guesses we just made work out in experiments. That is, the gravity force, evidenced by the spring scale reading, would be smaller if the mass of the earth were smaller, if the mass of the ball being held near the earth were of less mass, or if the ball were placed farther away from the earth.

Parts C and D: What Are the Effects of Gravity?

Explaining Falling Bodies

Part A was about "what gravity is not." That is, the effects of the surrounding fluid are not the cause of weight or gravity. But we ended up seeing that fluids such as air and water can have an effect on scale readings when we attempt to weigh objects. Part B was about the nature of gravitational force being one of the actions at a distance. And by analogy we concluded that the magnitude of the gravitational force depends on the masses of the two interacting objects and on the separation distance between them. Investigations into the nature of forces could stop here or could continue and focus on gaining a better understanding of the effects of gravity.

Subsequent investigations in my classes involve explaining the phenomena of falling bodies. Part of a rich understanding of falling bodies is to understand the effects of air (or fluid) resistance as well those of gravity.

Activities in these subunits are more consistent with what is presently suggested in curricula, so they are not described here. But students' preconceptions, such as "heavier falls faster," need to be addressed. More mature students can also quantify the acceleration of freely falling bodies and arrive at equations describing the motion in free fall. But younger students can gain a qualitative understanding of free fall as speeding up uniformly, and they can gain some understanding of factors affecting air resistance.

Explaining Motion of Projectiles

Next investigations, especially for older students, can involve understanding the motion of projectiles. Preconceptions, including "horizontal motion slows the vertical fall," will need to be addressed. Understanding the independence of horizontal and vertical motions is a learning goal. Again those activities are not discussed in detail here. Suffice it to say that additional investigations into the nature and effects of gravity will build a stronger relationship between ideas and increase the likelihood that what is learned will be understood and remembered.

SUMMARY

In this chapter, we have tried to make real the principles of *How People Learn* by writing from our experience and the experience of other teachers, researchers, and curriculum developers. The sequence of activities described is not the only one that could foster learning of the main ideas that have been the focus here. Likewise, the dialogues presented are just examples of the many conversations that might take place. Teaching and learning are complex activities that spawn multiple problems suggesting multiple solutions. What we have discussed here is just one set of solutions to exemplify one set of generalizations about how students learn.

That having been said, the activities described are ones that real teachers are using. But this chapter has not been just about activities that teachers can take away and use next week. Our main purpose is to give teachers and curriculum developers an idea of what it looks like when assessment, curriculum, and teaching act as a system consistent with the principles of *How People Learn*. We have tried to give the reader the flavor of what it means to teach in a way that is student-centered, knowledge-centered, and assessment-centered. By looking at the teacher's decision making, we have attempted to provide a glimpse of what it is like to be a teacher or a learner in a learning community that is respectful of members of the community while at the same time being critical of the ideas they voice. Students are encouraged to question each other by asking, "What do you mean by that?" "How do you know?" But they are also guided to listen and allow others in the community to speak and complete their thoughts.

Students' preconceptions are identified and addressed, and subsequent learning is monitored. This means assessment is used primarily for formative learning purposes, when learning is the purpose of the activities in the classroom. By listening to their students, teachers can discern the sorts of experiences that are familiar and helpful in fostering the learning of other students.

Learning experiences need to develop from first-hand, concrete experiences to the more distant or abstract. Ideas develop from experiences, and technical terms develop from the ideas and operations that are rooted in those experiences. When terms come first, students just tend to memorize so much technical jargon that it sloughs off in a short while. Students need opportunities to see where ideas come from, and they need to be held responsible for knowing and communicating the origins of their knowledge. The teacher should also allow critical questions to open the Pandora's box of issues that are critical to the content being taught. The better questions are those that raise issues about the big ideas important to deep understanding of the discipline. Some of the best questions are those that come from students as they interact with phenomena.

Students need opportunities to learn to inquire in the discipline. Teachers can model the sorts of questions that the students will later ask themselves. Free inquiry is desirable, but sometimes (e.g., when understanding requires careful attention and logical development) inquiry is best guided, especially when the teacher is responsible for the learning of 30 or more students. But the teacher does not need to tell students the answers; doing so often short-circuits their thinking. Instead, teachers can guide their students with questions—not just factual questions, such as "What did you see?", but the more important questions that foster student thinking, such as those that ask students to provide explanations or make sense of the phenomena observed. By listening respectfully and critically to their students, teachers can model appropriate actions in a learning community. Through questions, teachers can assist learners in monitoring their own learning. Finally, teachers also need the freedom to learn in their classrooms—to learn about both learning and about teaching.

NOTES

1. We use the term "benchmark lesson" to mean a memorable lesson that initiates students' thinking about the key content issues in the next set of activities.

2. The computer-based Diagnoser assessment system described is available on the web through www.FACETInnovations.com. Thus, it is accessible to teachers and students anytime from a computer with web access and appropriate browser. The concept and program were developed by the authors, Minstrell and Kraus, Earl Hunt, and colleagues at the University of Washington, FACET Innovations, Talaria Inc., and surrounding school districts. It includes sets of questions for students, reports for teachers, and suggested lessons to address problematic facets of thinking.

12

Developing Understanding Through Model-Based Inquiry

James Stewart, Jennifer L. Cartier, and
Cynthia M. Passmore

A classroom of students need only look at each other to see remarkable variation in height, hair color and texture, skin tone, and eye color, as well as in behaviors. Some differences, such as gender, are discrete: students are male or female. Others, such as hair color or height, vary continuously within a certain range. Some characteristics—10 fingers, 10 toes, and one head—do not vary at all except in the rarest of cases. There are easily observed similarities between children and their parents or among siblings, yet there are many differences as well. How can we understand the patterns we observe?

Students need only look through the classroom window to take these questions a next step. Birds have feathers and wings—characteristics on which they vary somewhat from each other but on which they are completely distinct from humans. Dogs, cats, and squirrels have four legs. Why do we have only two? As with much of science, students can begin the study of genetics and evolution by questioning the familiar. The questions mark a port of entry into more than a century of fascinating discovery that has changed our understanding of our similarities, our differences, and our diseases and how to cure them. That inquiry has never been more vital than it is today.

It is likely that people observed and wondered about similarities of offspring and their parents, and about how species of animals are similar and distinct, long before the tools to record those musings were available. But major progress in understanding these phenomena has come only relatively recently through scientific inquiry. At the heart of that inquiry is the careful collection of data, the observation of patterns in the data, and the generation of causal models to construct and test explanations for those patterns. Our goal in teaching genetics and evolution is to introduce students to the conceptual models and the wealth of knowledge that have been generated by that scientific enterprise. Equally important, however, we want to build students' understanding of scientific modeling processes more generally—how scientific knowledge is generated and justified. We want to foster students' abilities not only to understand, but also to use such understandings to engage in inquiry.

For nearly two decades, we have developed science curricula in which the student learning outcomes comprise both disciplinary knowledge and knowledge about the nature of science. Such learning outcomes are realized in classrooms where students learn by "doing science" in ways that are similar to the work scientists do in their intellectual communities. We have created classrooms in which students are engaged in discipline-specific inquiry as they learn and employ the causal models and reasoning patterns of the discipline. The topics of genetics and evolution illustrate two different discipline-specific approaches to inquiry. While causal models are central in both disciplines, different reasoning patterns are involved in the use or construction of such models. The major difference is that the reconstruction of past events, a primary activity in the practice of evolutionary biology, is not common in the practice of genetics. The first section of this chapter focuses on genetics and the second on evolution. The third describes our approach to designing classroom environments, with reference to both units.

Our approach to curriculum development emerged as a result of collaborative work with high school teachers and their students (our collaborative group is known as MUSE, or Modeling for Understanding in Science Education).[1] As part of that collaboration, we have conducted research on student learning, problem solving, and reasoning. This research has led to refinements to the instruction, which in turn have led to improved student understanding.

GENETICS

An important step in course design is to clarify what we want students to know and be able to do.[2] Our goal for the course in genetics is for students to come away with a meaningful understanding of the concepts introduced above—that they will become adept at identifying patterns in the variations and similarities in observable traits (phenotypes) found within family lines. We expect students will do this using realistic data that they generate themselves or, in some cases, that is provided. However, while simply being familiar with data patterns may allow students to predict the outcomes of future genetic crosses, it provides a very incomplete understanding of genetics because it does not have explanatory power. Explanatory power comes from understanding that there is a physical basis for those patterns in the transmission of genetic material (i.e., that there are genes, and those genes are "carried" on chromosomes from mother and father to offspring as a result of the highly specialized process of cell division known as meiosis) and as a result of fertilization.

To achieve this understanding, students must learn to explain the patterns they see in their data using several models in a consistent fashion. Genetics models (or inheritance pattern models) explain how genes interact to produce variations in traits. These models include Mendel's simple dominance model, codominance, and multiple alleles. But to understand how the observed pairings of genes (the genotype) came about in the first place, students must also understand models of chromosome behavior, particularly the process of segregation and independent assortment during meiosis (the meiotic model).

We have one additional learning outcome for students—that they will couple their understanding of the transmission of the genetic material and their rudimentary understanding of how alleles interact to influence phenotype with an understanding of the relationship of DNA to genes and the role played by DNA products (proteins) in the formation of an organism's phenotype (biomolecular models). DNA provides the key to understanding why there are different models of gene interaction and introduces students to the frontier of genetic inquiry today.

These three models (genetic, meiotic, and biomolecular) and the relationships among them form the basic conceptual framework for understanding genetics. We have designed our instruction to support students in putting this complex framework in place.

Attending to Students' Existing Knowledge

While knowledge of the discipline of genetics has shaped our instructional goals, students' knowledge—the preconceptions they bring to the classroom and the difficulties they encounter in understanding the new material—have played a major role in our instructional design as well.

The genetics course is centered around a set of scientific models. However, in our study of student learning we have found, as have others,[3] that students have misunderstandings about the origin, the function, and the very nature of causal models (see Box 12-1). They view models in a "naïve realistic" manner rather than as conceptual structures that scientists use to explain data and ask questions about the natural world.[4]

Following our study of student thinking about models, we altered the instruction in the genetics unit to take into consideration students' prior knowledge about models and particular vocabulary for describing model attributes. Most important, we recognized the powerful prior ideas students had brought with them about models as representational entities and explic-

BOX 12-1 Student Conceptions of Models

One early study of student learning in the genetics unit focused on identifying the criteria students used when assessing their models for inheritance phenomena.[5] The study was predicated on a commitment to developing with students early in the course the idea of consistency as a basis for model assessment. Students read a mystery scenario involving a car accident and evaluated several explanations of the cause of the accident. Each explanation was problematic because it was either (1) inconsistent with some of the information the students had been given, (2) inconsistent with their prior knowledge about the world, or (3) unable to account for all of the information mentioned in the original scenario. Students discussed these explanations and their shortcomings, and the teacher provided the language for talking about model assessment criteria: she instructed them to seek explanatory power, predictive power (which was discussed but not applied to the accident scenario), internal consistency (among elements within the model), and external consistency (between a model and one's prior knowledge or other models).

Throughout the genetics unit, students were prompted to use these criteria to evaluate their own inheritance models. Despite the explicit emphasis on consistency as a criterion for model assessment, however, we found that very few students actually judged their models this way. Instead, students valued explanatory adequacy, visual simplicity, and "understandability" more strongly. A closer look at the work of students in this study showed that most of them viewed models not as conceptual structures but as physical replicas, instructional tools, or visual representations. In fact, the common use of the term to describe small replicas—as in model airplanes—sometimes interferes with students' grasp of a causal model as a representation of a set of relationships. Similarly, when attempting to apply model assessment criteria to their explanations for data patterns in liquid poured from a box, several students treated "internal consistency" and "external consistency" literally: they evaluated the box's proposed internal components and the external phenomena (observations) separately. This confusion stemmed from students' prior understanding of concepts associated with the vocabulary we provided: clearly "internal" and "external" were already meaningful to the students, and their prior knowledge took precedence over the new meanings with which we attempted to imbue these terms. Given this misunderstanding of models, it was not surprising that our genetics students neither applied nor discussed the criterion of conceptual consistency within and among models.

itly addressed these ideas at the outset of the unit. In the genetics unit, teachers employ tasks early on that solicit students' ideas about scientific models and explicitly define the term "model" as it will be used in the science unit. Frequently, teachers present sample models that purport to explain the phenomena at hand and ask students to evaluate these models. Teachers create models that have particular shortcomings in order to prompt discussion by students. Most commonly, students will describe the need for a model to explain all the data, predict new experimental outcomes, and be realistic (their term for conceptual consistency). Throughout the course, teachers return to these assessment criteria in each discussion about students' own inheritance models.

A subsequent study has shown that these instructional modifications (along with other curricular changes in the genetics unit) help students understand the conceptual nature of scientific models and learn how to evaluate them for consistency with other ideas.[6] We now provide an example of an initial instructional activity—the black box—designed to focus students' attention on scientific modeling.

As Chapter 1 suggests, children begin at a very young age to develop informal models of how things work in the world around them. Scientific modeling, however, is more demanding. Students must articulate their model as a set of propositions and consider how those propositions can be confirmed or disconfirmed. Because this more disciplined modeling is different from what students do in their daily lives, we begin the course with an activity that focuses only on the process of modeling. No new scientific content is introduced. The complexity of the task itself is controlled to focus students on the "modeling game" and introduce them to scientific norms of argumentation concerning data, explanations, causal models, and their relationships. This initial activity prepares students for similar modeling pursuits in the context of sophisticated disciplinary content.

During the first few days of the genetics course, the teacher presents the students with a black box—either an actual box or a diagram and description of a hypothetical box—and demonstrates or describes the phenomenon associated with it. For example, one box is a cardboard detergent container that dispenses a set amount of detergent each time it is tipped, while another is a large wooden box with a funnel on top and an outlet tube at the bottom that dispenses water in varying amounts, shown in Figure 12-1. Once the students have had an opportunity to establish the data pattern associated with the particular box in question, the teacher explains that the students' task is to determine what mechanisms might give rise to this observable pattern. During this activity (which can take anywhere from 3 to 11 class periods, depending on the black box that is used and the extent to which students can collect their own data), the students work in small teams. At the conclusion of the task, each team creates a poster representing its explana-

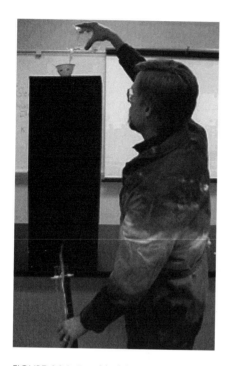

Black Box

A typical pattern of data would be:

Water In (ml)	Water Out (ml)
400	0
400	400
400	600
400	400
400	0
400	1000
400	0
400	400

and so forth.

FIGURE 12-1 One black box used in the MUSE science curriculum and typical data patterns associated with the box.

tion for the box mechanism and presents it to the class. Classmates offer criticism and seek clarification during these presentations.

As the dialogue below suggests, the exercise begins with students engaged in a central activity of scientists—making observations.

| Teacher | Making observations is important in science. I want you to observe this carton. Just call out what you notice and I will write it on the board. |

The students respond with a variety of observations:

Ian	The box is white with blue lettering.
Delia	The contents slosh around and it looks like liquid soap when we pour it.
Sarah	Hey, it stopped coming out! Try to pour it again so we can see what happens.
Owen	It always pours about the same amount then stops.

After several minutes of listening to the students, the teacher stops them and invites them to take a closer look at the carton, prompting them to identify patterns associated with their observations. Their reflection on these patterns leads the students to propose manipulations of the container, which in turn produce more observations. The teacher now interrupts them to guide their attention, saying:

Teacher	Okay, you've made some wonderful observations, ones that you are going to be using in just a few minutes. But, there is more to science than making observations. Scientists also develop ideas of what is not visible in order to explain that which is. These ideas are called models.

She goes on to challenge them:

Teacher	Imagine an invisible "world" inside the container that, if it existed in the way that you imagine, could be used to explain your observations. I want you to make drawings of your imagined world and maybe some groups will have time to develop a three-dimensional representation too. And, one last thing, I want each group to develop at least one test of your model. Ask yourself, "If the world inside the carton is as I imagine it and I do X to the carton, what result would I expect?"

Over the next two class periods, the students work in animated groups to develop models that can be used to explain their observations. They describe, draw, and create three-dimensional representations of what they think is in the carton. They argue. They negotiate. They revise. Then they share drawings of their models with one another.

Sarah	Hey Scott, you have a different idea than ours. How does that flap work?
Scott	The flap is what stops the detergent from gushing out all at once when you tip it.
Delia	Yeah, I get that, but does your design allow the same amount of detergent to come out every time? Because we tried a flap, too, but we couldn't figure out how to get the amount to be the same.

The students also propose tests of their models:

Sarah	Well, Scott is saying that the flap is like a trapdoor and it closes to keep the detergent in. But I think that if there is a trapdoor-like thing in there, then we should be able to hear it close if we listen with a stethoscope, right?
Delia	Hey, Mrs. S., can we get a stethoscope?

A visitor to the classroom would notice that Mrs. S. listens attentively to the descriptions that each group gives of its model and the observations the model is designed to explain. She pays special attention to the group's interactions with other groups and is skillful in how she converses with the students during their presentations. Through her comments she demonstrates how to question the models of others and how to present a scientific argument. To one group she says, "I think I follow your model, but I am not sure how it explains why you get 90 milliliters of liquid each time you tip the box." To another she comments, "You say that you have used something similar to a toilet bowl valve. But I don't understand how your valve allows soap to flow in both directions." And to a third group she asks, "Do you think that Ian's model explains the data? What question would you ask his group at this point?" By the end of the multiday activity, the students are explicit about how their prior knowledge and experiences influence their observations and their models. They also ask others to explain how a proposed model is consistent with the data and challenge them when a component of a model, designed to explain patterns in observations, does not appear to work as described.

This activity creates many opportunities to introduce and reinforce foundational ideas about the nature of scientific inquiry and how one judges scientific models and related explanations. As the class shares early ideas, the teacher leads discussion about the criteria they are using to decide whether and how to modify these initial explanations. Together, the class establishes that causal models must be able to explain the data at hand, accurately predict the results of future experiments, and be consistent with prior knowledge (or be "realistic") (see the example in Box 12-2). Through discussion and a short reading about scientific inquiry and model assessment, the teacher helps students connect their own work on the black boxes with that of scientists attempting to understand how the natural world works. This framework for thinking about scientific inquiry and determining the validity of knowledge claims is revisited repeatedly throughout the genetics unit.

Other modeling problems might serve just as well as the one we introduce here. What is key is for the problem to be complex enough so that students have experiences that allow them to understand the rigors of scien-

BOX 12-2 Assessing Knowledge Claims in Genetics

While working to revise Mendel's simple dominance model to account for an inheritance pattern in which there are five variations (rather than two), many students propose models in which each individual in the population has three alleles at the locus in question. However, such a model fails to hold up when evaluated according to the criteria established during the black box activity because it is inconsistent with the students' prior knowledge about meiosis and equal segregation of parental information during gamete formation:

Teacher	I'm confused. I'm just curious. I'm a newcomer to this research lab and I see you using two alleles in some areas and three in other areas.
David	We got rid of the three allele model.
Michelle	Cross that out. It didn't work.
David	We didn't know how two parents who each had three alleles could make kids with three alleles.
Michelle	When we tried to do the Punnett square and look at what was happening in meiosis, it didn't make sense.
Chee	Right. We thought maybe one parent would give the kid two alleles and the other parent would just give one. But we didn't like that.
David	We had to stick with only two alleles, so we just made it three different kinds of alleles in the population.
Chee	But now every person has only two alleles inside their cells. Right?
Teacher	In other words, you didn't like this first, three allele, model because it is inconsistent with meiosis?

tific modeling. In particular, the activity is designed to give students an opportunity to do the following:

- *Use prior knowledge to pose problems and generate data.* When science teaching emphasizes results rather than the process of scientific inquiry, students can easily think about science as truths to be memorized, rather than as understandings that grow out of a creative process of observing, imagining, and reasoning by making connections with what one already knows. This latter view is critical not only because it offers a view of science that is more engaging and inviting, but also because it allows students to grasp that what we understand today can be changed, sometimes radically, by tomorrow's new observations, insights, and tools. By carrying out a modeling activity they see as separate from the academic content they are studying in the unit, students are more likely to engage in understanding how models are generated rather than in learning about a particular model.

• *Search for patterns in data.* Often the point of departure between science and everyday observation and reasoning is the collection of data and close attention to its patterns. To appreciate this, students must take part in a modeling activity that produces data showing an interesting pattern in need of explanation.

• *Develop causal models to account for patterns.*[7] The data produced by the activity need to be difficult enough so that the students see the modeling activity as posing a challenge. If an obvious model is apparent, the desired discourse regarding model testing and consideration of the features of alternative models will not be realized.

• *Use patterns in data and models to make predictions.* A model that is adequate to explain a pattern in data provides relatively little power if it cannot also be used for predictive purposes. The activity is used to call students' attention to predictive power as a critical feature of a model.

• *Make ideas public, and revise initial models in light of anomalous data and in response to critiques of others.* Much of the schoolwork in which students engage ends with a completed assignment that is graded by a teacher. Progress in science is supported by a culture in which even the best work is scrutinized by others, in which one's observations are complemented by those of others, and in which one's reasoning is continually critiqued. For some students, making ideas public and open to critique is highly uncomfortable. A low-stakes activity like this introductory modeling exercise can create a relatively comfortable setting for familiarizing students with the culture of science and its expectations. A teacher might both acknowledge the discomfort of public exposure and the benefits of the discussion and the revised thinking that results in progress in the modeling effort. Students have ample opportunity to see that scientific ideas, even those that are at the root of our most profound advances, are initially critiqued harshly and often rejected for a period before they are embraced.

Learning Genetics Content

Having provided this initial exposure to a modeling exercise, we turn to instruction focused specifically on genetics. While the core set of causal models, assumptions, and argument structures generated the content and learning outcomes for our genetics unit, our study of student understanding and reasoning influenced both the design and the sequencing of instructional activities. For example, many high school students do not understand the interrelationships among genetic, meiotic, and biomolecular models, relationships that are key to a deep understanding of inheritance phenomena.[8] To deal with this problem, we identified learning outcomes that address the conceptual connections among these families of models, and the models are introduced in a sequence that emphasizes their relatedness. Initially, for example, we introduced genetic models, beginning with Mendel's model of simple dominance, first. This is typical of many genetics courses. In our early studies (as well as in similar studies on problem solving in genetics[9]), students often did not examine their inheritance models to see whether they were consistent with meiosis. In fact, students proposed models whereby offspring received unequal amounts of genetic information from their two parents or had fewer alleles at a particular locus than did their parents.[10] Because of their struggles and the fact that meiosis is central to any model of inheritance, we placed this model first in the revised curricular sequence. Students now begin their exploration of Mendelian inheritance with a firm understanding of a basic meiotic model and continue to refer to this model as they examine increasingly complex inheritance patterns.

A solid integration of the models does not come easily, however. In early versions of the course, it became apparent that students were solving problems, even sophisticated ones, without adequately drawing on an integrated understanding of meiotic and genetic models.[11] In response, we designed a set of data analysis activities and related homework that required students to integrate across models (cytology, genetics, and molecular biology) when conducting their genetic investigations and when presenting model-based explanations to account for patterns in their data. By providing tasks that require students to attend to knowledge across domains and by structuring classrooms so that students must make their thinking about such integration public, we have seen improvements in their understanding of genetics.[12]

We then focus on inheritance models, beginning with Mendel's model of simple dominance. Mendel, a nineteenth-century monk, grew generation after generation of pea plants in an attempt to understand how traits were passed from parent plants to their offspring. As Chapter 9 indicates, Mendel's work represented a major breakthrough in understanding inheritance, achieved in large part by selecting a subject for study—peas—that had discontinuous trait variations. The peas were yellow or green, smooth or wrinkled. Peas can be self-fertilized, allowing Mendel to observe that some offspring from a single genetic source have the same phenotype as the parent plants and some have a different phenotype. Mendel's work confirmed that individuals can carry alleles that are recessive—not expressed in the phenotype. By performing many such crosses, Mendel was able to deduce that the distribution of alleles follows the laws of probability when the pairing of alleles is random. These insights are fundamental to all the work in classical transmission genetics since Mendel. Students need ample opportunity to work with Mendel's model if they are to make these fundamental insights their own.

The development of modern genetic theory from its classical Mendelian origins has been the subject of much historical and philosophical analysis. Darden[13] draws on historical evidence to identify a set of strategies used by scientists to generate and test ideas while conducting early inquiries into the phenomenon of inheritance. She traces the development of a number of inheritance models that were seen at least originally to be at odds with those underlying a Mendelian (i.e., simple dominance) explanation of inheritance. Among these models are those based on the notions of linkage and multiple forms (alleles) of a single gene. In short, Darden provides a philosophical analysis of the history of model-based inquiry into the phenomenon of inheritance from a classical genetics perspective. Drawing on Darden's work and our own experiences as teachers and researchers, we made a primary feature of the course engaging students in building and revising Mendel's simple dominance model. Students thereby have rich opportunities to learn important genetics concepts, as well as key ideas about the practice of genetics.

Inheritance is considerably more complex than Mendel's simple dominance model suggests. Mendel was not wrong. However, simple dominance applies to only a subset of heritable traits. Just as geneticists have done, students need opportunities to observe cases that cannot be explained by a simple dominance model. We provide such opportunities and thus allow students to conclude that Mendel's model is not adequate to explain the data. Students propose alternatives, such as the codominance model, to explain these more complex patterns.

Once students have come to understand that there are multiple models of allele interaction, they are primed for an explanation of why we observe these different inheritance patterns. How can a recessive allele sometimes have an influence and sometimes not? With that question in mind, we introduce DNA and its role in protein production. What drives the instructional experience throughout is students' active engagement in inquiry, which we turn to in the next section.

Student Inquiry in Genetics

Early instruction in the genetics class includes a few days during which students learn about the meiotic model[14] and the phenomena this model can explain. In an introductory activity, students look at sets of pictures and are asked to determine which individuals are members of the same families. The bases for their decisions include physical similarities between parents and children and between siblings. Thus, instruction about meiosis focuses on how the meiotic model can account for these patterns: children resemble their parents because they receive information from both of them, and siblings resemble each other but are not exactly alike because of the random assortment of parental information during meiosis.

After students have developed some understanding of meiosis, they create, with guidance from the teacher, a representation of Mendel's model of simple dominance (see Figures 12-2a and 12-b) in an attempt to further explain why offspring look like parents. First, "Mendel" (a teacher dressed in a monk's habit) pays the class a visit and tells them he would like to share some phenomena and one important model from his own research with them. In character, "Mendel" passes out three packets of peas representing a parental generation and the F1 and F2 generations (the first and second filial generations, respectively). He asks the students to characterize the peas according to color and shape. For example, the parental generation includes round green peas and wrinkled yellow peas. The F1 generation contains only round yellow peas. Finally, the F2 generation contains a mix of round yellow, wrinkled yellow, round green, and wrinkled green peas in a ratio of approximately 9:3:3:1. Using what they already know about meiosis—particularly the fact that offspring receive information from both parents—the students reconstruct Mendel's model of simple dominance to explain these patterns (see Figures 12-2a and 12-b).

While Darden's work (discussed above) aides in the identification of important inheritance models and strategies used by scientists to judge those models, it is the work of Kitcher[15] that places the simple dominance model developed by students into context with comparable models of geneticists. According to Kitcher,[16] genetic models provide the following information:

> (a) Specification of the number of relevant loci and the number of alleles at each locus; (b) Specification of the relationships between genotypes and phenotypes; (c) Specification of the relations between genes and chromosomes, of facts about the transmission of chromosomes to gametes (for example, resolution of the question whether there is disruption of normal segregation) and about the details of zygote formation; (d) Assignment of genotypes to individuals in the pedigree.

Moreover, Kitcher[17] describes how such models might be used in inquiry:

> . . . after showing that the genetic hypothesis is consistent with the data and constraints of the problem, the principles of cytology and the laws of probability are used to compute expected distributions of phenotypes from crosses. The expected distributions are then compared with those assigned in part (d) of the genetic hypothesis.

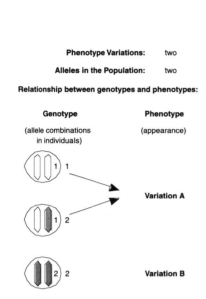

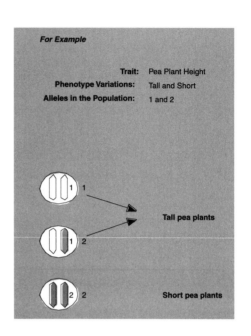

FIGURE 12-2 Mendel's model of simple dominance.

(a) Students' representation of Mendel's simple dominance model. This model accounts for the inheritance of discrete traits for which there are two variants (designated A and B). Each individual in the population possesses two alleles (designated 1 and 2) for the trait; one allele (here, allele 1) is completely dominant over the other. For plant height, for example, there are two phenotypic variants: short and tall. There are only two different alleles in the population. Plants with a genetic makeup of (1,1) or (1,2) will be tall, whereas plants with a genetic makeup of (2,2) will be short.

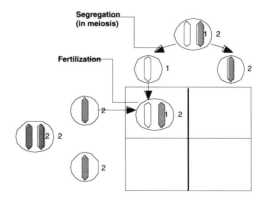

(b) Meiotic processes governing inheritance. The underlying processes governing simple dominance are Mendel's law of segregation (the meiotic process of sex cell formation during which half of all parental genetic information is packaged into sperm or egg cells) and fertilization (during which genetic information from both parents combines in the offspring).

With their teacher's guidance, students represent Mendel's simple dominance model in a manner consistent with Kitcher's description of the models of geneticists. They pay particular attention to (b) and (d) above: specifying the relationships between genotypes and phenotypes and identifying the genotypes of individuals in their experimental populations. Because our unit does not address multigene traits, one locus per trait is assumed (thus part of criterion (a) above is not applicable in this case), and students focus on determining the number of alleles at that locus. Finally, the students' prior understanding of meiosis—developed earlier in the unit—enables them to specify chromosomal transmission of genes for each particular case (item (c) above). The vignette below portrays students engaged in this type of inquiry.

Genetic Inquiry in the Classroom: A Vignette

Nineteen students are sitting at lab tables in a small and cluttered high school biology classroom. The demonstration desk at the front of the room is barely visible under the stacks of papers and replicas of mitotic cells. A human skeleton wearing a lab coat and a sign reading "Mr. Stempe" stands in a corner at the front of the room, and the countertops are stacked with books, dissecting trays, and cages holding snakes and gerbils.

During the previous few days, the students in this class have studied the work of Mendel. Years of work resulted in his publication of *Experiments on Plant Hybridization*,[18] a paper in which he presented his model explaining the inheritance of discontinuous traits in plants.[19] The students have read an edited version of this paper and refer to Mendel's idea as the "simple dominance model" because it explains the inheritance of traits derived from two alleles (or pieces of genetic information) when one of the alleles is completely dominant over the other (see Figures 12-2a and 12-2b).

During class on this day, the students' attention is drawn to the cabinet doors along the length of the room. These doors are covered with students' drawings of family pedigrees labeled "Summers: Marfan" (see Figure 12-3a), "Healey: Blood Types," "Jacques: Osteogenesis Imperfecta," and "Cohen: Achondroplasia." The teacher is standing at the side of the room facilitating a discussion about these family pedigrees.

Teacher	Now that we've learned about Mendel's model, can we use it to explain any of the patterns in our pedigrees?
Kelly	Well, I think Marfan is dominant.
Teacher	Okay. Since we are using 1's and 2's to show alleles in the Mendel model, can you put some numbers up there so we can see what you're talking about?

Kelly walks to one of the cabinets at the side of the room and begins to label each of the circles and squares on the pedigree with two alleles: some are assigned the genotype 1,2 (heterozygous or possessing two different alleles) and others 2,2 (homozygous recessive or possessing two recessive alleles) (see Figures 12-3a and 12-3b, respectively).

Teacher	Kelly thinks that the allele that causes Marfan syndrome is dominant and she's put some genotypes up there to help us see her idea. What do you all think about that?
Chee	Yeah, that's OK. That works.
Jamie	Yeah, because all the filled in ones, the ones who have Marfan, are all 1,2's, so it's dominant.
Curtis	Well, but we started off by saying that it's dominant. I mean, we made that assumption. If we say that the Marfan allele is recessive and switch all the affected genotypes to 2,2's then that would work too. Do you know what I'm saying?
Teacher	Wow! That's quite an idea. I think we need help thinking about that, Curtis, so can you write your genotypes next to Kelly's in a different color?

Curtis proceeds to label the same pedigree consistently with his idea that the Marfan allele is actually recessive (see Figure 12-3c).

Teacher	Well, that's very interesting.
David	I don't get it. Both of them work.
Teacher	You think they both work. Marfan could be dominant or recessive.
Lucy	Well, we can't tell right now.
Sarah	But if we could take two people with Marfan, like the grandmother and the son, and find out what kind of kids they'd have, then we could tell for sure.
Sam	That's sick, man!
Teacher	Wait a minute. Wait a minute. What's Sarah saying here?
Sarah	That if you got children from two affected people . . .

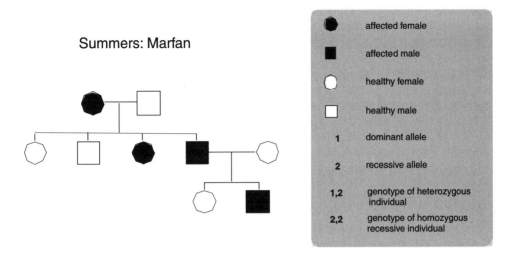

FIGURE 12-3 Pedigrees representing inheritance of Marfan symdrome in the Summers family. (a) The original pedigree, representing the inheritance pattern within the Summers family without specifying individual genotypes.

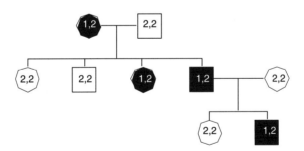

FIGURE 12-3 (b) Kelly's genotype assignments, assuming that Marfan syndrome is inherited as a dominant trait.

Curtis	. . . that you could tell if it was recessive or dominant.
Teacher	What would you see?
Sarah	Well, if it's recessive, then all the kids would be Marfan, too. But if it's dominant, then some of the kids might not be Marfan 'cause they could get like a 2 from both parents.

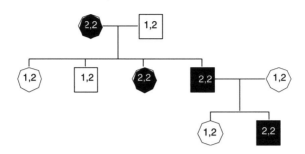

FIGURE 12-3 (c) Curtis' genotype assignments, assuming that Marfan syndrome is inherited as a recessive trait.

Teacher	Do you all see that? Sarah is saying that if the parents had what genotype?
Sam	They'd have to be a 1,2, right?
Teacher	A 1,2. Then if these parents had kids, their kids could be what?
Kelly	1,2 or 1,1 or 2,2.
Teacher	Right. So Sarah is actually proposing an experiment that we could do to find out more [see Box 12-3].
Teacher	Now what about the Healey pedigree? Can Mendel explain that one?
Chee	I don't think so.
Chris	Why not?
Chee	Because there's four things. And Mendel only saw two.
Teacher	Four things?
Sarah	Yeah. Like phenotypes or traits or whatever.
David	There's people who have type A and people who have B and some who have AB or O.
Tanya	But isn't AB the most dominant or something?
Teacher	What do you mean by "most dominant," Tanya?
Tanya	I don't know. It's just like . . .
Chee	. . . like it's better or stronger or something.
Tanya	Like you're gonna see that showing up more.
Lee	Well even if that's true, you still can't really explain why there're A's and B's, too. It's not just AB is dominant to O, right? You still have

BOX 12-3 Sarah's Thought Experiment

In Sarah's thought experiment, two individuals with Marfan's syndrome would produce sex cells, and those sex cells would recombine during fertilization (see Figure
12-3). Looking at the children from such a mating would enable the students to
determine whether Marfan's syndrome is inherited as a dominant or recessive trait
because the only situation in which one would expect to see both unaffected and
affected children would be if Marfan's is inherited as a dominant trait (see below).

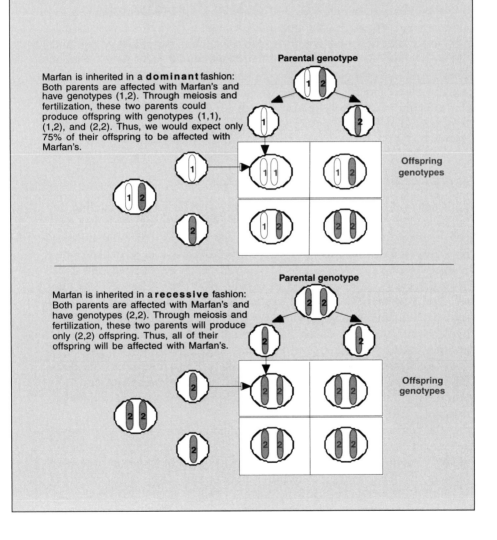

Marfan is inherited in a **dominant** fashion:
Both parents are affected with Marfan's and
have genotypes (1,2). Through meiosis and
fertilization, these two parents could
produce offspring with genotypes (1,1),
(1,2), and (2,2). Thus, we would expect only
75% of their offspring to be affected with
Marfan's.

Marfan is inherited in a **recessive** fashion:
Both parents are affected with Marfan's and
have genotypes (2,2). Through meiosis and
fertilization, these two parents will produce
only (2,2) offspring. Thus, all of their
offspring will be affected with Marfan's.

	four different things to explain and Mendel didn't see that.
Teacher	OK, so Mendel's model of simple dominance isn't going to be enough to explain this pattern is it?
Chris	Nope.

The students in this high school biology class are engaged in genetic inquiry: they are examining data and identifying patterns of inheritance for various traits. They are also attempting to use a powerful causal model, Mendel's model of simple dominance, to explain the patterns they see. And just as scientists do, they recognize the limitations of their model when it simply cannot explain certain data patterns. These students are poised to continue their inquiry in genetics by revising Mendel's model such that the resulting models will be able to explain a variety of inheritance patterns, including the multiple allele/codominance pattern within the Healey pedigree.

Multiple Examples in Different Contexts

Chapter 1 argues that learning new concepts with understanding requires multiple opportunities to use those concepts in different contexts. Our course is designed to provide those opportunities. Once the students have represented and used the simple dominance model to explain phenomena such as the inheritance of characteristics in peas and disease traits in humans, they use the model to explain data they generate using the software program Genetics Construction Kit or GCK.[20] This program enables students to manipulate populations of virtual organisms (usually fruit flies) by performing matings (or crosses) on any individuals selected. Each cross produces a new generation of organisms whose variations for particular traits (e.g., eye color, wing shape) are described. Thus, the students develop expertise using the simple dominance model to explain new data, and they also design and perform crosses to test their initial genotype-to-phenotype mappings within these populations.

The beginning of this process is illustrated in Figure 12-4, which shows an excerpt from one student's work with GCK and the simple dominance model. After the student's model is discussed, the teacher presents or revisits phenomena that the simple dominance model cannot explain. For example, students realize when applying the model to explain their human pedigrees that it is inadequate in some cases: it cannot account for the inheritance of human blood types or achondroplasia. The next step for the class is to study these "anomalous" inheritance patterns using GCK. They begin with achondroplasia, a trait for which there are three variations rather than two. Students revise the simple dominance model to account for the codominant

Field Population

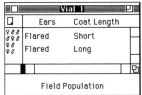

So we can only tell that there is one variation for ears but two for coat length. Another variation for ears might show up.

F1: Cross a female Flared Short with a male Flared Long from the Field Population

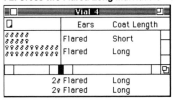

Since a Flared was crossed with another Flared, and the result was both Flared and Narrow, Flared must be dominant since it carried alleles for both variations. Both Flared parents must have been (1,2) for both variations to show. I can't tell if Long or Short is dominant but one of them must be recessive, a (2,2), and the other parent must have been a (1,2) in order to get a mix of both Long and Short in the kids.

F2: Cross two Narrow Short individuals from F1

Both Narrow and Short must be recessive. I already determined that Flared was dominant, so crossing two Narrow and getting all Narrows confirms that their parents were (2,2) because if Short was dominant the parents would have been both (1,2)'s, given their heritage. So the only way to get all Short would be to cross 2 (2,2)'s.

F2: Cross two Flared Long individuals from F1

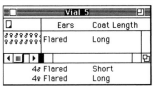

The parent Flareds must have been either both (1,1)'s or a (1,1) and a (1,2) in order to get all Flareds. The Short is a (2,2) and the Long must have been a (1,1) in order to get all Longs. The children Longs must be all (1,2)'s.

F3: Cross a Flared Short male with a Flared Long female from F2

Again, the Flareds must have been both (1,1)'s or (1,1) and (1,2) in order to get all Flareds. The Short is a (2,2), and the Long must have been a (1,1) in order to get all Longs. The children Longs must be all (1,2)'s.

What might the offspring phenotypes be if you were to cross a Flared-eared, Long-coat individual from Vial 5 with a Flared-eared, Short-coat individual from Vial 2? Describe the genetic reasoning behind your answer.

The offspring will either be all Flared, if the parents are (1,1) and (1,1) or (1,2) and (1,1) or there will be a mix Flared and Narrow if the parents are (1,2) and (1,2). Since the Longs in Vial 5 are all (1,2), when they are crossed with a Short, the offspring will be both Long and Short.

FIGURE 12-4 Example of student work on a GCK homework assignment. Students were asked to infer as much as possible from each successive cross within this population. The student's work is shown to the right of each cross.

inheritance pattern observed for this trait. While solving GCK problems such as this, students propose models that specify some or all of the information (a through d) noted above and then test their models for fit with existing data, as well as for the ability to predict the results of new experiments accurately.

Since most students ultimately explain the inheritance of achondroplasia using a codominant model (whereby each possible genotype maps to a distinct phenotype), they must also revise their understanding of dominance and recessiveness. Up to this point, most students tend to associate recessiveness with either (1) a phenotype, (2) any genotype that contains a recessive allele (designated with the number 2), or (3) both. It is quite common for students to conclude that the phenotypes associated with (1,1) and (1,2) genotypes are both "recessive."[21] However, this conclusion is inconsistent with the students' prior concept of recessiveness as it was developed under the simple dominance model. Thus, it is at this point in the unit that we emphasize the need for models to be consistent with other knowledge in a scientific discipline. In other words, geneticists must assess a new inheritance model in part on the basis of how well it fits within an existing family of related models, such as those for meiosis (including cytological data) and molecular biology (which specifies the relationships between DNA and proteins, as well as protein actions in cells). After explicit instruction about DNA transcription, translation, and protein function, students attempt to reconcile their codominance models with this new model of protein action in cells. In the case of codominance, doing so requires them to conceptualize recessiveness at the level of alleles and their relationships to one another, rather than at the level of phenotypes or genotypes.[22] In the process, students construct meanings for dominance and recessiveness that are consistent across various inheritance models (e.g., simple dominance, codominance, multiple alleles, etc.), as well as models of meiosis and molecular biology.

For the final GCK inquiry, the students are organized into two research teams, each of which consists of four small research groups. Each team is assigned a population of virtual fruit flies and told to explain the inheritance of four traits within this population (see Figure 12-5). The work is divided such that each research group studies two of the traits. Consequently, there is some overlap of trait assignments among the groups within a team. The teams hold research meetings periodically, and a minimal structure for those meetings is imposed: two groups present some data and tentative explanations of the data, one group moderates the meeting, and one group records the proceedings. The roles of individual groups alternate in successive meetings.

Each of the fly populations in this last problem contains traits that exhibit the following inheritance patterns: (1) Mendelian simple dominance; (2) codominance; (3) multiple alleles (specifically, three different alleles with varying dominant/codominant relationships between pairs of alleles); and

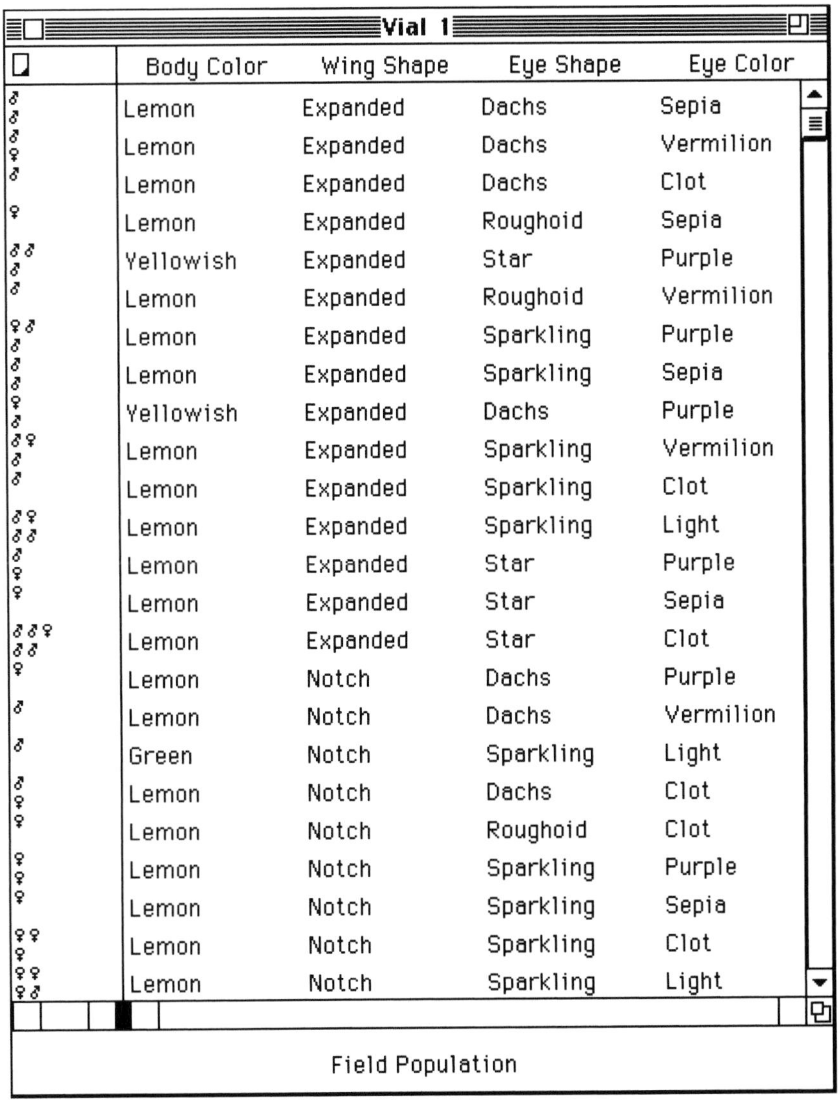

	Body Color	Wing Shape	Eye Shape	Eye Color
	Lemon	Expanded	Dachs	Sepia
	Lemon	Expanded	Dachs	Vermilion
	Lemon	Expanded	Dachs	Clot
	Lemon	Expanded	Roughoid	Sepia
	Yellowish	Expanded	Star	Purple
	Lemon	Expanded	Roughoid	Vermilion
	Lemon	Expanded	Sparkling	Purple
	Lemon	Expanded	Sparkling	Sepia
	Yellowish	Expanded	Dachs	Purple
	Lemon	Expanded	Sparkling	Vermilion
	Lemon	Expanded	Sparkling	Clot
	Lemon	Expanded	Sparkling	Light
	Lemon	Expanded	Star	Purple
	Lemon	Expanded	Star	Sepia
	Lemon	Expanded	Star	Clot
	Lemon	Notch	Dachs	Purple
	Lemon	Notch	Dachs	Vermilion
	Green	Notch	Sparkling	Light
	Lemon	Notch	Dachs	Clot
	Lemon	Notch	Roughoid	Clot
	Lemon	Notch	Sparkling	Purple
	Lemon	Notch	Sparkling	Sepia
	Lemon	Notch	Sparkling	Clot
	Lemon	Notch	Sparkling	Light

Vial 1

Field Population

FIGURE 12-5 *Initial GCK population for the final GCK inquiry.*

(4) x-linkage. After about a week of data collection, model testing, and team meetings, each small research group is usually able to describe a model of inheritance for at least one of the traits in its population, and most groups can describe inheritance models for both of the traits on which they chose to focus. The entire class then gathers for a final conference during which students create posters that summarize their research findings, take turns

making formal presentations of their models, and critique their classmates' models.

This high school biology curriculum is designed to give students opportunities to learn about genetic inquiry in part by providing them with realistic experiences in conducting inquiry in the discipline. As a primary goal of practicing scientists is to construct causal models to explain natural phenomena, involving students in the construction of their own models is given major emphasis in the classroom. The students work in groups structured like scientific communities to develop, revise, and defend models for inheritance phenomena. The overall instructional goals include helping students to understand mechanistic explanations for inheritance patterns in fruit flies and humans, and to appreciate the degree to which scientists rely on empirical data as well as broader conceptual knowledge to assess models.

Metacognition: Engaging Students in Reflective Scientific Practice

Ultimately, students need to learn to reflect on and judge their own work rather than relying solely on assessments from others. Several early studies of students' GCK work in our genetics unit revealed that students assessed their tentative models primarily on the basis of empirical rather than conceptual criteria.[23] Even when conceptual inconsistencies occurred between the students' proposed models and other models or biological knowledge, their primary focus was usually on how well a given model could explain the data at hand. They frequently had difficulty recognizing specific inconsistencies between their models and meiosis or other biological knowledge, such as the method of sex determination in humans. In some instances, students recognized that their models were inconsistent with other knowledge but were willing to overlook such inconsistencies when they judged their models to have adequate explanatory power. (For example, students sometimes proposed models to account for x-linkage inheritance patterns wherein a male organism simply could never be heterozygous. They gave no explanation consistent with independent assortment in meiosis for this model.) Thus, students paid more attention to empirical than conceptual issues and tended to value empirical power over conceptual consistency in models when both criteria were brought to bear.

White and Frederiksen[24] describe a middle school science curriculum designed to teach students about the nature of inquiry generally and the role of modeling in specific scientific inquiries. One aspect of the curriculum that had a measurable effect on its success was the emphasis on students' reflective (metacognitive) assessment. Following modeling activities, students were asked to rate themselves and others in various categories, including "understanding the science," "understanding the processes of inquiry," "being systematic," and "writing and communicating well." Involving the students in

BOX 12-4 Simple Dominance Homework Assignment

Students are asked to use Mendel's simple dominance model to explain a realistic data pattern. They are also asked to justify their reasoning explicitly, in a manner similar to that in which they argue in support of their ideas in regular classroom activities.

Inheritance of PKU in the Samsom Family

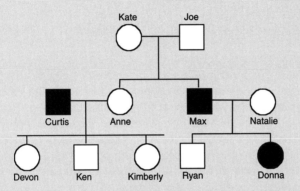

1. Use Mendel's simple dominance model to assign genotypes to the individuals in this pedigree.

2. Do the affected individuals in this pedigree show a dominant or recessive variation of the trait? Pick two family groups (a group is one set of parents and their offspring), and describe how those groups helped you make that decision.

3. Describe how you would convince another student who had no knowledge of how PKU is inherited that you understand the inheritance of this trait. As the student is not easily convinced, you must carefully show how the Mendel model can be used to support your idea.

such an explicit evaluation task helped emphasize the importance of learning about inquiry and modeling in addition to learning how to do inquiry.

Our work in developing tasks for students is also predicated on the importance of metacognitive reflection on the students' part. Influenced by our research in the genetics unit, we built into the curriculum more tasks that require students to reflect upon, write about, and discuss conceptual aspects of genetic modeling. These tasks include journal writing, written self-assessments, homework assignments that require students to explain their reasoning (see Box 12-4), and class presentations (both formal and informal). Most important, we created a complex problem involving several different inheritance patterns and asked the students to account for these new data while working in cooperative laboratory teams. As described above, the regular team interactions required students to be critical of their own thinking and that of others. Moreover, situating the study of these inheritance patterns within the context of a single population of organisms helped emphasize the need for each inheritance model to be basically consistent with other models within genetics. We have found that in this new context, students are more successful at proposing causal models and have a better understanding of the conceptual nature of such scientific models.[25]

Summary

The structure of the genetics class that we have described reflects important aspects of scientific practice: students are engaged in an extended inquiry into inheritance in which they collect data, seek patterns, and attempt to explain those patterns using causal models. The models proposed by students are also highly similar to those of practicing geneticists in that they specify allelic relationships and genotype-to-phenotype mappings for particular traits. In the next section, we describe a course in evolutionary biology that provides opportunities for students to participate in realistic inquiry within another subdiscipline of biology.

DEVELOPING DARWIN'S MODEL OF NATURAL SELECTION IN HIGH SCHOOL EVOLUTION

Hillary and Jerome are sitting next to each other in their sixth-hour science class waiting for the bell to ring.

Jerome	What are we doing in here today?
Hillary	I think we will be starting the next case study.

The bell rings, and their teacher announces that the class will start work on the last of three case studies designed to allow the students to continue to develop and use Darwin's model of natural selection. She tells the students that there are two parts to this third case. First, they will need to use their knowledge of the natural selection model to develop an explanation for the bright coloration of the male ring-necked pheasant. Second, they will have to write a research proposal that will then be considered by the rest of the students in a research grant competition.

Teacher	Each of you has seen during the past two cases that there are aspects of your explana-

tion that you would like to explore further or confirm in some way. This is your opportunity to imagine how you might do that. Each group will need to think about their explanation and identify areas that could use a bit more evidence.

As the teacher passes out the eight pages of case materials, she asks the students to get to work. Each group receives a file folder containing the task description and information about the ring-necked pheasant. There are color pictures that show adult males, adult females, and young. Some of the pages contain information about predators, mating behavior, and mating success. Hillary, Jerome, and their third group member, Grace, begin to shuffle through the pages in the folder.

Hillary	The males look completely different from the females!
Jerome	Okay, so what are we supposed to be doing here?
Grace	It is similar to the last case. We need to come up with a Darwinian explanation for why the males look brighter than the females.
Hillary	How can this be? It seems like being bright would be a problem for the males, so how can it fit with Darwin's ideas?
Grace	Well, I guess we need to look at the rest of the stuff in the folder.

The three students spend the remainder of the period looking over and discussing various aspects of the case. By the middle of the period on Tuesday, this group is just finalizing their explanation when Casey, a member of another group, asks if she can talk to them.

Casey	What have you guys come up with? Our group was wondering if we could talk over our ideas with you.
Grace	Sure, come over and we can each read our explanations.

These two groups have very different explanations. Hillary's group is thinking that the males' bright coloration distracts predators from the nest, while Casey's group has decided that the bright coloration confers an advantage on the males by helping them attract more mates. A lively discussion ensues.

Ed	But wait, I don't understand. How can dying be a good thing?
Jerome	Well, you have to think beyond just survival of the male himself. We think that the key is the survival of the kids. If the male can protect his young and give them a better chance of surviving then he has an advantage.
Claire	Even if he dies doing it?
Grace	Yeah, because he will have already passed on his genes and stuff to his kids before he dies.
Casey	How did you come up with this? Did you see something in the packets that we didn't see?
Grace	One reason we thought of it had to do with the last case with the monarchs and viceroy.
Hillary	Yeah, we were thinking that the advantage isn't always obvious and sometimes what is good for the whole group might not seem like it is good for one bird or butterfly or whatever.
Jerome	We also looked at the data in our packets on the number of offspring fathered by brighter versus duller males. We saw that the brighter males had a longer bar.
Grace	See, look on page 5, right here.
Jerome	So they had more kids, right?
Casey	We saw that table too, but we thought that it could back up our idea that the brighter males were able to attract more females as mates.

The groups agree to disagree on their interpretation of this piece of data and continue to compare their explanations on other points.

The students in the above vignette are using Darwin's model of natural selection and realistic data to create arguments about evolution in a population of organisms. In doing so, they attend to and discuss such ideas as selective advantage and reproductive success that are core components of the Darwinian model. Early in the course, students have opportunities to *learn about* natural selection, but as the course progresses, they are required to *use* their understanding to develop explanations (as illustrated in the vignette). As was true in teaching genetics, our goals for student learning include both deep understanding of evolution and an understanding of how knowledge in evolution is generated and justified. And once again we want students to be able to use their understanding to engage in scientific inquiry—to construct their own Darwinian explanations.

There is an important difference between the two units, however, that motivated the decision to include both in this chapter. The nature of the scientific inquiry involved in the study of evolution is different from that involved in the study of genetics—or in some other scientific disciplines for that matter. The difference arises because of the important role that history plays in evolution and the inability of biologists to "replay the tape of the earth's history." Engaging students in authentic inquiry therefore presents a new set of challenges. Mayr[26] suggests that "there is probably no more original, more complex, and bolder concept in the history of ideas than Darwin's mechanistic explanation of adaptation." Our teacher/researcher collaborative took on the challenge of designing a course that would allow students to master this powerful concept and to use it in ways that are analogous to those of evolutionary biologists.

Attending to Significant Disciplinary Knowledge

The choices we make when designing curricula are determined in part by an examination of the discipline under study. In the case of evolution, it is clear that a solid understanding of natural selection provides a foundation upon which further knowledge depends—the knowledge-centered conceptual framework referred to in the principles of *How People Learn* (see Chapter 1). But that foundation is hard won and takes time to develop because the concepts that make up the natural selection model are difficult for students to understand and apply. To understand natural selection, students must understand the concept of random variation. They must understand that while some differences are insignificant, others confer an advantage or a disadvantage under certain conditions. The length of a finch's beak, for example, may give it access to a type of food that allows it to survive a drought. Survivors produce offspring, passing their genes along to the next generation. In this way, nature "selects" for particular characteristics within species.

Equally important in our instructional approach is that students understand how Darwinian explanations are generated and justified. Kitcher[27] describes a Darwinian history as a "narrative which traces the successive modifications of a lineage of organisms from generation to generation in terms of various factors, most notably that of natural selection." The use of narrative explanation is a key means of distinguishing evolutionary biology from other scientific disciplines. "Narratives fix events along a temporal dimension, so that prior events are understood to have given rise to subsequent events and thereby explain them."[28] Thus, our concept of a Darwinian explanation draws together the components of the natural selection model and a narrative structure that demands attention to historical contingency. Textbook examples of explanations for particular traits frequently take the form of "state explanations"—that is, they explain the present function of particular character states without reference to their history.[29] In contrast, what we call a Darwinian explanation attempts to explain an event or how a trait might have come into being. This type of explanation is summarized by Mayr:[30]

> *When a biologist tries to answer a question about a unique occurrence such as "Why are there no hummingbirds in the Old World?" or "Where did the species Homo sapiens originate?" he cannot rely on universal laws. The biologist has to study all the known facts relating to the particular problem, infer all sorts of consequences from the recon-structed constellation of factors, and then attempt to construct a scenario that would explain the observed facts in this particular case. In other words, he constructs a historical narrative.*

Providing opportunities for students to use the natural selection model to develop narrative explanations that are consistent with the view described above is a central goal of the course.

Attending to Student Knowledge

Anyone who has ever taught evolution can attest to the fact that students bring a wide range of conceptions and attitudes to the classroom. During the past two decades, researchers have documented student ideas both before and after instruction.[31] These studies have confirmed what teachers already know: students have very tenacious misconceptions about the mechanism of evolution and its assumptions.

As Mayr suggests, the scientific method employed by evolutionary biologists in some respects resembles history more than it does other natural sciences. This resemblance can be problematic. In disciplines such as history, for example, we look for motivations. While students may struggle to understand that in different times and under different circumstances, the motivations of others may be different from our motivations today, motivation itself is a legitimate subject for inquiry. But in the Darwinian model, naturally occurring, random variation within species allows some individuals to survive the forces of nature in larger numbers. The random nature of the variation, the role of natural phenomena in selecting who flourishes and who withers, and the absence of motivation or intent make Darwinian narrative antithetical to much of the literary or historical narrative that students encounter outside the science classroom.

We have found that replacing this familiar approach to constructing a narrative with the scientific approach used in evolutionary biology requires a significant period of time and multiple opportunities to try out the Darwinian model in different contexts. Many courses or units in evolutionary biology at the high school level require far shorter periods of time than the 9 weeks described here and also include additional sophisticated concepts, such as genetic drift and speciation. With a large number of concepts being covered in a short period of time, however, the likelihood that students will develop a deep understanding of any concept is diminished; a survey of content is not sufficient to support the required conceptual change.

In the next section, we highlight key instructional activities that we have developed over time to support students in acquiring an understanding of evolution and an ability to engage in evolutionary inquiry.

Instruction

The three principles of *How People Learn* are interwoven in the design of the instructional activities that make up the course in evolutionary biology. For example, the related set of concepts that we consider to be central to students' understanding (Principle 2) was expanded when we realized that students' preconceptions (about variation, for example) or weak foundational knowledge (about drawing inferences and developing arguments) served as barriers to learning. Instructional activities designed to support students' ability to draw inferences and make arguments at the same time strengthen their metacognitive abilities. All three principles are tightly woven in the instruction described below.

Laying the Groundwork

Constructing and defending Darwinian explanations involves drawing inferences and developing arguments from observed patterns in data. In early versions of the course, we found that students' ability to draw inferences was relatively weak, as was their ability to critique particular arguments. Our course has since been modified to provide opportunities for students to develop a common framework for making and critiquing arguments. As with the black box activity at the beginning of the genetics course, we use a cartoon sequencing activity that does not introduce course content, thus allowing students to focus more fully on drawing inferences and developing arguments.

Students are given a set of 13 cartoon frames (see Box 12-5) that have been placed in random order. Their task is to work with their group to reconstruct a story using the information they can glean from the images. Students are enthusiastic about this task as they imagine how the images relate to one another and how they can all be tied together in a coherent story. The whole class then assembles to compare stories and discuss how

BOX 12-5 Cartoon Sequencing Activity

Below are the differing interpretations and sequencing of the same cartoon images by two different groups of students. There are images in the complete set that the students worked with for this activity. The 13 images are given to the students in random order, and the students are asked to create narrative stories.

Group One

"We think that in this first frame little red riding hood is telling the pigs that she is going to visit her sick grandmother. In the second scene, the pigs are telling the wolf about little red riding hood and her sick grandmother and showing him which way she went. In the next frame, the pigs see that the grandmother is tied up in the woods and they feel bad that they gave the wolf the information earlier."

Group Two

"The pigs have discovered grandma tied up in the woods and they try to throw the wolf off the track by telling him that he must get away before the hunter comes. In the last frame, little red riding hood is thanking the pigs for saving the grandmother and they feel bashful."

decisions were made. The sequences presented by different groups usually vary quite a bit (see Box 12-5 for two examples). This variation provides a context for discussing how inferences are drawn.

The initial discussion centers on students' observations about the images. However, it quickly becomes apparent that each person does not place the same importance on specific observations and that even though groups may have observed the same thing, they may not have made the same decisions about the order of the cards. What ensues is a conversation about considerations that entered into the students' decision making. Students realize that they are all examining the same images (the data), but that each also brings a lifetime of experience with cartoons and stories to the table. Together the students establish that the process of drawing inferences about the order of the cards is influenced by both what they observe (the data) and their own prior knowledge and beliefs. This notion is then generalized, and students see that all inferences can be thought of as having these two bases. They discuss how scientific arguments are usually a collection of several inferences, all of which are dependent on data and prior knowledge and beliefs. The teacher supports this discussion by pointing out examples of fruitful questioning and encouraging the students to think about what it means to foster a community in which communication about important ideas is expected.

In addition to introducing general norms for classrooms in which scientific argumentation is central, the cartoon activity serves to orient students to a framework for critiquing arguments in evolution. At one level, this framework is common to all science disciplines. In this capacity, the emphasis is on the importance of being explicit about how prior knowledge and beliefs influence the inferences drawn from particular data. At this general level, the activity is linked to the common MUSE framework of models and modeling as the teacher connects the ideas concerning inferences to those concerning models. The teacher does this by explaining that a causal model is an idea that is used to create explanations for some set of phenomena and that models are based on several inferences. Students then read some material on models and as a class discuss the ways in which models can be assessed. Through examples in the reading and from their own experience, the group settles on criteria for judging models: explanatory power and consistency with other knowledge. Note that, in contrast with the genetics course, there is no mention of predictive adequacy here as a major assessment criterion because explanation is much more central than prediction in the evolution course. This is one example of the assertion we have made previously: disciplines do rely on differing methods for making and evaluating claims. The demonstrative inference that is common in the genetics course gives way to a greater reliance on nondemonstrative inference in the evolution course. This occurs as students create Darwinian explanations. Such explanations, with their characteristic narrative structure, are developed to make sense out of the diverse data (structural and behavioral characteristics of organisms, patterns in their molecular biology, patterns of distribution in both time and geography, and so on) that are characteristic of evolutionary argumentation.

A second evolution-specific function served by the cartoon activity is to introduce students to one of the more important undertakings of evolutionary biologists—the reconstruction of past events (the development of a trait, such as the vertebrate eye, or the speciation events that led to the "tree of life"). Such historical reconstructions do not have close analogues in genetic inquiry.

A second instructional component was added to the course when we observed students' difficulties in understanding the concept of variation. These difficulties have been documented in the literature,[32] and we have encountered them in our own classrooms. Because of the experiences students have with variability in most genetics instruction—in which they usually examine traits with discrete variations—the concept of continuous variation can be a significant challenge for them. We have seen that an incomplete understanding of variation in populations promotes students' ideas that adaptations are a result of a single dramatic mutation and that selection is an all-or-none event operating on one of two to three possible phenotypes. Recognition of these problems has led us to incorporate explicit instruction on variability in populations and, perhaps more important, to provide opportunities for students to examine and characterize the variability present in real organisms before they begin using the concept in constructing Darwinian explanations.

One of the activities used for this purpose is a relatively simple one, but it provides a powerful visual representation on which students can draw later when thinking about variation in populations. Typically, students do not recognize the wide range of variation that is present even in familiar organisms. To give them experience in thinking about and characterizing variation, we have them examine sunflower seeds. Their task is to count the stripes on a small sample of seeds (but even this simple direction is less than straightforward since the class must then negotiate such matters as what counts as a stripe and whether to count one side or two).

Once they have come up with common criteria and have sorted their sample into small piles, the teacher has them place their seeds into correspondingly numbered test tubes. The result, once the test tubes have been lined up in a row, is a clear visual representation of a normal distribution. The subsequent discussion centers on ways to describe distributions using such concepts as mean, median, and mode. This activity takes place before students need to draw on their understanding of variation to construct explanations using the natural selection model.

Understanding the Darwinian Model

The second major section of the course engages students in examining three historical models that account for species' adaptation and diversity. The students must draw on the framework established during the cartoon activity to accomplish this comparison. This means that as they examine each argument, they also identify the major inferences drawn and the data and prior knowledge and beliefs that formed the basis for those inferences. The three models are (1) William Paley's model of intelligent design, which asserts that all organisms were made perfectly for their function by an intelligent creator; (2) Jean Baptiste de Lamarck's model of acquired characteristics, which is based on a view that adaptations can result from the use or disuse of body parts and that changes accumulated during an organism's lifetime will be passed on to offspring; and (3) Darwin's model of natural selection. The models of Paley and Lamarck were chosen because each represents some of the common ideas students bring with them to the classroom. Specifically, it is clear that many students attribute evolutionary change to the needs of an organism and believe that extended exposure to particular environments will result in lasting morphological change. Many students are also confused about the role of supernatural forces in evolution. Darwin's model is included in the analysis so students can see how the underlying assumptions of his model compare with those of the Paley and Lamarck models.

For students to compare the prior knowledge and beliefs of the authors, however, they must first become familiar with the models. To this end, each model is examined in turn, and students are discouraged from making comparisons until each model has been fully explored. All three models are presented in the same way. Students read edited selections of the author's original writing, answer questions about the reading, and participate in a class discussion in which the proposed explanation for species diversity and adaptation is clarified and elaborated. In the following example, Claire and Casey are working with Hillary in a group during class. They are trying to analyze and understand an excerpt of original writing by Lamarck. Hillary is looking over the discussion questions:

Hillary	It seems like Lamarck did think that species changed over time, so I can see that as an underlying assumption of his, but I'm having a hard time figuring out how he thought that happened.
Casey	I agree, he is definitely different from Paley who didn't think things had changed at all.
Claire	But how did the change happen? It seems like

	Lamarck puts it on the organisms themselves, that they try to change.
Hillary	I'm not sure what you mean.
Claire	Well, he talks a lot about the usefulness of particular traits for an animal and about repeated use of a body part causing a change.

Students are also given an opportunity to explore the natural phenomena or data that served as an inspiration for each author: they examine fossils as discussed by Lamarck, dissect an eye to examine the structure/function relationships that so fascinated Paley, and are visited by a pigeon breeder who brings several of the pigeon varieties that Darwin described in his *Origin of Species*. Once students have developed an understanding of the explanation that each author proposed and some familiarity with the observations on which it was based, they examine the readings again to identify the prior knowledge and beliefs that each author may have held.

Following this discussion, the students compare the three models. First, they assess the explanatory power of the models, using each to explain phenomena other than those described in the original writings. For example, they attempt to use Paley's model to explain the presence of fossils and Lamarck's model to explain the structure of the eye. Sometimes the model can easily account for new phenomena; Lamarck's model of use inheritance, for example, is easily adapted to explaining the diversity of pigeon varieties. In other instances, the students recognize the limitations of the model; Paley's model, for instance, cannot easily account for the presence of fossils or extinct organisms. The students then compare the underlying assumptions or beliefs of the authors. Even if a model can account for diverse phenomena on its own terms, it is still necessary to examine and critique the underlying assumptions. Many students question the necessity of the supernatural force underlying Paley's model, and still more find the role of need to be a questionable assumption in Lamarck's model.

These explicit discussions of some of the major views students bring to the study of evolution lay the groundwork for the future use and extension of Darwin's model. Comparing the assumptions of the three models enables students to distinguish between those beliefs that underlie the model of natural selection and those that do not. Unlike some classroom contexts, however, in which it is the students' ideas that are laid bare and examined for inconsistencies, here we have developed a situation in which students' ideas are represented by the models of Paley and Lamarck. We have found that through this approach, students are willing to attend to the differences between ideas rather than spending their time and energy being defensive; because they do not feel that their own ideas are being criticized, the discussions are fruitful.

These two activities foster a classroom community that operates from a common set of commitments. For our purposes, the most important of these is that Darwin proposed a naturalistic mechanism of species change that acts on variation among individuals within a species and that assumptions of supernatural influence and individual need are not a part of his model. Keeping this distinction in mind while using the natural selection model later in the course enables students to avoid some common misconceptions, or at least makes identification of those misconceptions more straightforward. For example, when students use the natural selection model to explain the bright coloration of the monarch butterfly, they often challenge each other when need-based or Lamarckian language is used.

Using the Darwinian Model

During the final weeks of the course, students are engaged in creating Darwinian explanations using the components of the natural selection model to make sense of realistic data they have been given. Each scenario is presented to the students as a case study, and they are given materials that describe the natural history of the organism. Photographs, habitat and predator information, mating behavior and success, and phylogenetic data are examples of the types of information that may be included in a given case. Students then weave the information into a narrative that must take into account all of the components of a natural selection model and describe the change over time that may have occurred (see Box 12-6 for one group's Darwinian explanation). As students hone their abilities to develop and assess evolutionary arguments over three successive case studies, they are able to participate in realistic evolutionary inquiry.

In the first case study, students develop a Darwinian explanation for differences in seed coat characteristics among populations of a hypothetical plant species. The second case study involves explaining the bright, and similar, coloration of monarch and viceroy butterflies. The final case requires that students develop an explanation for how the sexual dimorphism exhibited by ring-necked pheasants might have arisen.

During each case study, the time is structured so that a group will consult with at least one other group as they develop their explanations. This task organization reinforces the nature of argumentation in evolutionary biology, as it includes the expectation that students will attend to the central feature of any Darwinian explanation—that it have a historical component. But it is not enough to just have a history. In tracing the possible historical development of a trait, students must weave a complex story that draws on available data, as well as their understanding of an array of biological models (e.g., genetic models), to explain the role of heritable variation, superfecundity, competition, and agents of selection. Within their research

BOX 12-6 Darwinian Explanation Written by a Group of Students at the End of the Monarch/Viceroy Case

Monarchs and viceroys are very similar in appearance, although this has not always been true. The brightness in both butterflies is viewed as an advantage in their environment—where a main predator is the blue jay—an advantage that may be explained by the Darwinian model.

Each butterfly lays many more eggs than can survive on the limited resources in its environment. As a result of this limit, there is a struggle among the offspring for survival. As within all species, there exists natural variation among the populations of monarchs and viceroys, including variations of color. In the past populations, some butterflies were brightly colored and others were dull. Blue jays, a main predator of the monarch, rely on movement and coloration to identify their prey when hunting. They can vomit up bad-tasting or poisonous food, and exhibit an ability to learn to avoid such food in the future.

As caterpillars, monarchs have as a source of food milkweed leaves, which contain cardenolides—poisonous or unpalatable substances. As the larva are growing, they ingest a large amount of cardenolides. When they become butterflies, these substances remain in their bodies, making them unpalatable to their predators.

When blue jays eat monarchs, they react to the cardenolides by vomiting up their prey. They learn from this experience that they should avoid the brightly colored monarchs to avoid the cardenolides. The dull monarchs, although poisonous, were still consumed by their predators more because they more closely resembled nonpoisonous prey such as moths, grasshoppers, and lacewings. The brightly colored monarchs survived more than the dull ones and were more prolific. After many generations, most monarchs were bright because of their success in the environment. Because of the blue jays' association of bright colors with bad food, the brightly colored viceroys, although not poisonous like the monarch, were also avoided, and this advantageous variation was passed on as with the monarch.

groups, meetings between research groups, and whole-class discussions, students question one another using a variety of sophisticated stances. These include ensuring that there is consistency among the data, the natural selection model, and claims; that the history of the shift in a trait is feasible (i.e., consistent with genetics); and that the proposed selection agent could have brought about the change in the trait between times 1 and 2. The students question one another to ensure that their explanations are both internally and externally consistent. In so doing, they normally propose more than a single explanation, thus recognizing that, in evolution at least, it is important to consider multiple interpretations. As they examine competing Darwinian explanations for the same phenomena, they invoke an evolution-specific argument-analysis norm—that the explanation of the history of a trait has to be consistent with the natural selection model. For example, the second case requires students to provide a Darwinian explanation for the similarity in color between the monarch and viceroy butterflies. Frequently students will say such things as "the viceroy needs to look like the monarch so that the birds won't eat it." When statements such as these are made, other students will often challenge the speaker to use Darwinian rather than Lamarckian language. The work on the cases allows students to practice using the Darwinian model in appropriate ways, and the interactive nature of all of the work in class affords them opportunities to think explicitly about and defend their own ideas.

The culminating activities for each of the three cases require public sharing of ideas in a forum where the expectation is that the presenting groups and audience members will consider thoughtfully the ideas before them. Each case has a different type of final presentation. The first case ends with a poster session, the second with a roundtable discussion, and the last with a research proposal and an oral presentation.

One particularly powerful experience students have occurs during the final case study. For the first two case studies, students use their understanding of the Darwinian model to account for the changes that may have occurred in particular populations and to explicitly tie data from the case materials to their claims. For the final case study, they must construct a Darwinian explanation for the sexual dimorphism observed between male and female ring-necked pheasants, and in addition, they must produce a research proposal to shed light on their explanation. Typically, students choose to focus their research proposal on a single aspect of their explanation. This activity requires that they think carefully about the components of their explanation and the confidence they place in each of those components. Thus in this instance they are not evaluating the entire explanation as a single entity, but are considering each part in relation to the others. Once they have decided on a research proposal, they must determine how their proposed research would strengthen their argument. Being able to examine an argument as a whole and according to its parts is an important skill that this task helps develop. This case also stimulates interesting conversations among groups. The nonpresenting groups act as a proposal review panel and interact with the presenting groups in an attempt to understand the proposal. Once all groups have presented, the students discuss the merits and shortcomings of each proposal and then decide individually which proposal should be funded.

CLASSROOM ENVIRONMENTS THAT SUPPORT LEARNING WITH UNDERSTANDING

We have found that much of what students learn in genetics and evolutionary biology units grounded in model-based inquiry depends on their active and thoughtful participation in the classroom community.[33] To learn about the process of modeling and about discipline-specific patterns of argumentation, students must be critically aware of the elements that influence their own knowledge generation and justification. The MUSE curricula are designed to facilitate this type of student thinking through explicit discussion of students' expectations for engaging in argumentation, the design of student tasks, and the use of various tools for interacting with and representing abstract concepts.

Knowledge-Centered

By the end of our courses, students are able to reason in sophisticated ways about inheritance patterns and about evolutionary phenomena. Realizing that goal, we believe, is due in large measure to careful attention to the core disciplinary knowledge, as well as persistent attention to students' preconceptions and the supports required for effective conceptual change. The instructional activities we have described highlight a classroom environment that is knowledge-centered in putting both the core concepts and scientific approaches to generating and justifying those concepts at the center of instruction.

Learner-Centered

The classrooms are also learner-centered in several respects. The curriculum was designed to address existing conceptions that we had observed were creating problems for students as they tried to master new material. We also identified weaknesses in students' knowledge base—such as their understanding of models and their ability to draw inferences and develop arguments—and designed activities to strengthen those competencies. The use of frequent dialogue in our courses allows an attentive teacher to continuously monitor students' developing thinking.

Assessment-Centered

We have attempted to embed formative and authentic assessments throughout our courses. Assessment of student understanding needs to be undertaken with an eye to the various types of prior knowledge described above (misconceptions of science concepts, ideas about what science is, and the extent to which students' knowledge is integrated). We have seen, time and again, teachers becoming aware of students' common struggles and beginning to "hear" their own students differently. Thus, an important feature of instructional activities that give students opportunities to make their thinking and knowledge public and therefore visible to teachers is that they make assessment and instruction seamless. This becomes possible when students articulate the process of arriving at a solution and not simply the solution itself.

Because students struggle with conceptual problems in the genetics unit, for example, we incorporate a number of assessments that require them to describe the relationships between models or ideas that they have learned (see Box 12-7). Whenever possible, we design formal assessments as well as written classroom tasks that reflect the structure of students' work in the classroom. Our students spend a great deal of their class time working in groups, pouring over data, and talking with one another about their ideas. Thus, assessments also require them to look at data, propose explanations, and describe the thinking that led to particular conclusions.

In the evolution course, students are required during instruction to use the natural selection model to develop Darwinian explanations that account for rich data sets. To then ask them about data or the components of natural selection in a multiple-choice format that would require them to draw on only bits and pieces of knowledge for any one question appears incomplete at best. Instead, we provide them with novel data and ask them to describe their reasoning about those data using the natural selection model—a task analogous to what they have been doing in class. An instance of this type of assessment on the final exam asks students to write a Darwinian explanation for the color of polar bear fur using information about ancestral populations. In this way, during assessment we draw on students' ideas and skills as they were developed in class rather than asking students to simply recall bits of information in contrived testing situations.

While assessments provide teachers with information about student understanding, students also benefit from assessments that give them opportunities to see how their understanding has changed during a unit of study. One method we have used is to require each student to critique her or his own early work based on what she or he knows at the conclusion of a course. Not only does this approach give teachers insights into students' knowledge, but it also allows students to glimpse how much their knowledge and their ability to critique arguments have changed. Students' consideration of their own ideas has been incorporated into the assessment tasks in both units. On several occasions and in different ways, students examine their own ideas and explicitly discuss how those ideas have changed. For example, one of the questions on the final exam in evolution requires students to read and critique a Darwinian explanation they created on the first

BOX 12-7 Sample Exam Question: Consistency Between Models

This exam question is one of several tasks designed to produce evidence of students' understandings about the need for models to be consistent with one another and with the data they purport to explain.

*Below is a concept map that represents the relationships among
specific models, models in general, and data. Use the map to
respond to the tasks below.*

*a. Remember that a <u>line</u> in a concept map represents a relationship
between two terms (concepts, ideas, etc.) in the map. Write <u>a few</u>
<u>sentences</u> that describe the numbered relationships between the
terms given. Be as specific as you can: use the appropriate vocabulary of genetics to make your point as clearly as possible.*

*b. Draw a line (not necessarily a straight one) to separate the world
of ideas from that of observations on this map. Please label both
sides. Justify your placement of that line.*

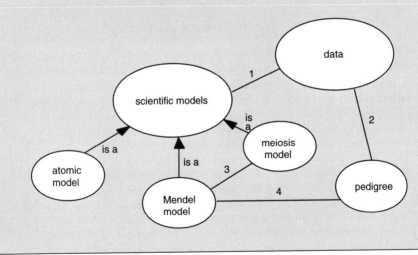

day of class (see Box 12-8). We have found this to be one of the most
powerful moments for many students, as they recognize how much their
own ideas have changed. Many students are critical of the need-based language that was present in their original explanation, or they find that they
described evolutionary change as having happened at the individual rather
than the population level.

BOX 12-8 Examples of Students' Critiques of Their Own Darwinian Explanations

On the first day of class, students were asked to explain how the carapace of Galapagos tortoises may have changed from the dome shape to the saddleback shape. As part of the final exam for the class, students were asked to critique the explanation they had given on the first day. Below are the original explanation and critique offered by one student.

Original Answer

The saddleback carapace came into being due to the need of migrating tortoises to adjust to a new environment. On Albermarle Island the domed shaped carapaces served well for shedding rain and eating ground vegetation. However, when the tortoises began to migrate to a smaller, drier island with less ground vegetation, they had to adapt in order to survive. The majority of the food was now higher up and the domed shell served as a hindrance. Over time, the saddleback carapace developed to allow the neck to extend further, thereby allowing the tortoises to reach the fleshy green parts of the prickly pear cactus. This evolutionary process created a new species of giant tortoise that could live successfully in a new environment.

Critique on Final Exam

In my original answer, I used an almost exclusive Lamarckian definition of evolution. In my introductory statement I stated that the saddleback carapace came into being due to the need of the tortoise to fit its environment. I needed to acknowledge the existence of variation within the tortoise population of the shape of the shell. My original explanation makes the evolutionary process sound like a physical change taking place during the life of the tortoise and then being passed on to the offspring. I now know that variations that are advantageous give animals a better chance of survival (survival of the fittest!) and allow them a better chance of passing on their advantageous trait to their offspring. In my original explanation I also touched on ideas of use and disuse to explain how the saddleback carapace came to be, this is a Lamarkian model of evolution which is incorrect. I did explain how the saddleback carapace was an advantage because it allowed the tortoise to eat higher vegetation. Since I didn't understand evolution through the generations, I wasn't able to describe how the species changed over time. Overall, I would say I had a basic but flawed understanding of evolution but I lacked the tools to explain evolution from a scientific and Darwinian perspective, until now.

Community-Centered

As Chapter 1 suggests, the knowledge-centered, learner-centered, and assessment-centered classrooms come together in the context of a classroom community. The culture of successful scientific communities includes both collaboration and questioning among colleagues. It involves norms for making and justifying claims. At the source of the productivity of such a community is an understanding of central causal models, the ability to use such models to conduct inquiry, and the ability to engage in the assessment of causal models and related explanations. We have found that these outcomes can be realized in classrooms where students are full participants in a scientific community.[34] Interestingly, one unexpected outcome of structuring classrooms so that students are expected to participate in the intellectual work of science has been increased involvement and achievement by students not previously identified as successful in science.

In addition to establishing expectations for class participation and a shared framework for knowledge assessment, MUSE curricula promote metacognitive reflection on the part of students by incorporating tasks that require discourse (formal and informal) at all stages of student work. While working in groups and presenting results to the class as a whole, students are required to share their ideas even when those ideas may not be fully formed. Moreover, recall that the context for idea sharing is one in which discipline-specific criteria for assessment of ideas have been established. Thus, discourse is anchored in norms of argumentation that reflect scientific practice to the extent possible.

Learning with Understanding

While the four features of classroom environments can be described individually, in practice they must interact if students are to deeply engage in learning for understanding. High school students have had more than 9 years of practice at playing the "game of school." Most have become quite adept at memorizing and reiterating information, seeking answers to questions or problems, and moving quickly from one topic to another. Typically during the game of school, students win when they present the correct answer. The process by which one determines the answer is irrelevant or, at best, undervalued. The students described here are quite typical in this regard: they enter our genetics and evolution classes anticipating that they will be called upon to provide answers and are prepared to do so. In fact, seeking an end product is so ingrained that even when we design tasks that involve multiple iterations of modeling and testing ideas, such as within the genetics course, students frequently reduce the work to seeking algorithms that have predictive power instead of engaging in the much more difficult task of evaluating models on the basis of their conceptual consistency within a family of related ideas.[35]

After studying how people solved problems in a variety of situations, Klayman and Ha[36] noted the frequent use of what they call a "positive test strategy." That is, solvers would propose a model (or solution) and test it by attempting to apply it to the situation most likely to fit the model in the first place. If the idea had explanatory or predictive power, the solver remained satisfied with it; if not, the solver would quickly test another idea. The positive test strategy was frequently applied by students in early versions of our genetics course.[37] This method of problem solving does not map well to scientific practice in most cases, however: it is the absence of disproving evidence, and not the presence of confirming evidence that is more commonly persuasive to scientists. Moreover, testing a model in limited situations in which one expects a data–model match would be considered "confirmation bias" within scientific communities. Nevertheless, Klayman and Ha point out that this positive test strategy is often quite useful in real-life situations.

Given our students' facility with the game of school and the general tendency to apply less scientific model-testing strategies when problem solving, we were forced to create tasks that not only afford the opportunity for reflection, but actually *require* students to think more deeply about the ways in which they have come to understand science concepts, as well as what is involved in scientific argumentation. We want students to realize that the models and explanations they propose are likely to be challenged and that the conflicts surrounding such challenges are the lifeblood of science. Thus, we explicitly discuss with our students the expectations for their participation in the course. Teachers state that the students' task is not simply to produce an "answer" (a model in genetics or a Darwinian explanation in evolutionary biology), but also to be able to defend and critique ideas according to the norms of a particular scientific discipline. In other words, we ask the students to abandon the game of school and begin to play the game of science.

Examination of ideas requires more than simply providing space for reflection to occur; it also involves working with students to develop systematic ways of critiquing their own ideas and those of others. This is why we begin each course with an activity whose focus is the introduction of discipline-specific ways of generating and critiquing knowledge claims. These activities do not require that students will come to understand any particular scientific concepts upon their completion. Rather, they will have learned about the *process* of constructing and evaluating arguments in genetics or evolutionary biology. Specific criteria for weighing scientific explanations are revisited throughout each course as students engage in extended inquiries within these biological disciplines.

SUMMARY

For students to develop understanding in any scientific discipline, teachers and curriculum developers must attend to a set of complex and interrelated components, including the nature of practice in particular scientific disciplines, students' prior knowledge, and the establishment of a collaborative environment that engages students in reflective scientific practice. These design components allow educators to create curricula and instructional materials that help students learn about science both *as* and *by* inquiry.

The students in the biology classrooms described in this chapter have developed sophisticated understandings of some of the most central explanatory frameworks in genetics and evolutionary biology. In addition, they have, unlike many high school students, shown great maturity in their abilities to reason about realistic biological data and phenomena using these models. Moreover, they have accomplished this in classrooms that are structured along the lines of scientific communities. This has all been made possible by a concerted collaboration involving high school teachers and their students, university science educators, and university biologists. That MUSE combined this collaboration with a research program on student learning and reasoning was essential. With the knowledge thus gained, we believe it is possible to help others realize the expectations for improving science education that are set forth in reform documents such as the *National Science Education Standards*.[38] In particular, there has been a call for curricular reforms that allow students to be "engaged in inquiry" that involves "combin[ing] processes and scientific knowledge as they use scientific reasoning and critical thinking to develop their understanding of science."[39] Recommendations for improved teaching of science are solidly rooted in a commitment to teaching both *through* and *about* inquiry. Furthermore, the *National Science Education Standards* do not simply suggest that science teachers incorporate inquiry in classrooms; rather, they demand that teachers embrace inquiry in order to:

- Plan an inquiry-based science program for their students.
- Focus and support inquiries while interacting with students.
- Create a setting for student work that is flexible and supportive of science inquiry.
- Model and emphasize the skills, attitudes, and values of scientific inquiry.

It is just these opportunities that have been described in this chapter.

NOTES

1. We encourage readers to visit our website (www.wcer.wisc.edu/ncusla/muse/). The site includes discussions of student knowledge and reasoning, intended learning outcomes, instructional activities, instructional notes, assessments, examples of student work, teachers' reflections, and connections to the *National Science Education Standards* and *Benchmarks for Science Literacy.*
2. Wiggins and McTighe, 1998, Chapter 1.
3. Grosslight et al., 1991.
4. Grosslight et al., 1991; Harrison and Treagust, 1998.
5. Cartier, 2000a.
6. Cartier, 2000b.
7. We consider a causal model to be an idea or set of ideas that can be used to explain particular natural phenomena. Models are complex constructions that consist of conceptual objects (e.g., alleles, populations) and processes (e.g., selection, independent assortment) in which the objects participate or interact.
8. Cartier, 2000a; Kindfield, 1994; Wynne et al., 2001.
9. Kindfield, 1994.
10. Cartier, 2000a.
11. Cartier, 2000a; Wynne et al., 2001.
12. Cartier, 2000b.
13. Darden, 1991.
14. Meiosis is the process by which sperm and egg cells are formed. During meiosis, chromosomal replication is followed by two rounds of cell division. Thus, one cell undergoing meiosis produces four new cells, each of which contains half the number of chromosomes of the original parent cell.
15. Kitcher, 1984, 1993.
16. Kitcher, 1984, p. 356.
17. Kitcher, 1984, p. 356.
18. Mendel, 1959.
19. Discontinuous traits are those for which two or more distinct categories of phenotypes (or variants) are identified. For example, Mendel studied the trait of height in pea plants. He noted that the pea plants were either short (18 in.) or tall (84 in.). In contrast, height is not a discontinuous trait in humans: human height is best characterized as continuously variable, or nondiscrete, because humans are not simply either 18 or 84 in. tall. Thus, the phenotype categories for height in humans are not clear-cut.
20. Calley and Jungck, 2002.
21. Achondroplasia is inherited in a codominant fashion. Individuals with two disease alleles (2,2) are severely dwarfed and seldom survive. Individuals who are heterozygous (1,2) are achondroplastic dwarfs, having disproportionately short arm and leg bones relative to their torsos. Thus while these two phenotypes differ from normal stature, they are distinct from one another.
22. In the past, our students have developed the following explanations for protein action in traits inherited in a codominant fashion:

- One allele (designated 1) codes for an active protein. The other allele codes for an inactive protein. Thus, individuals with genotype (1,1) have the greatest amount (or dose) of active protein and the associated phenotype at the organismal level. Individuals who are (2,2) have little or no measurable protein activity, and this is reflected in the phenotype. Heterozygous individuals (1,2) have an intermediate level of protein activity and a phenotype that is also intermediate. For example, in the case of achondroplasia, (1,1) individuals would have two alleles for a growth receptor and a phenotype of normal stature; (2,2) individuals would have few or no functional receptors and suffer from severe growth retardation; and heterozygotes (1,2) would have half as much growth receptor activity as the (1,1) individuals and consequently be short-statured achondroplastic dwarves without the additional health problems of the (2,2) individuals. This example of codominance is admittedly simplified, as students do not study the systemic effects of achondroplasia. However, this model is applied widely in genetics and sometimes referred to as the "dosage" model.

- Both alleles code for active proteins, giving rise to observable phenotypes at the macroscopic level. Heterozygotes display the phenotypes associated with both alleles. For example, in human blood types, individuals carrying alleles for protein A and protein B have both of these proteins on their blood cells. The phenotype is not blended or dosage dependent as in the achondroplasia example above. Instead, both proteins are detected intact in heterozygous individuals.

23. Cartier, 2000a, 2000b.
24. White and Frederiksen, 1998, p. 25.
25. Cartier 2000a, 2000b.
26. Mayr, 1982, p. 481.
27. Kitcher, 1993, pp. 20-21.
28. Richards, 1992, p. 23.
29. O'Hara, 1988.
30. Mayr, 1997, p. 64.
31. Bishop and Anderson, 1990; Demastes et al., 1992, 1995, 1996.
32. Bishop and Anderson, 1990.
33. Cartier, 2000a, 2000b; Passmore and Stewart, 2002.
34. Cartier, 2000b; Passmore and Stewart, 2000.
35. Cartier, 2000a.
36. Klayman and Ha, 1987.
37. Cartier, 2000a.
38. National Research Council, 1996.
39. National Research Council, 1996, p. 105.

REFERENCES

Bishop, B.A., and Anderson, C.W. (1990). Student conceptions of natural selection and its role in evolution. *Journal of Research in Science Teaching, 27*(5), 415-427.

Calley, J., and Jungck, J.R. (2002). *Genetics construction kit.* (The BioQUEST Library IV, version 1.1B3) [Computer software]. New York: Academic Press.

Cartier, J.L. (2000a). *Assessment of explanatory models in genetics: Insights into students' conceptions of scientific models.* Research report 98-1 for the National Center for Improving Student Learning and Achievement in Mathematics and Science. Available: http://www.wcer.wisc.edu/ncisla/publications/main.html#reports/RR98-1.pdf [accessed February 3, 2003].

Cartier, J.L. (2000b). *Using a modeling approach to explore scientific epistemology with high school biology students.* Research report 99-1 for the National Center for Improving Student Learning and Achievement in Mathematics and Science. Available: http://www.wcer.wisc.edu/ncisla/publications/reports/RR99-1.pdf [accessed February 3, 2003].

Darden, L. (1991). *Theory change in science: Strategies from Mendelian genetics.* New York: Oxford University Press.

Demastes, S., Good, R., and Peebles, P. (1995). Students' conceptual ecologies and the process of conceptual change in evolution. *Science Education, 79*(6), 637-666.

Demastes, S., Good, R., and Peebles, P. (1996). Patterns of conceptual change in evolution. *Journal of Research in Science Teaching, 33*(4), 407-431.

Demastes, S.S., Trowbridge, J.E., and Cummins, C.L. (1992). Resource paper on evolution education research. In R.G. Good, J.E. Trowbridge, S.S. Demastes, J.H. Wandersee, M.S. Hafner, and C.L. Cummins (Eds.), *Proceedings of the 1992 Evolution Education Conference,* Louisiana State University, Baton Rouge, LA.

Grosslight, L., Unger, C., Jay, E., and Smith, C.L. (1991). Understanding models and their use in science: Conceptions of middle and high school students and experts. *Journal of Research in Science Teaching, 28,* 799-822.

Harrison, A.G., and Treagust, D.F. (1998). Modeling in science lessons: Are there better ways to learn with models? *School Science and Mathematics, 98*(8), 420-429.

Kindfield, A.C.H. (1994). Understanding a basic biological process: Expert and novice models of meiosis. *Science Education, 78*(3), 255-283.

Kitcher, P. (1984). 1953 and all that: A tale of two sciences. *The Philosophical Review, 93,* 335-373.

Kitcher, P. (1993). *The advancement of science: Science without legend, objectivity without illusions.* New York: Oxford University Press.

Klayman, J., and Ha, Y. (1987). Confirmation, disconfirmation, and information in hypothesis testing. *Psychological Review, 94,* 211-228.

Mayr, E. (1982). *The growth of biological thought: Diversity, evolution, and inheritance.* Cambridge, MA: Belknap Press of Harvard University Press.

Mayr, E. (1997). *This is biology: The science of the living world.* Cambridge, MA: Belknap Press of Harvard University Press.

Mendel, G. (1959; Original publication date 1865). Experiments on plant hybridization. In J. Peters (Ed.), *Classic papers in genetics.* Upper Saddle River, NJ: Prentice Hall.

National Research Council. (1996). *National science education standards.* National Committee on Science Education Standards and Assessment, Center for Science, Mathematics, and Engineering Education. Washington, DC: National Academy Press.

O'Hara, R.J. (1988). Homage to Clio, or, toward a historical philosophy for evolutionary biology. *Systematic Zoology, 37,* 142-155.

Passmore, C.M., and Stewart, J. (2002). A modeling approach to teaching evolutionary biology in high schools. *Journal of Research in Science Teaching, 39,* 185-204.

Richards, R.J. (1992). The structure of narrative explanation in history and biology. In M.H. Nitecki and D.V. Nitecki (Eds.), *History and evolution* (pp. 19-53). Albany, NY: State University of New York Press.

White, B.Y., and Frederiksen, J.R. (1998). Inquiry, modeling, and metacogntion: Making science accessible to all students. *Cognition and Instruction, 16,* 3-118.

Wiggins, G., and McTighe, J. (1998). *Understanding by design.* Upper Saddle River, NJ: Merrill/Prentice-Hall.

Wynne, C., Stewart, J., and Passmore, C. (2001). High school students' use of meiosis when solving genetics problems. *The International Journal of Science Education, 23*(5), 501-515.

A FINAL SYNTHESIS:
REVISITING THE THREE LEARNING PRINCIPLES

13

Pulling Threads

M. Suzanne Donovan and John D. Bransford

What ties the chapters of this volume together are the three principles from *How People Learn* (set forth in Chapter 1) that each chapter takes as its point of departure. The collection of chapters in a sense serves as a demonstration of the second principle: that a solid foundation of detailed knowledge and clarity about the core concepts around which that knowledge is organized are both required to support effective learning. The three principles themselves are the core organizing concepts, and the chapter discussions that place them in information-rich contexts give those concepts greater meaning. After visiting multiple topics in history, math, and science, we are now poised to use those discussions to explore further the three principles of learning.

ENGAGING RESILIENT PRECONCEPTIONS

All of the chapters in this volume address common preconceptions that students bring to the topic of focus. Principle one from *How People Learn* suggests that those preconceptions must be engaged in the learning process, and the chapters suggest strategies for doing so. Those strategies can be grouped into three approaches that are likely to be applicable across a broad range of topics.

1. Draw on knowledge and experiences that students commonly bring to the classroom but are generally not activated with regard to the topic of study.

This technique is employed by Lee, for example, in dealing with students' common conception that historical change happens as an *event*. He points out that students bring to history class the everyday experience of "nothing much happening" until an event changes things. Historians, on the other hand, generally think of change in terms of the *state of affairs*. Change in this sense may include, but is not equivalent to, the occurrence of events. Yet students have many experiences in which things change gradually— experiences in which "nothing happening" is, upon reflection, a mischaracterization. Lee suggests, as an example, students might be asked to "consider the change from a state of affairs in which a class does not trust a teacher to one in which it does. There may be no event that could be singled out as marking the change, just a long and gradual process."

There are many such experiences on which a teacher could draw, such as shifting alliances among friends or a gradual change in a sports team's status with an improvement in performance. Each of these experiences has characteristics that support the desired conception of history. Events are certainly not irrelevant. A teacher may do particular things that encourage trust, such as going to bat for a student who is in a difficult situation or postponing a quiz because students have two other tests on the same day. Similarly, there may be an incident in a group that changes the dynamic, such as a less popular member winning a valued prize or taking the blame for an incident to prevent the whole group from being punished. But in these contexts students can see, perhaps with some guided discussion, that single events are rarely the sole explanation for the state of affairs.

It is often the case that students have experiences that can support the conceptions we intend to teach, but instructional guidance is required to bring these experiences to the fore. These might be thought of as "recessive" experiences. In learning about rational number, for example, it is clear that whole-number reasoning—the subject of study in earlier grades—is dominant for most students (see Chapter 7). Yet students typically have experience with thinking about percents in the context of sale items in stores, grades in school, or loading of programs on a computer. Moss's approach to teaching rational number as described in Chapter 7 uses that knowledge of percents to which most students have easy access as an alternative path to learning rational number. She brings students' recessive understanding of proportion in the context of reasoning about percents to the fore and strengthens their knowledge and skill by creating multiple contexts in which proportional reasoning is employed (pipes and tubes, beakers, strings). As with events in history, students do later work with fractions, and that work at times presents them with problems that involve dividing a pizza or a pie into discrete parts—a problem in which whole-number reasoning often dominates. Because a facility with proportional reasoning is brought to bear, however, the division of a pie no longer leads students so easily into whole-number traps.

Moss reinforces proportional reasoning by having students play games in which fractions (such as $\frac{1}{4}$) must be lined up in order of size with decimals (such as .33) and percents (such as 40 percent). A theme that runs throughout the chapters of this volume, in fact, is that students need many opportunities to work with a new or recessive concept, especially when doing so requires that powerful preconceptions be overturned or modified.

Bain, for example, writes about students' tendency to see "history" and "the past" as the same thing: "No one should think that merely pointing out conceptual distinctions through a classroom activity equips students to make consistent, regular, and independent use of these distinctions. Students' habits of seeing history and the past as the same do not disappear overnight." Bain's equivalent of repeated comparisons of fractions, decimals, and percents is the ever-present question regarding descriptions and materials: is this "history-as-event"—the description of a past occurrence—or "history-as-account"—an explanation of a past occurrence. Supporting conceptual change in students requires repeated efforts to strengthen the new conception so that it becomes dominant.

2. Provide opportunities for students to experience discrepant events that allow them to come to terms with the shortcomings in their everyday models.

Relying on students' existing knowledge and experiences can be difficult in some instances because everyday experiences provide little if any opportunity to become familiar with the phenomenon of interest. This is often true in science, for example, where the subject of study may require specialized tools or controlled environmental conditions that students do not commonly encounter.

In the study of gravity, for example, students do not come to the classroom with experiences that easily support conceptual change because gravity is a constant in their world. Moreover, experiences they have with other forces often support misconceptions about gravity. For example, students can experience variation in friction because most have opportunities to walk or run an object over such surfaces as ice, polished wood, carpeting, and gravel. Likewise, movement in water or heavy winds provide experiences with resistance that many students can easily access. Minstrell found his students believed that these forces with which they had experience explained why they did not float off into space (see Chapter 11). Ideas about buoyancy and air pressure, generally not covered in units on gravity, influenced these students' thinking about gravity. Television images of astronauts floating in space reinforced for the students the idea that, without air to hold things down, they would simply float off.

Minstrell posed to his students a question that would draw out their thinking. He showed them a large frame from which a spring scale hung and placed an object on the scale that weighed 10 pounds. He then asked the students to consider a situation in which a large glass dome would be placed over the scale and all the air forced out with a vacuum pump. He asked the students to predict (imprecisely) what would happen to the scale reading. Half of Minstrell's students predicted that the scale reading would drop to zero without air; about a third thought there would be no effect at all on the scale reading; and the remainder thought there would be a small change. That students made a prediction and the predictions differed stimulated engagement. When the experiment was carried out, the ideas of many students were directly challenged by the results they observed.

In teaching evolution, Stewart and colleagues found that students' everyday observations led them to underestimate the amount of variation in common species. In such cases, student observations are not so much "wrong" as they are insufficiently refined. Scientists are more aware of variation because they engage in careful measurement and attend to differences at a level of detail not commonly noticed by the lay person. Stewart and colleagues had students count and sort sunflower seeds by their number of stripes as an easy route to a discrepant event of sorts. The students discovered there is far more variation among seeds than they had noticed. Unless students understand this point, it will be difficult for them to grasp that natural selection working on natural variation can support evolutionary change.

While discrepant events are perhaps used most commonly in science, Bain suggests they can be used productively in history as well (see Chapter 4). To dislodge the common belief that history is simply factual accounts of events, Bain asked students to predict how people living in the colonies (and later in the United States) would have marked the anniversary of Columbus's voyage 100 years after his landing in 1492 and then each hundred years after that through 1992. Students wrote their predictions in journals and were then given historical information about the changing Columbian story over the 500-year period. That information suggests that the first two anniversaries were not really marked at all, that the view of Columbus's "discovery of the new world" as important had emerged by 1792 among former colonists and new citizens of the United States, and that by 1992 the Smithsonian museum was making no mention of "discovery" but referred to its exhibit as the "Columbian Exchange." If students regard history as the reporting of facts, the question posed by Bain will lead them to think about *how* people might have celebrated Columbus's important discovery, and not *whether* people would have considered the voyage a cause for celebration at all. The discrepancy between students' expectation regarding the answer to the question and the historical accounts they are given in the classroom lecture cannot help but jar the conception that history books simply report events as they occurred in the past.

3. Provide students with narrative accounts of the discovery of (targeted) knowledge or the development of (targeted) tools.

What we teach in schools draws on our cultural heritage—a heritage of scientific discovery, mathematical invention, and historical reconstruction. Narrative accounts of how this work was done provide a window into change that can serve as a ready source of support for students who are being asked to undergo that very change themselves. How is it that the earth was discovered to be round when nothing we casually observe tells us that it is? What is place value anyway? Is it, like the round earth, a natural phenomenon that was discovered? Is it truth, like e = mc², to be unlocked? There was a time, of course, when everyday notions prevailed, or everyday problems required a solution. If students can witness major changes through narrative, they will be provided an opportunity to undergo conceptual change as well.

Stewart and colleagues describe the use of such an approach in teaching about evolution (see Chapter 12). Darwin's theory of natural selection operating on random variation can be difficult for students to grasp. The beliefs that all change represents an advance toward greater complexity and sophistication and that changes happen in response to use (the giraffe's neck stretching because it reaches for high leaves, for example) are widespread and resilient. And the scientific theory of evolution is challenged today, as it was in Darwin's time, by those who believe in intelligent design—that all organisms were made perfectly for their function by an intelligent creator. To allow students to differentiate among these views and understand why Darwin's theory is the one that is accepted scientifically, students work with three opposing theories as they were developed, supported, and argued in Darwin's day: William Paley's model of intelligent design, Jean Baptiste de Lamarck's model of acquired characteristics based on use, and Darwin's theory of natural selection. Students' own preconceptions are generally represented somewhere in the three theories. By considering in some depth the arguments made for each theory, the evidence that each theorist relied upon to support his argument, and finally the course of events that led to the scientific community's eventually embracing Darwin's theory, students have an opportunity to see their own ideas argued, challenged, and subjected to tests of evidence.

Every scientific theory has a history that can be used to the same end. And every scientific theory was formulated by particular people in particular circumstances. These people had hopes, fears, and passions that drove their work. Sometimes students can understand theories more readily if they learn about them in the context of those hopes, fears, and passions. A narrative that places theory in its human context need not sacrifice any of the technical material to be learned, but can make that material more engaging and meaningful for students.

The principle, of course, does not apply only to science and is not restricted to discovery. In mathematics, for example, while some patterns and relationships were discovered, conventions that form our system of counting were *invented*. As the mathematics chapters suggest, the use of mathematics with understanding—the engagement with problem solving and strategy use displayed by the best mathematics students—is undermined when students think of math as a rigid application of given algorithms to problems and look for surface hints as to which algorithm applies. If students can see the nature of the problems that mathematical conventions were designed to solve, their conceptions of what mathematics is can be influenced productively.

Historical accounts of the development of mathematical conventions may not always be available. For purposes of supporting conceptual change, however, fictional story telling may do just as well as history. In *Teaching as Story Telling,* Egan[1] relates a tale that can support students' understanding of place value:

> *A king wanted to count his army. He had five clueless counselors and one ingenious counselor. Each of the clueless five tried to work out a way of counting the soldiers, but came up with methods that were hopeless. One, for example, tried using tally sticks to make a count, but the soldiers kept moving around, and the count was confused. The ingenious counselor told the king to have the clueless counselors pick up ten pebbles each. He then had them stand behind a table that was set up where the army was to march past. In front of each clueless counselor a bowl was placed. The army then began to march past the end of the table.*
>
> *As each soldier went by, the first counselor put one pebble into his bowl. Once he had put all ten pebbles into the bowl, he scooped them up and then continued to put one pebble down for each soldier marching by the table. He had a very busy afternoon, putting down his pebbles one by one and then scooping them up when all were in the bowl. Each time he scooped up the ten pebbles, the clueless counselor to his left put one pebble into her bowl [gender equity]. When her ten pebbles were in her bowl, she too scooped them out again, and continued to put one back into the bowl each time the clueless counselor to her right picked his up.*
>
> *The clueless counselor to her left had to watch her through the afternoon, and he put one pebble into his bowl each time she picked*

hers up. And so on for the remaining counselors. At the end of the afternoon, the counselor on the far left had only one pebble in his bowl, the next counselor had two, the next had seven, the next had six and the counselor at the other end of the table, where the soldiers had marched by, had three pebbles in his bowl. So we know that the army had 12,763 soldiers. The king was delighted that his ingenious counselor had counted the whole army with just fifty pebbles.[2]

When this story is used in elementary school classrooms, Egan encourages the teacher to follow up by having the students count the class or some other, more numerous objects using this method.

The story illustrates nicely for students how the place-value system allows the complex problem of counting large numbers to be made simpler. Place value is portrayed not as a truth but as an invention. Students can then change the base from 10 to other numbers to appreciate that base 10 is not a "truth" but a "choice." This activity supports students in understanding that what they are learning is designed to make number problems raised in the course of human activity manageable.

That imaginative stories can, if effectively designed, support conceptual change as well as historical accounts is worth noting for another reason: the fact that an historical account is an *account* might be viewed as cause for excluding it from a curriculum in which the nature of the account is not the subject of study. Historical accounts of Galileo, Newton, or Darwin written for elementary and secondary students can be contested. One would hope that students who study history will come to understand these as accounts, and that they will be presented to students as such. But the purpose of the accounts, in this case, is to allow students to experience a time when ideas that they themselves may hold were challenged and changed, and that purpose can be served even if the accounts are somewhat simplified and their contested aspects not treated fully.

ORGANIZING KNOWLEDGE AROUND CORE CONCEPTS

In the *Fish Is Fish* story discussed in Chapter 1, we understand quite easily that when the description of a human generates an image of an upright fish wearing clothing, there are some key missing concepts: adaptation, warm-blooded versus cold-blooded species, and the difference in mobility challenges in and out of water. How do we know which concepts are "core?" Is it always obvious?

The work of the chapter authors, as well as the committee/author discussions that supported the volume's development, provides numerous insights about the identification of core concepts. The first is observed most explicitly in the work of Peter Lee (see Chapter 2): that two distinct types of core concepts must be brought to the fore simultaneously. These are concepts about the nature of the discipline (what it means to engage in doing history, math, or science) and concepts that are central to the understanding of the subject matter (exploration of the new world, mathematical functions, or gravity). Lee refers to these as first-order (the discipline) and second-order (the subject) concepts. And he demonstrates very persuasively in his work that students bring preconceptions about the discipline that are just as powerful and difficult to change as those they bring about the specific subject matter.

For teachers, knowing the core concepts of the discipline itself—the standards of evidence, what constitutes proof and disproof, and modes of reasoning and engaging in inquiry—is clearly required. This requirement is undoubtedly at the root of arguments in support of teachers' course work in the discipline in which they will teach. But that course work will be a blunt instrument if it focuses only on second-order knowledge (of subject) but not on first-order knowledge (of the discipline). Clarity about the core concepts of the discipline is required if students are to grasp what the discipline— history, math, or science—is about.

For identifying both first- and second-order concepts, the obvious place to turn initially is to those with deep expertise in the discipline. The concepts that organize experts' knowledge, structure what they see, and guide their problem solving are clearly core. But in many cases, exploring expert knowledge directly will not be sufficient. Often experts have such facility with a concept that it does not even enter their consciousness. These "expert blind spots" require that "knowledge packages"[3]—sets of related concepts and skills that support expert knowledge—become a matter for study.

A striking example can be found in Chapter 7 on elementary mathematics. For those with expertise in mathematics, there may appear to be no "core concept" in whole-number counting because it is done so automatically. How one first masters that ability may not be accessible to those who did so long ago. Building on the work of numerous researchers on how children come to acquire whole-number knowledge, Griffin and Case's[4] research conducted over many years suggests a core conceptual structure that supports the development of the critical concept of *quantity*. Similar work has been done by Moss and Case[5] (on the core conceptual structure for rational number) and by Kalchman, Moss, and Case[6] (on the core conceptual structure for functions). The work of Case and his colleagues suggests the important role cognitive and developmental psychologists can play in extending understanding of the network of concepts that are "core" and might be framed in less detail by mathematicians (and other disciplinary experts).

The work of Stewart and his colleagues described in Chapter 12 is another case in which observations of student efforts to learn help reshape understanding of the package of related core concepts. The critical role of natural selection in understanding evolution would certainly be identified as a core concept by any expert in biology. But in the course of teaching about natural selection, these researchers' realization that students underestimated the variation in populations led them to recognize the importance of this concept that they had not previously identified as core. Again, experts in evolutionary biology may not identify population variation as an important concept because they understand and use the concept routinely—perhaps without conscious attention to it. Knowledge gleaned from classroom teaching, then, can be critical in defining the connected concepts that help support core understandings.

But just as concepts defined by disciplinary experts can be incomplete without the study of student thinking and learning, so, too, the concepts as defined by teachers can fall short if the mastery of disciplinary concepts is shallow. Liping Ma's study of teachers' understanding of the mathematics of subtraction with regrouping provides a compelling example. Some teachers had little conceptual understanding, emphasizing procedure only. But as Box 13-1 suggests, others attempted to provide conceptual understanding without adequate mastery of the core concepts themselves. Ma's work provides many examples (in the teaching of multidigit multiplication, division of fractions, and calculation of perimeter and area) in which efforts to teach for understanding without a solid grasp of disciplinary concepts falls short.

SUPPORTING METACOGNITION

A prominent feature of all of the chapters in this volume is the extent to which the teaching described emphasizes the development of metacognitive skills in students. Strengthening metacognitive skills, as discussed in Chapter 1, improves the performance of all students, but has a particularly large impact on students who are lower-achieving.[7]

Perhaps the most striking consistency in pedagogical approach across the chapters is the ample use of classroom discussion. At times students discuss in small groups and at times as a whole class; at times the teacher leads the discussion; and at times the students take responsibility for questioning. A primary goal of classroom discussion is that by observing and engaging in questioning, students become better at monitoring and questioning their own thinking.

In Chapter 5 by Fuson, Kalchman, and Bransford, for example, students solve problems on the board and then discuss alternative approaches to solving the same problem. The classroom dialogue, reproduced in Box 13-2, supports the kind of careful thinking about why a particular problem-solv-

BOX 13-1 Conceptual Explanation Without Conceptual Understanding

Liping Ma explored approaches to teaching subtraction with regrouping (problems like 52 – 25, in which subtraction of the 5 ones from the 2 ones requires that the number be regrouped). She found that some teachers took a very procedural approach that emphasized the order of the steps, while others emphasized the concept of composing a number (in this case into 5 tens and 2 ones) and decomposing a number (into 4 tens and 12 ones). Between these two approaches, however, were those of teachers whose intentions were to go beyond procedural teaching, but who did not themselves fully grasp the concepts at issue. Ma[8] describes one such teacher as follows:

> *Tr. Barry, another experienced teacher in the procedurally directed group, mentioned using manipulatives to get across the idea that "you need to borrow something." He said he would bring in quarters and let students change a quarter into two dimes and one nickel: "a good idea might be coins, using money because kids like money. . . . The idea of taking a quarter even, and changing it to two dimes and a nickel so you can borrow a dime, getting across that idea that you need to borrow something."*
>
> *There are two difficulties with this idea. First of all, the mathematical problem in Tr. Barry's representation was 25 – 10, which is not a subtraction with regrouping. Second, Tr. Barry confused borrowing in everyday life—borrowing a dime from a person who has a quarter—with the "borrowing" process in subtraction with regrouping—to regroup the minuend by rearranging within place values. In fact, Tr. Barry's manipulative would not convey any conceptual understanding of the mathematical topic he was supposed to teach.*

Another teacher who grasps the core concept comments on the idea of "borrowing" as follows:[9]

> *Some of my students may have learned from their parents that you "borrow one unit form the tens and regard it as 10 ones". . . . I will explain to them that we are not borrowing a 10, but decomposing a 10. "Borrowing" can't explain why you can take a 10 to the ones place. But "decomposing" can. When you say decomposing, it implies that the digits in higher places are actually composed of those at lower places. They are exchangeable . . . borrowing one unit and turning it into 10 sounds arbitrary. My students may ask me how can we borrow from the tens? If we borrow something, we should return it later on.*

ing strategy does or does not work, as well as the relative benefits of different strategies, that can support skilled mathematics performance.

Similarly, in the science chapters students typically work in groups, and the groups question each other and explain their reasoning. Box 13-3 reproduces a dialogue at the high school level that is a more sophisticated version of that among young mathematics students just described. One group of students explains to another not only what they concluded about the evolutionary purpose of different coloration, but also the thinking that led them to that conclusion and the background knowledge from an earlier example that supported their thinking. The practice of bringing other knowledge to bear in the reasoning process is at the heart of effective problem solving, but can be difficult to teach directly. It involves a search through one's mental files for what is relevant. If teachers simply give students the knowledge to incorporate, the practice and skill development of doing one's own mental search is shortchanged. Group work and discussions encourage students to engage actively in the mental search; they also provide examples from other students' thinking of different searches and search results. The monitoring of consistency between explanation and theory that we see in this group discussion (e.g., even if the male dies, the genes have already been passed along) is preparation for the kind of self-monitoring that biologists do routinely.

Having emphasized the benefits of classroom discussion, however, we offer two cautionary notes. First, the discussion cited in the chapters is *guided* by teachers to achieve the desired learning. Using classroom discussion well places a substantial burden on the teacher to support skilled discussion, respond flexibly to the direction the discussion is taking, and steer it productively. Guiding discussion can be a challenging instructional task. Not all questions are good ones, and the art of questioning requires learning on the part of both students and teachers.[10] Even at the high school level, Bain (see Chapter 4) notes the challenge a teacher faces in supporting good student questioning:

Sarena	Does anyone notice the years that these were written? About how old are these accounts? Andrew?
Andrew	They were written in 1889 and 1836. So some of them are about 112 years old and others are about 165 years old.
Teacher	Why did you ask, Sarena?
Sarena	I'm supposed to ask questions about when the source was written and who wrote it. So, I'm just doing my job.

BOX 13-2 Supporting Skilled Questioning and Explaining in Mathematics Problem Solving

In the dialogue below, young children are learning to explain their thinking and to ask questions of each other—skills that help students guide their own learning when those skills are eventually internalized as self-questioning and self-explaining.

Teacher	Maria, can you please explain to your friends in the class how you solved the problem?
Maria	Six is bigger than 4, so I can't subtract here [pointing] in the ones. So I have to get more ones. But I have to be fair when I get more ones, so I add ten to both my numbers. I add a ten here in the top [pointing] to change the 4 to a 14, and I add a ten here in the bottom in the tens place, so I write another ten by my 5. So now I count up from 6 to 14, and I get 8 ones (demonstrating by counting "6, 7, 8, 9, 10, 11, 12, 13, 14" while raising a finger for each word from 7 to 14). And I know my doubles, so 6 plus 6 is 12, so I have 6 tens left. [She thought, "1 + 5 = 6 and 6 + ? = 12 tens. Oh, I know 6 + 6 = 12, so my answer is 6 tens."]
Jorge	I don't see the other 6 in your tens. I only see one 6 in your answer.
Maria	The other 6 is from adding my 1 ten to the 5 tens to get 6 tens. I didn't write it down.
Andy	But you're changing the problem. How do you get the right answer?
Maria	If I make both numbers bigger by the same amount, the difference will stay the same. Remember we looked at that on drawings last week and on the meter stick.
Michelle	Why did you count up?

Palincsar[11] has documented the progress of students as they move beyond early, unskilled efforts at questioning. Initially, students often parrot the questions of a teacher regardless of their appropriateness or develop questions from a written text that repeat a line of the text verbatim, leaving a blank to be filled in. With experience, however, students become productive questioners, learning to attend to content and ask genuine questions.

Maria	Counting down is too hard, and my mother taught me to count up to subtract in first grade.
Teacher	How many of you remember how confused we were when we first saw Maria's method last week? Some of us could not figure out what she was doing even though Elena and Juan and Elba did it the same way. What did we do?
Rafael	We made drawings with our ten-sticks and dots to see what those numbers meant. And we figured out they were both tens. Even though the 5 looked like a 15, it was really just 6. And we went home to see if any of our parents could explain it to us, but we had to figure it out ourselves and it took us 2 days.
Teacher	Yes, I was asking other teachers, too. We worked on other methods too, but we kept trying to understand what this method was and why it worked.
	And Elena and Juan decided it was clearer if they crossed out the 5 and wrote a 6, but Elba and Maria liked to do it the way they learned at home. Any other questions or comments for Maria? No? Ok, Peter, can you explain your method?
Peter	Yes, I like to ungroup my top number when I don't have enough to subtract everywhere. So here I ungrouped 1 ten and gave it to the 4 ones to make 14 ones, so I had 1 ten left here. So 6 up to 10 is 4 and 4 more up to 14 is 8, so 14 minus 6 is 8 ones. And 5 tens up to 11 tens is 6 tens. So my answer is 68.
Carmen	How did you know it was 11 tens?
Peter	Because it is 1 hundred and 1 ten and that is 11 tens.

Similarly, students' answers often cannot serve the purpose of clarifying their thinking for classmates, teachers, or themselves without substantial support from teachers. The dialogue in Box 13-4 provides an example of a student becoming clearer about the meaning of what he observed as the teacher helped structure the articulation.

BOX 13-3 Questioning and Explaining in High School Science

The teacher passes out eight pages of case materials and asks the students to get to work. Each group receives a file folder containing the task description and information about the natural history of the ring-necked pheasant. There are color pictures that show adult males, adult females, and young. Some of the pages contain information about predators, mating behavior, and mating success. The three students spend the remainder of the period looking over and discussing various aspects of the case. By the middle of the period on Tuesday, this group is just finalizing their explanation when Casey, a member of another group, asks if she can talk to them.

Casey	What have you guys come up with? Our group was wondering if we could talk over our ideas with you.
Grace	Sure, come over and we can each read our explanations.

These two groups have very different explanations. Hillary's group is thinking that the males' bright coloration distracts predators from the nest, while Casey's group has decided that the bright coloration confers an advantage on the males by helping them attract more mates. A lively discussion ensues.

Ed	But wait, I don't understand. How can dying be a good thing?
Jerome	Well, you have to think beyond just survival of the male himself. We think that the key is the survival of the kids. If the male can protect his

Group work and group or classroom discussions have another potential pitfall that requires teacher attention: some students may dominate the discussion and the group decisions, while others may participate little if at all. Having a classmate take charge is no more effective at promoting metacognitive development—or supporting conceptual change—than having a teacher take charge. In either case, active engagement becomes unnecessary. One approach to tackling this problem is to have students rate their group effort in terms not only of their product, but also of their group dy-

	young and give them a better chance of surviving then he has an advantage.
Claire	Even if he dies doing it?
Grace	Yeah, because he will have already passed on his genes and stuff to his kids before he dies.
Casey	How did you come up with this? Did you see something in the packets that we didn't see?
Grace	One reason we thought of it had to do with the last case with the monarchs and viceroy.
Hillary	Yeah, we were thinking that the advantage isn't always obvious and sometimes what is good for the whole group might not seem like it is good for one bird or butterfly or whatever.
Jerome	We also looked at the data in our packets on the number of offspring fathered by brighter versus duller males. We saw that the brighter males had a longer bar.
Grace	See, look on page 5, right here.
Jerome	So they had more kids, right?
Casey	We saw that table too, but we thought that it could back up our idea that the brighter males were able to attract more females as mates.

The groups agree to disagree on their interpretation of this piece of data and continue to compare their explanations on other points. While it may take the involvement of a teacher to consider further merits of each explanation given the data, the students' group work and dialogue provide the opportunity for constructing, articulating, and questioning a scientific hypothesis.

namics.[12] Another approach, suggested by Bain (Chapter 4), is to have students pause during class discussion to think and write individually. As students discussed the kind of person Columbus was, Bain asked them to write a 2-minute essay before discussing further. Such an exercise ensures that students who do not engage in the public discussion nonetheless formulate their ideas.

Group work is certainly not the only approach to supporting the development of metacognitive skills. And given the potential hazard of group

BOX 13-4 Guiding Student Observation and Articulation

In an elementary classroom in which students were studying the behavior of light, one group of students observed that light could be both reflected and transmitted by a single object. But students needed considerable support from teachers to be able to articulate this observation in a way that was meaningful to them and to others in the class:

Ms. Lacey	I'm wondering. I know you have a lot of see-through things, a lot of reflect things. I'm wondering how you knew it was see-through.
Kevin	It would shine just, straight through it.
Ms. Lacey	What did you see happening?
Kevin	We saw light going through the . . .
Derek	Like if we put light . . .
Kevin	Wherever we tried the flashlight, like right here, it would show on the board.
Derek	And then I looked at the screen [in front of and to the side of the object], and then it showed a light on the screen. Then he said, come here, and look at the back. And I saw the back, and it had another [spot].
Ms. Lacey	Did you see anything else happening at the material?
Kevin	We saw sort of a little reflection, but we, it had mostly just see-through.
Derek	We put, on our paper we put reflect, but we had to decide which one to put it in. Because it had more of this than more of that.
Ms. Lacey	Oh. So you're saying that some materials . . .
Derek	Had more than others . . .

dynamics, using some individual approaches to supporting self-monitoring and evaluation may be important. For example, in two experiments with students using a cognitive tutor, Aleven and Koedinger[13] asked one group to explain the problem-solving steps to themselves as they worked. They found that students who were asked to self-explain outperformed those who spent the same amount of time on task but did not engage in self-explanation on transfer problems. This was true even though the common time limitation meant that the self-explainers solved fewer problems.

Ms. Lacey	. . . are doing, could be in two different categories.
Derek	Yeah, because some through were really reflection and see-through together, but we had to decide which.
	[Intervening discussion takes place about other data presented by this group that had to do with seeing light reflected or transmitted as a particular color, and how that color compared with the color of the object.]
	[at the end of this group's reporting, and after the students had been encouraged to identify several claims that their data supported among those that had been presented previously by other groups of students]
Ms. Lacey	There was something else I was kinda convinced of. And that was that light can do two different things. Didn't you tell me it went both see-through and reflected?
Kevin & Derek	Yeah. Mm-hmm.
Ms. Lacey	So do you think you might have another claim there?
Derek	Yeah.
Kevin	Light can do two things with one object.
Ms. Lacey	More than one thing?
Kevin	Yeah.
Ms. Lacey	Okay. What did you say?
Kevin & Derek	Light can do two things with one object.

See Chapter 10 for the context of this dialogue.

Another individual approach to supporting metacognition is suggested by Stewart (Chapter 12). Students record their thinking early in the treatment of a new topic and refer back to it at the unit's end to see how it has changed. This brings conscious attention to the change in a student's own thinking. Similarly, the reflective assessment aspect of the ThinkerTools curriculum described in Chapter 1 shifts students from group inquiry work to evaluating their group's inquiry individually. The results in the ThinkerTools case suggest that the combination of group work and individual reflective assessment is more powerful that the group work alone (see Box 9-5 in Chapter 9).

PRINCIPLES OF LEARNING AND CLASSROOM ENVIRONMENTS

The principles that shaped these chapters are based on efforts by researchers to uncover the rules of the learning game. Those rules as we understand them today do not tell us how to play the best instructional game. They can, however, point to the strengths and weakness of instructional strategies and the classroom environments that support those strategies. In Chapter 1, we describe effective classroom environments as learner-centered, knowledge-centered, assessment-centered, and community-centered. Each of these characteristics suggests a somewhat different focus. But at the same time they are interrelated, and the balance among them will help determine the effectiveness of instruction.

A community-centered classroom that relies extensively on classroom discussion, for example, can facilitate learning for several reasons (in addition to supporting metacognition as discussed above):

• It allows students' thinking to be made transparent—an outcome that is critical to a learner-centered classroom. Teachers can become familiar with student ideas—for example, the idea in Chapter 7 that two-thirds of a pie is about the same as three-fourths of a pie because both are missing one piece. Teachers can also monitor the change in those ideas with learning opportunities, the pace at which students are prepared to move, and the ideas that require further work—key features of an assessment-centered classroom.

• It requires that students explain their thinking to others. In the course of explanation, students develop a disposition toward productive interchange with others (community-centered) and develop their thinking more fully (learner-centered). In many of the examples of student discussion throughout this volume—for example, the discussion in Chapter 2 of students examining the role of Hitler in World War II—one sees individual students becoming clearer about their own thinking as the discussion develops.

• Conceptual change can be supported when students' thinking is challenged, as when one group points out a phenomenon that another group's model cannot explain (knowledge-centered). This happens, for example, in a dialogue in Chapter 12 when Delia explains to Scott that a flap might prevent more detergent from pouring out, but cannot explain why the amount of detergent would always be the same.

At the same time, emphasizing the benefits of classroom discussion in supporting effective learning does not imply that lectures cannot be excellent pedagogical devices. Who among us have not been witness to a lecture from which we have come away having learned something new and important? The Feynman lectures on introductory physics mentioned in Chapter 1, for example, are well designed to support learning. That design incorporates a strategy for accomplishing the learning goals described throughout this volume.[14] Feynman anticipates and addresses the points at which students' preconceptions may be a problem. Knowing that students will likely have had no experiences that support grasping the size of an atom, he spends time on this issue, using familiar references for relative size that allow students to envision just how tiny an atom is.

But to achieve effective learning by means of lectures alone places a major burden on the teacher to anticipate student thinking and address problems effectively. To be applied well, this approach is likely to require both a great deal of insight and much experience on the part of the teacher. Without such insight and experience, it will be difficult for teachers to anticipate the full range of conceptions students bring and the points at which they may stumble.[15] While one can see that Feynman made deliberate efforts to anticipate student misconceptions, he himself commented that the major difficulty in the lecture series was the lack of opportunity for student questions and discussion, so that he had no way of really knowing how effective the lectures were. In a learner-centered classroom, discussion is a powerful tool for eliciting and monitoring student thinking and learning.

In a knowledge-centered classroom, however, lectures can be an important accompaniment to classroom discussion—an efficient means of consolidating learning or presenting a set of concepts coherently. In Chapter 4, for example, Bain describes how, once students have spent some time working on competing accounts of the significance of Columbus's voyage and struggled with the question of how the anniversaries of the voyage were celebrated, he delivers a lecture that presents students with a description of current thinking on the topic among historians. At the point at which this lecture is delivered, student conceptions have already been elicited and explored. Because lectures can play an important role in instruction, we stress once again that the emphasis in this volume on the use of discussion to elicit students' thinking, monitor understanding, and support metacognitive development—all critical elements of effective teaching—should not be mistaken for a pedagogical recommendation of a single approach to instruction. Indeed, inquiry-based learning may fall short of its target of providing students with deep conceptual understanding if the teacher places the full burden of learning on the activities. As Box 1-3 in Chapter 1 suggests, a lecture that consolidates the lessons of an activity and places the activity in the conceptual framework of the discipline explicitly can play a critical role in supporting student understanding.

How the balance is struck in creating a classroom that functions as a learning community attentive to the learners' needs, the knowledge to be mastered, and assessments that support and guide instruction will certain vary from one teacher and classroom to the next. Our hope for this volume, then, is that its presentations of instructional approaches to addressing the key principles from *How People Learn* will support the efforts of teachers to play their own instructional game well. This volume is a first effort to elaborate those findings with regard to specific topics, but we hope it is the first of many such efforts. As teachers and researchers become more familiar with some common aspects of student thinking about a topic, their attention may begin to shift to other aspects that have previously attracted little notice. And as insights about one topic become commonplace, they may be applied to new topics.

Beyond extending the reach of the treatment of the learning principles of *How People Learn* within and across topics, we hope that efforts to incorporate those principles into teaching and learning will help strengthen and reshape our understanding of the rules of the learning game. With physics as his topic of concern, Feynman[16] talks about just such a process: "For a long time we will have a rule that works excellently in an overall way, even when we cannot follow the details, and then some time we may discover a *new rule*. From the point of view of basic physics, the most interesting phenomena are of course in the *new* places, the places where the rules do not work—not the places where they *do* work! That is the way in which we discover new rules."

We look forward to the opportunities created for the evolution of the science of learning and the professional practice of teaching as the principles of learning on which this volume focuses are incorporated into classroom teaching.

NOTES

1. Egan, 1986.
2. Story summarized by Kieran Egan, personal communication, March 7, 2003.
3. Liping Ma's work, described in Chapter 1, refers to the set of core concepts and the connected concepts and knowledge that support them as "knowledge packages."
4. Griffin and Case, 1995.
5. Moss and Case, 1999.
6. Kalchman et al., 2001.
7. Palincsar, 1986; White and Fredrickson, 1998.
8. Ma, 1999, p. 5.
9. Ma, 1999, p. 9.

10. Palincsar, 1986.
11. Palincsar, 1986.
12. National Research Council, 2005 (Stewart et al., 2005, Chapter 12).
13. Aleven and Koedinger, 2002.
14. For example, he highlights core concepts conspicuously. In his first lecture, he asks, "If, in some cataclysm, all of scientific knowledge were to be destroyed, and only one sentence passed on to the next generation of creatures, what statement would contain the most information in the fewest words? I believe it is the atomic hypothesis that all things are made of atoms—little particles that move around in perpetual motion, attracting each other when they are a little distance apart, but repelling upon being squeezed into one another.
15. Even with experience, the thinking of individual students may be unanticipated by the teacher.
16. Feynman, 1995, p. 25.

REFERENCES

Aleven, V., and Koedinger, K. (2002). An effective metacognitive strategy: Learning by doing and explaining with a computer-based cognitive tutor. *Cognitive Science, 26*, 147-179.

Egan, K. (1986). *Teaching as story telling: An alternative approach to teaching and curriculum in the elementary school* (vol. iii). Chicago, IL: University of Chicago Press.

Feynman, R.P. (1995). *Six easy pieces: Essentials of physics explained by its most brilliant teacher*. Reading, MA: Perseus Books.

Griffin, S., and Case, R. (1995). Re-thinking the primary school math curriculum: An approach based on cognitive science. *Issues in Education, 3*(1), 1-49.

Kalchman, M., Moss, J., and Case, R. (2001). Psychological models for the development of mathematical understanding: Rational numbers and functions. In S. Carver and D. Klahr (Eds.), *Cognition and instruction: Twenty-five years of progress* (pp. 1-38). Mahwah, NJ: Lawrence Erlbaum Associates.

Ma, L. (1999). *Knowing and teaching elementary mathematics*. Mahwah, NJ: Lawrence Erlbaum Associates.

Moss, J., and Case, R. (1999). Developing children's understanding of rational numbers: A new model and experimental curriculum. *Journal for Research in Mathematics Education, 30*(2).

Palincsar, A.S. (1986). *Reciprocal teaching: Teaching reading as thinking*. Oak Brook, IL: North Central Regional Educational Laboratory.

Stewart, J., Cartier, J.L., and Passmore, C.M. (2005). Developing understanding through model-based inquiry. In National Research Council, *How students learn: History, mathematics, and science in the classroom*. Committee on How People Learn, A Targeted Report for Teachers, M.S. Donovan and J.D. Bransford (Eds.). Division of Behavioral and Social Sciences and Education. Washington, DC: The National Academies Press.

White, B., and Fredrickson, J. (1998). Inquiry, modeling and metacognition: Making science accessible to all students. *Cognition and Instruction, 6*(1), 3-117.

OTHER RESOURCES

National Academy of Sciences. (1998). *Teaching about evolution and the nature of science.* Working Group on Teaching Evolution. Washington, DC: National Academy Press: Available: http://books.nap.edu/catalog/5787.html.

National Academy of Sciences. (2004). *Evolution in Hawaii: A supplement to teaching about evolution and the nature of science* by Steve Olson. Washington, DC: The National Academies Press. Available: http://www.nap.edu/books/0309089913/html/.

Biographical Sketches of Committee Members and Contributors

Rosalyn Ashby is a lecturer in education in the History in Education Unit in the School of Arts and Humanities in the University of London Institute of Education. Her work focuses on designing history curricula, assessment systems, and support materials for teachers. She now leads a history teacher-training course. Prior to becoming a university lecturer, Ashby taught history, politics and economics, and then worked as a history adviser with primary and secondary teachers. She has published numerous articles and book chapters, including many coauthored with Peter Lee regarding children's ideas about history. She is an editor of the *International Review of History Education*. She has a degree in American history and government from the University of Essex.

Robert B. Bain is assistant professor in the school of education at the University of Michigan. He teaches social studies education and investigates history education, the intersection between the disciplines and social studies instruction, and professional development. Previously, he spent more than 25 years as a high school history teacher. Among other publications, he has coauthored an article on professional development of elementary school teachers.

John D. Bransford (*Chair*) is James W. Mifflin university professor and professor of education at the University of Washington in Seattle. Previously, he was centennial professor of psychology and education and codirector of the Learning Technology Center at Vanderbilt University. Early work by Bransford and his colleagues in the 1970s included research in the areas of human learning and memory and problem solving; this research helped shape the "cognitive revolution" in psychology. An author of seven books and hundreds of articles and presentations, Bransford's work focuses on the areas of cognition and technology. He served as cochair of the National Research Council (NRC) committee that authored *How People Learn: Brain, Mind, Experience, and School.* He received a Ph.D. in cognitive psychology from the University of Minnesota.

Susan Carey is a professor of psychology at Harvard University. Carey's research concerns the evolutionary and ontogenetic origins of human knowledge in a variety of domains, including number, lexical semantics, physical reasoning, and reasoning about intentional states. She studies conceptual change involving older children, and focuses on three domains of knowledge: number, intuitive biology, and intuitive physics. She received a Ph.D. from Harvard University.

Jennifer L. Cartier is an assistant professor in the Department of Instruction and Learning at the University of Pittsburgh. Her research interests include student learning in classrooms where modeling is a focus and teacher education—particularly the ways in which hands-on curriculum materials can be implemented to engage elementary school students in realistic scientific practices. She has published articles describing students' reasoning in genetics in *Science and Education* and *BioQUEST Notes* and she has coauthored a book chapter describing the use of black-box activities to introduce students to aspects of scientific argumentation.

M. Suzanne Donovan (*Study Director*) is also director of the NRC's Strategic Education Research Partnership (SERP) and coeditor of the project's two reports, *Strategic Education Research Partnership* and *Learning and Instruction: A SERP Research Agenda.* At the NRC, she served as director of the previous study that produced *How People Learn: Bridging Research and Practice,* and she was coeditor for the NRC reports *Minority Students in Special and Gifted Education* and *Eager to Learn: Educating Our Preschoolers.* Previously, she was on the faculty of Columbia University. She has a Ph.D. in public policy from the University of California at Berkeley.

Kieran Egan is a professor in the Faculty of Education at Simon Fraser University in Burnaby, Canada. Dr. Egan was the 1991 winner of the Grawemeyer Award in Education for his analyses of children's imaginations. His recent books include *The Educated Mind: How Cognitive Tools Shape Our Understanding* (University of Chicago Press) and *Getting It Wrong from the Beginning: Our Progressivist Inheritance from Herbert Spencer, John Dewey, and Jean Piaget* (Yale University Press).

Karen C. Fuson is a professor emeritus in the School of Education and Social Policy and in the Psychology Department at Northwestern University. After teaching high school mathematics to Chicago inner-city African-American students for 3 years, she began research to ascertain how to help all students enter high school with more knowledge of mathematics. She has conducted extensive research regarding children's learning of mathematical concepts from ages 2 through 12, focusing in on the development of effective teaching and learning materials, including the "Children's Math World's K through 5" curriculum, supporting effective learning for children from various backgrounds, and ambitious accessible learning paths through school mathematics. Fuson was a member of the NRC committee that authored *Adding It Up: Helping Children Learn Mathematics.*

Sharon Griffin is an associate professor of education and an adjunct associate professor of psychology at Clark University. She is coauthor of "Number Worlds," a research-based mathematics program for young children, coauthor of *What Develops in Emotional Development?* (Plenum), and author of several articles on cognitive development and mathematics education. For the past 10 years, she has sought to improve mathematics learning and achievement for young children by developing and evaluating programs to "provide the central conceptual prerequisites for success in school math to children at risk for school failure." Griffin is currently participating in an advisory capacity on national projects, in Canada and the United States, to enhance the cognitive, mathematical, and language development of "high-need" preschool children, from birth to 5 years.

Mindy Kalchman is an assistant professor in the School of Education at DePaul University. Her research interests include children's learning of mathematics, theory-based curriculum design, and the effect of discoveries from the field of developmental cognitive psychology on classroom practice. She has coauthored numerous articles regarding mathematics education and curriculum and has conducted workshops on how to teach functions. Kalchman also served as a consulting content editor for the development of the Ontario mathematics curriculum for grades 9–12. She received her Ph.D. from the Ontario Institute for Studies in Education, University of Toronto.

Kenneth R. Koedinger is an associate professor in the Human Computer Interaction Institute and Psychology Department at Carnegie Mellon University. His research interests include cognitive modeling, problem solving and learning, intelligent tutoring systems, and educational technology. Earlier in his career, Koedinger was a teacher in an urban high school. He has developed computer simulations of student thinking that are used to guide the construction of educational materials and are the core of intelligent software systems that provide students with individualized interactive learning assistance. He has developed such "cognitive tutors" for mathematics that are now in use in over 1700 schools.

Pamela Kraus is a research scientist and cofounder of FACET Innovations. She is currently working on the Diagnoser projects and related professional development projects and she is helping conduct the research and organize the facet clusters in the physical sciences. In addition, Kraus works closely with the resource teachers from across the state as they produce assessment tools. She received a Ph.D. from the University of Washington.

Peter J. Lee is a senior lecturer in education in the History Education Unit of the School of Arts and Humanities at the Institute of Education of The University of London. Previously, he taught history in primary and secondary schools. Lee has directed several research and curriculum development projects (the latter with Denis Shemilt). He has edited five books on history education, and published numerous chapters and articles exploring children's ideas about history, many of them coauthored with Rosalyn Ashby. He is an editor of the *International Review of History Education*. He received a history degree at Oxford University.

Shirley J. Magnusson is the Cotchett Professor of Science and Mathematics Teacher Education at the California Polytechnic State University. She has taught science to students at the elementary, middle school, high school, and college levels since 1980. She joined the faculty at the University of Michigan in 1991 as a science teacher educator, specializing in learning and instruction in science at the elementary school level. She collaborated with Annemarie Palincsar on a program of research that has sought to define and study the outcomes from an approach to inquiry-based science instruction known as Guided Inquiry supporting Multiple Literacies (GIsML). Publications of Magnusson's work have appeared in the *Journal of the Learning Sciences, Teaching and Teacher Education*, the *Journal of Science Education and Technology*, and *Learning Disabilities Quarterly*, as well as a number of books such as *Science Teacher Knowledge, Cognition and Instruction: Twenty-five Years of Progress*, and *Translating Educational Theory into Practice*.

James Minstrell is cofounder and research scientist at FACET Innovations, LLC. This position followed a lengthy career as a science and mathematics teacher and classroom researcher in the learning of physical science and mathematics. He received the Presidential Award for Excellence in Science and Mathematics Teaching from the National Science Foundation. Minstrell served on the U.S. Department of Education's Expert Panel on Science and

Mathematics Education. He has published numerous articles, with a major focus on understanding of mathematics and physics.

Joan Moss is an assistant professor in the Department of Human Development and Applied Psychology at the Ontario Institute for Studies in Education at the University of Toronto. Previously she worked as a master teacher at the Institute of Child Study Laboratory School. Her research interests include children's development and understanding of rational numbers and proportional reasoning. More recently, Moss has been working on classroom-based studies of children's development of algebraic thinking. Her work in professional development includes preservice training, as well as coordination of learning opportunities with novice elementary school mathematics teachers using a Japanese lesson study approach. She has published widely and is an author of a mathematics textbook series. Moss carried out postdoctoral research at the University of California at Berkeley.

Annemarie Sullivan Palincsar is the Jean and Charles Walgreen professor of reading and literacy at the University of Michigan's School of Education. She has conduced extensive research on peer collaboration in problem-solving activity, instruction to promote self-regulation, acquisition and instruction of literacy with primary students at risk for academic difficulty, and how children use literacy in the context of guided inquiry experiences. She was a member of the NRC committees that produced the reports *How People Learn: Bridging Research and Practice,* and *Preventing Reading Difficulties in young Children.* Palincsar is currently coeditor of *Cognition and Instruction.*

Cynthia M. Passmore is an assistant professor in the School of Education at the University of California, Davis. She specializes in science education and is particularly interested in student learning and reasoning about scientific models. Her research also focuses on preservice and in-service teacher professional development. She teaches the science methods courses for single and multiple subjects credential candidates, as well as graduate courses in science education. Earlier in her career she worked as a high school science teacher in East Africa, Southern California, and Wisconsin.

Denis Shemilt has worked at the University of Leeds for more than 25 years, where he has been evaluator of the Schools History Project 13-16, and codirector of the Cambridge History Project. Until recently, he was head of the School of Education at Trinity and All Saints, a constituent college of the university, devoting time to educational management at the expense of real work. He is now focusing on training history teachers and pursuing a long-postponed interest in the development of students' historical frameworks.

He has published numerous contributions to history education, including the *History 13-16 Evaluation Study* and papers on students' ideas about change, evidence, and empathy in history. He received a degree in education from the University of Manchester.

James Stewart is a professor in the School of Education's Department of Curriculum and Instruction at the University of Wisconsin-Madison. His research interests include student understanding, reasoning, and problem solving in science, particularly in the biological sciences. Stewart's recent publications include articles on student understanding in genetics and evolutionary biology in *Science Education* and the *Journal of Research in Science Teaching* and a book chapter, "Teaching Science in a Multicultural Perspective."

Suzanne M. Wilson is a professor in the Department of Teacher Education and director of the Center for the Scholarship of Teaching at Michigan State University. She was a history and mathematics teacher for 6 years; directed the Teacher Assessment Project at Stanford University; taught third-grade social studies in a professional development school; and has directed several research projects exploring the relationship of teachers' practice to curriculum mandates. Wilson teaches prospective and practicing teachers, as well as prospective teacher educators and researchers.

Samuel S. Wineburg is professor of education at Stanford University, where he directs the Ph.D. program in History Education. His research explores the development of historical thinking among adolescents and the nature of historical consciousness. Wineburg's book, *Historical Thinking and Other Unnatural Acts: Charting the Future and Past,* was awarded the 2002 Frederic W. Ness Prize for the "most important contribution to the understanding and improvement of liberal education" by the Association of American Colleges and Universities. He was a member of the NRC committee that wrote *How People Learn: Brain, Mind, Experience, and School.* He received his Ph.D. from Stanford University.

Index

This index includes the text of the full version of *How Students Learn: History, Mathematics, and Science*, which can be found on the CD attached to the back cover.

T